Tailwater Trout

in the

South

An Angler's Guide

Jimmy Jacobs

Backcountry Publications
Woodstock, Vermont

An invitation to the reader

With time, access points may change, and road numbers, signs, and landmarks referred to in this book may be altered. If you find that such changes have occurred near waters described in this book, please let the author and publisher know, so that corrections can be made in future editions. Other comments and suggestions are also welcome. Address all correspondence to:

Fishing Editor
Backcountry Publications
PO Box 748
Woodstock, Vermont 05091

Library of Congress Cataloging-in-Publication Data

Jacobs, Jimmy.
    Tailwater trout in the South : an angler's guide / Jimmy Jacobs.
        p.   cm.
    Includes index.
    ISBN 0-88150-335-5 (alk. paper)
    1. Trout fishing—Southern States—Guidebooks. 2. Southern States—Guide books. I. Title.
SH688.U6J32   1996
796.1'4'755—dc20   96-12520
                                                                        CIP

10 9 8 7 6 5 4 3 2 1
Printed in the United States of America.

Cover design by Sally Sherman and Susan Wheeler.
Text design by Rachel Kahn.
Cover photo by Steve Wright.
Interior photos by the author unless otherwise noted.
Maps by XNR Productions, © 1996 The Countryman Press.

Published by Backcountry Publications
A division of The Countryman Press
PO Box 748
Woodstock, VT 05091

Distributed by
W.W. Norton & Company, Inc.
500 Fifth Avenue
New York, NY 10110

To Glenda

For providing a place where I could finish the book
and for putting me in my place when needed.

ACKNOWLEDGMENTS

Special thanks go out to all of the members of Trout Unlimited and the Federation of Fly Fishers who provided information, guidance, and support as I put this book together. Without their help, such a wide-ranging project could not have been possible.

Contents

	Introduction	7
1	Tailwater Tactics	18
2	Tackling Tailwaters	27

Section One: Alabama   35

3	Sipsey Fork Black Warrior River	37

Section Two: Arkansas   43

4	Little Missouri River	47
5	Little Red River	53
6	North Fork River	64
7	White River—Beaver Tailwater	72
8	White River—Bull Shoals Tailwater	81

Section Three: Georgia   95

9	Chattahoochee River	97
10	Toccoa River	105

Section Four: Kentucky   111

11	Barren River	113
12	Carr Fork	116
13	Cumberland River	119
14	Dix River	125
15	Johns Creek	128
16	Licking Creek	131
17	Licking River	133
18	Little Sandy River	136
19	Martins Fork	139
20	Middle Fork Kentucky River	142
21	Nolin River	145
22	Paint Creek	147
23	Rough River	150

SECTION FIVE: MISSOURI 153

24 White River   155

SECTION SIX: NORTH CAROLINA 163

25 Linville River   166
26 Nantahala River   169

SECTION SEVEN: SOUTH CAROLINA 175

27 Saluda River   177
28 Savannah River   182

SECTION EIGHT: TENNESSEE 187

29 Caney Fork River   189
30 Clinch River   195
31 Duck River   201
32 Elk River   205
33 Hiwassee River   209
34 Holston River   214
35 Obey River   217
36 South Holston River   221
37 Watauga River   227

SECTION NINE: VIRGINIA 231

38 Back Creek   233
39 Jackson River   237
40 Smith River   242

41 The Murky Crystal Ball   247

APPENDIX: MAP SOURCES 249

INDEX 251

Introduction

A LOOK BACK

When discussing trout fishing in the southeastern United States, the natural tendency is to think of the highlands of the Cumberland Plateau or the Blue Ridge and Appalachian Mountains. With regard to wild populations of trout, these are in fact the correct places to look.

The only species of trout native to the region is the brook trout, which is actually a member of the char family. Even in humanity's earliest encounters with the South's trout, the brookies were found in a quite limited range in the mountainous areas of the Carolinas, Georgia, Tennessee, Virginia, and possibly eastern Kentucky. Pressure from human activities and competition from introduced trout species relentlessly pushed the native brookies farther into the high headwater streams. Today, rainbow and brown trout dominate the region's trout fishery.

A milestone in southern trout fishing took place in the 1930s, when the United States Army Corps of Engineers and the Tennessee Valley Authority (TVA) began erecting dams on rivers throughout the region traditionally known as Dixie. The two stated purposes of these efforts were to produce power at hydroelectric facilities at these dams, and to control floods on downstream areas. Another driving force of that period was the creation of jobs during the depths of the Great Depression.

Even prior to this great dam-building drive, private power companies had been damming the region's rivers since the early part of the 20th century. Georgia's Tallulah River, for example, had been stifled by a string of dams as early as the 1920s. Eventually, the dam-building frenzy produced reservoirs whose mission statements targeted water-supply storage or even recreational uses.

Although none of the dam construction was begun with the idea of providing more trout fishing in the South, sporting and, in some cases, economic boons to the area have resulted from the creation of exceptional fishing resources. The waters impounded in the new lakes were the first to have an impact on southern fishing, as great largemouth bass fisheries developed in them. Fisheries managers were much slower to recognize the possibilities offered by the tailwaters below the dams. When it was realized, beginning in the 1940s, that the cold waters released through tailraces of these dams could support trout, a new era of angling dawned in the southeastern states.

Today the range of trout in Dixie has—thanks to tailwaters—expanded to include northern Alabama and portions of Arkansas, as well as western Kentucky and Tennessee. More than three dozen tailwaters are recognized by the various states in the region as trout fisheries. They run the gamut from large brawling flows to modest streams. More important, they provide some of the best trout fishing in the South and constitute the waters of this region most likely to give up a trophy-sized trout.

ANATOMY OF A TAILWATER

To take full advantage of the exceptional trout fishing found in the tailwater rivers of the South, it is necessary to have an understanding of these flows. Knowing the characteristics common to such rivers provides the first hints as to how to fish them. Although at first glance the entire river may look very similar, distinct portions can be identified. Each of these stretches presents different challenges and opportunities to the trout angler.

While some of the tailwater streams of the Southeast do not fit the following description exactly, most will have the sections described. Due, however, to some individual eccentricities, a few of the rivers will lack a portion of the standard run. These exceptions are noted later, when discussing the various streams.

To qualify as a tailwater fishery, the river must, of course, have a reservoir located on it. This impoundment, for our purposes, must create the trout fishery, or at least greatly improve it. This latter qualification is added because there are some hydroelectric stations on rivers, especially in North Carolina, whose rivers support trout downstream, but whose dams do not affect the flow or the fishery. One example of this situation is the Cheoah River. The dam at Santeetlah Lake releases virtually no water to the river downstream, but instead diverts the flow through a pipeline to a powerhouse at Cheoah Lake on the Little Tennessee River. Below Santeetlah Dam the Cheoah's

Earthen or concrete dams are key to creating
tailwater trout fisheries in the South.

flow is provided by feeder streams only, as are its trout, which move down into what is left of the river.

Other examples of dammed—but nontailwater—trout rivers in North Carolina are the West Fork of the Tuckaseegee below Thorpe Reservoir, and the main branch of the Tuckaseegee, which goes through four impoundments (the last being the Cedar Hill Reservoir). These rivers do not go through the surge and ebb cycles usually associated with tailwaters (described later in this chapter), but they are stocked with trout. Yet, the fisheries here are not greatly improved by their dams. They are simply trout waters both above and below the structures. Another place this is found is on the South Saluda River below South Carolina's Table Rock Reservoir.

Finally, some impoundments in the region do not create tailwater trout fisheries because they dump directly into other lakes. The best example of this is on the Little Tennessee River along its course through North Carolina and Tennessee. The river runs through Fontana, Cheoah, Calderwood, Chilhowee, and Tellico Lakes. The first four of these reservoirs support trout, but do not fit the standard tailwater description because they have no riverine flow.

Now that we have established what a tailwater trout fishery is not, it is time to describe what does make up such a resource. The first essential is a dam constructed to impound the river and regulate the downstream flow. In most cases this will be a huge earth-and-concrete structure that also has a hydroelectric powerhouse for the generation of electricity. Water released from the lake turns the generators within this complex, and immediately below the dam is a tailrace into which this water is released. This flow varies from gentle-to-nonexistent during nongeneration hours to a raging torrent at peak releases. The tailrace often has a concrete-and-rock riprap along its shore, along with a deep hole under the water and immediately below the dam. This hole is created by the violent surges of water through the dam. Often a 100-foot or longer safety zone is imposed directly downstream of the dam, in which boats and wading are forbidden.

The next characteristic section of a tailwater is a portion of the river that may be quite short or many miles long, and is heavily influenced by the water released during power-generation surges. During generation hours, this part of the river is subjected to huge volumes of water that scour the bottom and sometimes erode steep banks. This portion of a tailwater can be dangerous, as the turbulent water can sweep away a wade-angler or overturn an anchored boat. It is also fairly infertile trout habitat: The scouring of the bottom destroys virtually all aquatic weeds and insect life as well as other food sources on which trout depend. Great caution is needed when fishing on or in the water of this predominantly put-and-take trout fishery.

Next, the standard tailwater goes through several miles of intermediate water. Here the scouring effects of the river surges have lessened. Some insects and aquatic weeds begin to appear, allowing a portion of the trout population to carry over from year to year. Through this part of the river, which will encompass several miles of water, one is likely to see larger fish appearing. Brush heaps, snags, and blown-down trees in the water along the shore are less likely to be swept away by the river's force, providing more cover in which the fish can hide.

The third characteristic area of the tailwater could be called the *prime fishing portion*. Here the water level still fluctuates with the release schedule of the upstream dam, but the effects have lessened to the point that insects and cover structure are basically unaffected. Trout have a much more constant food supply and plenty of places to hide, so here one will find better, more dependable fishing—particularly around shallow riffle or shoal areas. These areas serve as nurseries for the aquatic insects and crustaceans that make up the lower rungs of the food chain, and provide easy and enjoyable angling. Since this prime fishing area is generally several miles removed from the dam site, it becomes possible—by timing the downstream flow of the released water—to predict times of low water and plan angling excursions to utilize the prime fishing hours.

The final portion of the tailwater is the marginal trout fishing areas. This is typically found far downstream and has water temperatures during summer months that make trout survival a dicey proposition. This area may begin anywhere from only a mile or two downriver from the dam on some tailwaters to as much as 60 or 70 miles distant on others.

Through this portion of the flow, insect life is usually present in great abundance, forage fish are readily available, and fishy-looking cover is widespread. Trout, however, are scarce, and share the habitat with warm-water species such as smallmouth or largemouth bass and bream. As a rule, the trout found in this marginal habitat tend to be large specimens—with a decided tendency to be brown trout. These European immigrants do better in turbid, marginal flows than other trout, plus they have an advantage when it comes to competing with warm-water species. Larger brown trout are basically carnivores, so they handle the competition by simply eating their rivals! As a result of this diet, the few trout present grow large and quickly, and come to dominate their home waters.

CREATING A FISHERY

As mentioned earlier, tailwater streams provide some of the most outstanding trout fishing opportunities in the South. There are several reasons why these rivers have proven so productive for cold-water anglers. The first has to do with the temperatures of the rivers' waters.

The reservoirs created by the dams are often deep, ranging from as little as 60 to 80 feet in depth to as many as several hundred. The water released through the turbines of the powerhouses is drawn from near the bottom of the lakes and is quite cold. This fact explains the very existence of trout in most of the tailwater streams in the South. They were at best marginal trout water before the dams; more often, they were turbid, warm-water flows.

Below the dams, though, not only is the temperature ideal for trout (between 45 and 60 degrees), but the water is of a constant temperature year-round. This means that the fish are not only present but they are also enjoying a 12-month growing period, regardless of the air temperatures of the region. Growth rates of ½ inch a month are common, and in some rivers they have been documented at more than 1 inch a month! Such phenomenal growth produces large fish in a hurry. Thus, these tailwaters have a well-earned reputation for yielding large fish as well as large numbers of trout.

Two other facets of these water releases are the dissolved oxygen and the nutrients that the flow carries out of the lakes and into the river downstream. Both are conducive to aquatic weeds, insects, and crustaceans. As a result, the rivers produce great quantities of food for trout downstream of the areas swept clean by the surging water. In some cases, stunned baitfish sucked through the turbines add to the food base near the tailrace. This large supply of biomass is the reason that tailwater fisheries are able to support enormous numbers of fish while producing some truly impressive lunker trout at the same time.

While tailwaters seem to provide excellent habitat for trout, this is not to say that no problems occur. At certain times of the year the levels of dissolved oxygen in the depths of the reservoirs can fall so low that the water will not support life. When this water is drawn through the dam and released to the river below, fish kills can take place. This is a particular concern during late summer to early fall and—as is noted in the river descriptions—has occurred on several streams with disturbing regularity.

A related problem that also affects the fisheries at times is high water temperatures, especially in times of drought. The period when electric power demand is at its lowest in most southern states is early fall, when air-conditioning season ends. This, however, is also the period when rainfall is at its scarcest. This means that powerhouses do not need to release as much water, and often there is simply less water to be released. In years of drought, the water levels in some reservoirs have fallen to the point that downstream releases were so infrequent and small that the total trout fishery was placed in peril.

Fortunately, more attention is now being paid to the quality of water introduced into these trout rivers. In particular, the TVA began a 5-year, $55 million program in 1991 designed to correct the problems and prevent harm to the fisheries. In some cases weir dams are installed just downstream of the main dams. These weirs create artificial waterfalls to oxygenate the water, lessening the danger of fish kills farther downstream. Another method being used is the placement at some dams of tower intakes, which draw water not just from the bottom of the lake where oxygen levels may be low, but also in part from several other levels. Thus, even if one stratum of water is depleted of oxygen, others will provide a minimum supply for the trout in the tailwater. Finally, the Corps of Engineers, the TVA, and private power companies are making greater efforts (often due to pressure from the angling community) to maintain minimum flows of water through the dams year-round.

Given the large size of most tailwater rivers and the abundant food they carry, the final ingredient making them fisheries is, of course, the fish. It is an unfortunate fact that southern tailwaters generally support almost no natural reproduction of trout. The scouring effect of water releases is not conducive to fish-spawning areas. Additionally, most of the feeder streams are low-altitude, warm-water flows that offer the trout no opportunities for spawning either. While some rivers show indications of very minor spawning activity, even there it is insufficient to support a fishery.

As a result, virtually all trout in tailwater rivers of the South are stocked. While many are caught quickly by anglers in the tradition of put-and-take streams, a couple of circumstances set these rivers apart from standard hatchery-supported waters. To begin with, the size of the rivers and the volume of the stocking virtually guarantee that a significant portion of the fish will avoid immediately ending up in a creel. These carryover trout gain weight and inches at phenomenal rates, providing the base for trophy fisheries.

Also, on some of the rivers the management scheme employed is one of put-grow-and-take. The trout are stocked as fingerlings, so that they reach maturity in the rivers. In many cases these fish act like wild, stream-bred trout and are less susceptible to anglers. This is especially true of brown trout.

Tailwater stockings range from a few thousand fish released seasonally on some minor flows of the region to hundreds of thousands of trout planted year-round on the major rivers. The stockings usually consist of rainbow trout, with some browns added. From time to time, brook trout and—in the case of Arkansas's tailwaters—even cutthroat trout are stocked.

As a result of the excellent conditions of the rivers and the often massive infusions of fish, the tailwater rivers of the Southeast have

Mary Borgwat shows off an average-sized rainbow trout from the Bull Shoals tailwater on Arkansas's White River.

become established as the premier trout waters in nearly every state of the region. Indeed, as we shall see in the descriptions of individual rivers, they also lay claim to being some of the most productive trophy trout waters in the world.

In the following chapters each of the streams recognized as a tailwater trout fishery in Alabama, Arkansas, Georgia, Kentucky, Missouri, North Carolina, South Carolina, Tennessee, and Virginia is discussed. Some of these waters do not fully fit the above description for a number of reasons. Some do not always have hydroelectric facilities, but rather originate in flood-control dams. Others are quite small flows below the dams, instead of large rivers. But all have waters drawn from the depths of a reservoir, are stocked with trout at some period of the year, and are managed as trout fisheries by the state authorities.

One final note is worth mentioning. With regard to the information provided in the following chapters, I do not claim to be an expert on fishing all, or even any, of the tailwaters discussed. Nor is this book intended to be the ultimate word on how to extract trout from them. Complete volumes could be written on the peculiarities and joys of wetting a hook in several of the rivers. Obviously, no one angler could produce a book that definitively speaks to the subject of how to fish all these tailwaters from his or her own experiences. Such knowledge would require several lifetimes.

What this book is designed to do is provide a brief overview of each tailwater. Much of the information was gleaned from fisheries biologists, state publications, and picking the brains of anglers, along with some firsthand fishing experiences by the author. The other aim of this book is to provide some information on where the public access areas are located, and on what rules and regulations apply to specific rivers. Be aware, however, that regulations can and will change in all of the states. Get a copy of the most current state fishing regulations before heading to any of the rivers, and read them with an eye toward recent rules changes.

MAPS

Of course, even the best fishing is useless to the sportsman unable to locate the river or its access points. The key to this is having some good maps. Unfortunately, the only standardized maps that cover all the states in this book are the United States Geological Survey (USGS) 7.5-minute quadrangle maps. While these are good at showing the topography of the area, they can be as much as 15 to 20 years old. This makes them useless for finding many of the newer secondary roads needed to reach access points on various rivers.

Other sources of directions are the official road maps available from all of the states covered. While the major federal and state highways are shown on these, again, secondary roads are lacking. Not a great deal of attention is paid to the exact locations of waterways, either. After all, these are road maps.

The best maps available for finding tailwaters and access points are in the *Atlas & Gazetteers* published by the DeLorme Mapping Company of Freeport, Maine. These multipage map books show secondary and dirt roads, as well as river locations, in enough detail to make locating the covered streams quite easy. On the downside, the company presently publishes editions of the *Gazetteer* only for North Carolina, Tennessee, and Virginia among the states in this volume.

Another option is the *South Carolina Wildlife Facilities Atlas,* produced by that state's Wildlife and Marine Resources Department. Broken down by county, the maps in this book are detailed enough to help locate the access points to both of that state's described tailwaters.

In a similar vein, the Arkansas Game and Fish Commission publishes a map book showing every county in that state, and detailing the fishing resources within them. Entitled *Fishing in Arkansas: A Fisherman's Guide to Public Access Facilities in Arkansas Counties,* it is a key to finding tailwater access points in the Natural State.

Thomas Publications, Ltd., of Lyndon, Wisconsin, produces books of county road maps for Arkansas, Kentucky, North Carolina, South Carolina, and Tennessee. The strong suit of these books is their detail when it comes to the positions and numbers of secondary roads. In the case of Kentucky, the book is the best resource presently available in the search for river access.

Finally, in the remaining states of Alabama, Georgia, and Missouri, a road map from each one's Department of Transportation is about the most useful tool available. Alabama and Missouri have only one tailwater each; both are short and relatively easy to access from major thoroughfares. The same can be said for Georgia's Toccoa River tailwater. The Peach State's Chattahoochee River is another question altogether. It has a number of access points over a 45-mile length, most of which are located within metropolitan Atlanta. A detailed map is needed for this tailwater.

Fortunately, the National Park Service comes to the rescue. Due to the location of the Chattahoochee River National Recreation Area along this flow, the park service publishes a brochure with a detailed map showing all public access to the tailwaters.

Beneath the name of each river in this book, the USGS quadrangle map on which it appears is identified. For North Carolina, Tennessee, and Virginia, the page number from the appropriate DeLorme *Gazetteer* where the river is found also is mentioned. In the case of Arkansas, the appropriate page number from the *Fishing in Arkansas (FIA)* map book is listed. Similarly, page numbers for the *South Carolina Wildlife Facilities Atlas (SCWFA)* are supplied for each of that state's rivers.

More information on what the various maps provide and how to contact the publishers of each is contained in the Map Appendix at the end of this book.

The maps accompanying each chapter in this book show roads, towns, and landmarks that should aid in locating access points on the various tailwaters. They are most helpful when used in conjunction with the maps suggested above.

One final note with regard to directions provided in this book is worth mentioning. All of the road names, numbers, and other landmarks used here were current when this book went to press. Be aware, however, that town, county, and state authorities often rearrange these. In particular, state departments of transportation are seemingly forever at work on the road systems. This often entails placing, replacing, removing—and at times neglecting to install—street, road, or highway signs at intersections. At other times road widening ends up removing some prominent landmark or sign that is mentioned in the directions to a river. Such instances are unavoidable, since the only thing that can be counted on is that things will change.

1

Tailwater Tactics

It takes but a couple of fishing trips to a tailwater river to discover that the trout angling on these flows is quite different from that found on small mountain streams. Being an accomplished trout stalker on mountain brooks does not ensure success when the action moves to one of these magnum-sized, trout-rich habitats. There is a transition period involved for most anglers in which they must unlearn some old lessons while absorbing some new ones.

As a result, some trout enthusiasts never develop a taste for tailwaters, despite the numbers and size of the fish available. It is not unusual to run into anglers who spend inordinate amounts of time chasing high-land trout, but shun the tailwaters. On the other hand, someone who learns trout fishing on large tailwater rivers is just as likely to express disdain for those "little fish" found in mountain habitats.

With tailwater fishing—as with fishing in any southern stream—a variety of tackle is found in the hands of the angling public, and the easiest way to define the various types of anglers is by their terminal tackle. The percentage of fly-fishers is usually a bit higher on tailwaters, due to the open fishing conditions. The overhanging foliage found on mountain brooks is not a problem here: Though some bushes line the rivers, there are also vast expanses of open water over which to let out some line. These are streams that beg for the graceful poetry of classic fly-casting.

Still, bait-fishers or anglers armed with spinning gear and small artificial lures heavily outnumber the fly-casters. In the case of the bait-anglers, the South's tradition of "meat-fishing" is usually the driving force. Catching the state limit of trout, to be cleaned and served at suppertime, is what brings them to the river. This is not to say that fly-fishers or spinning-lure fanciers do not also take home some fish for the skillet. A number of them, however, simply fish for the fun of the sport, releasing most or all of their catches. Such altruism is rarely found in bait-fishers.

There is also a "hybrid" or crossover category of anglers on the tailwater rivers of Dixie. The big water and the possibility of big fish attract a number of folks who could be called "converted" bass anglers. The "converted" part of the description is used with tongue in cheek, however, since these anglers are unlikely to give up their pursuit of the South's favorite fish, the largemouth bass. It is just that the chance of hooking into a huge trout is enough to make them backslide a bit and spend some time on a tailwater. These anglers are unlikely to use fly-rods or even light or ultralight spinning tackle. Instead, expect to see them fishing from boats (their standard bass boat if boat ramps and water levels permit) and using bait-casting equipment with natural baits—often minnows, where these are legal—or perhaps a jerkbait or crankbait, as for bass.

Crossover anglers usually concentrate their fishing directly below the dams and tailraces of the larger rivers, in order to take advantage of the dependable "hatches" of baitfish sucked through the turbines of the dam during power generation. These stunned shad and other forage fish litter the surface, weakly twitching, providing the larger trout with a dependable and abundant food source. Anglers who present live minnows or minnow-imitating lures at these times can fool some magnum-sized rainbows and browns.

GEARING UP

FLY-FISHING

As mentioned, the number of fly-fishers is higher on tailwaters than on most other southern streams. The open water is part of the appeal to these folks, but since the release of the movie version of Norman Maclean's *A River Runs Through It,* the urge to fly-cast has stricken even more people, especially novice anglers. Since many of the tailwaters are quite close to the metropolitan areas where most of these new fly-casters live, the rivers attract inordinate numbers of them. Of course, the excellent quality of the fly-fishing in the tailwater streams might have something to do with the phenomenon as well.

The gear used by fly-casters is more important to success on tailwaters than it is on smaller streams. On a mountain creek, an angler simply needs a rod he or she can handle, a floating line, and a reel of any description to store the line. On a large tailwater, however, a number of situations arise that call for specific reels, lines, or rods.

In the case of rods, longer and heavier-weight models are preferable. These open waters can make punching a cast into the wind a necessity. Another consideration is that weighted streamers, which are often productive flies, are difficult to cast with light, short rods. Six- to 7-weight rods that are 8 to 9 feet long are ideal for tailwater angling.

In the arena of fly-lines, tailwaters contain deep runs and river bends where it is necessary to get a streamer or nymph down deep to where the fish are holding. This may call for sinking or sink-tip lines—which are virtually never needed on smaller mountain waters. Some nylon backing for the fly-line is also advisable, since hooking a truly big trout in water where it has plenty of room to run is possible.

For the same reason, it is important to have a fly-reel with a good drag system. When that magnum trout-of-a-lifetime takes your fly, you need a reel that helps rather than hinders the fight. The reel should have enough line capacity for 100 yards of backing, since a large fish can find open water into which it can make 50- or 100-yard runs.

Undoubtedly the biggest difference between fly-casting on a southern mountain stream and the same sport on a tailwater is the selection of flies. Mountain-stream fish are opportunistic in their feeding habits because of their infertile habitat. They eat whatever is available, in most cases, and they eat it whenever possible. Matching the hatch is irrelevant when pursuing trout in this environment.

The reverse is ordinarily true on the tailwaters of the South. Many of these are big waters and quite fertile. Fish grow large here because they have plenty to eat and their menu has plenty of variety. As a result they can be picky eaters, sometimes keying on a few insects, or even a single variety. The fly-caster who does not present a proper imitation of that food item is likely to come away without having fooled many fish.

While each river has its idiosyncrasies, there are several classes of trout foods common to most of them. The insect and invertebrate life that is important in the individual rivers is mentioned in later sections. Here the emphasis is on covering the broad classes of trout foods common to many of the rivers. These are covered in lay terms rather than in a form designed to send entomologists into fits of ecstasy. Providing enough information about the insects to aid fishing success is the main concern here.

Among the most important and widespread insect forms in southern waters are the caddis flies of the order Trichoptera. These critters come in a wide variety of sizes and colors across the Southeast, with the common trademark of the order being the way the insects' wings lie on their backs—swept to the rear when folded.

The nymphs (actually the larval stage of the insect's life cycle, but ordinarily referred to as "nymphs" by anglers) of the caddis fly are case-builders that actually mold homes for themselves by gluing together tiny pebbles, sticks, or other materials to create a tube in which to live. Although trout will eat these worms, case and all, they are not usually imitated by southern fly-casters, since the cases are often stuck to rocks along the bottom. When you hear an old-time angler in the South speak of using "stickbait" for trout, he is referring to baiting up with these tiny larvae or the entire nymph cases.

Caddis nymphs are vulnerable to predation when they begin moving to the surface of the water to hatch into the adult version of the bug. Trout feed on the nymphs swimming to the surface, on the emergers shucking their shells as they float in the surface film, and on the adults trying to take off from the surface.

A number of nymph-pattern flies will take trout from tailwater streams when the fish are feeding on caddis. In this type of fishing, exactly matching the food source seems to be unimportant. Just getting close in size ordinarily does the trick. Gold-Ribbed Hare's Ears or Tellico Nymphs in sizes 12 to 20 have produced fish from nearly all of the South's tailwaters when the fish were keying on immature caddis.

Once the caddis reach the surface, both the size and the color of the flies become more important. Often trout will ignore any size or color fly that does not match the size or color of what they are feeding on at the moment. Elk Hair Caddis and Chuck Caddis patterns tied in a number of sizes and colors are good choices for this fishing.

The second broad category of aquatic insects of importance is mayflies of the order Ephemeroptera. Suffice it to say that these bugs, which have an adult life span of little more than a day, are about as widespread and abundant as caddis flies in the region. The easiest way to differentiate mayfly from caddis adults is to look at their wings. Mayflies have wings that stand upright, unlike the caddis's wings, which lie on its back.

While in the nymph stage, mayflies come in four distinct varieties. Some are free-ranging, swimming as they feed. Others are usually found crawling on the undersides of rocks on the streambed. Still others spend their time clinging to the tops of the rocks on the river bottom. Finally, some are burrowers, making their nymphal home in the mud and silt of slow-water areas. Since they are not glued to the bottom like some caddis nymphs, they are more likely to be available to the fish while in this stage of their life cycle. This is especially true of the free-swimming and clinging varieties.

As with caddis flies, mayflies are vulnerable to trout when hatching. As nymphs swimming to the surface, as emergers, and as adults, they present appetizing targets. In size they also resemble the caddis, so hooks in the size 12 to 16 range are in order. Standard flies to match the mayfly nymphs are the popular Hare's Ear and the Pheasant Tail.

Adult mayflies come in a wide variety of colors, so matching the hue of the bugs the trout are feeding on is again important. Patterns that work well at times are the Light Cahill, the Adams (regular and female), and the Hendricksons.

Although quite tiny in size, midges (order Diptera) are a more important food source for trout in tailwaters than they are in smaller streams. These minute insects favor slow currents and slick surfaces, as opposed to rough-and-tumble shoal water. Trout often feed on them in the spring through fall, as well as on warm winter days.

Describing the shape of midges is pretty much an exercise in futility, since they usually appear as just swarms of specks on or over the water. While true midges are of the family Chironomidae, most anglers refer to any extremely small flies as "midges." In fact, tiny dry flies that imitate mayflies, such as the Adams, Light Cahill, or Blue-Winged Olive in hook sizes 18 down to 22, are often the choice of anglers casting to midge hatches; the Griffith's Gnat and Olive Midge are also popular. Many times, more than one of these flies will catch fish during a single hatch, since fly color seems to mean less than size when it comes to midge fishing.

Next among the insects important as trout food is the order Plecoptera—the stone flies. While several hundred species of these bugs have been identified in southern tailwaters, their life cycle makes them a bit less vulnerable to the fish than the insects I mentioned above. But since they tend to be larger morsels, the trout are attracted to them when they are available.

During the nymphal stage, stone flies are bottom-dwellers, crawling on and under the rocks on the streambed. Fish will grab them when they are on exposed surfaces, or when they are dislodged and floating in the current. Eventually the nymphs climb out onto rocks or sticks above the surface to hatch into adults. Their drying nymphal cases are often found sticking to rocks or driftwood along the shore during these periods. Because the nymphs do not swim to the surface, they are more difficult for trout to catch at this stage. Still, flies such as the Ted's Stonefly or Montana Nymph can attract the attention of feeding fish. Larger hooks in sizes 6 to 10 are called for when tying stone fly nymph patterns.

When the adult stone flies have hatched and are laying eggs on the water's surface, their large size will attract trout. The fish attack these insects with great gusto, often creating noisy, violent rises. These hatches usually occur in rocky shoal areas, since the stone fly inhabits areas of the stream that have moving currents and are well oxygenated.

The key to catching trout feeding on stone fly adults is to put a big fly on the water. Elk Hair Caddis and Royal Trudes are two choices; the size should be 6 to 12. Speaking frankly, however, such surface action for stone flies is a rarely encountered novelty on southern tailwaters.

Terrestrial insects are another common item on the tailwater trout's menu. These are land-dwelling or flying insects that spend no part of their life cycle in the water. It is simply bad luck that finds them falling or being blown into the rivers. Once there, they become fair game for the hungry trout.

Grasshoppers, beetles, and ants (both crawling and flying) comprise the bulk of this category. Hoppers can provoke splashy surface action during the summer, as can Japanese beetles on some waters. There are a number of popular grasshopper-pattern flies—any of which is a good choice when the fish are explosively rising to the critters—as well as Japanese beetle imitations. Size 10 or 12 is about right for either of these. Good all-around choices to imitate other types of beetles are the Humpy and Goofus Bug series of flies. These are tied in a variety of colors; sizes 12 to 14 are good.

However, the most dependable of the terrestrials is the common ant. It is almost impossible to find a trout that does not have ants in its stomach if these insects are present. Red and black are the standard colors and sizes 16 down to 22 are preferable.

Another category of trout appetizers found in tailwater streams is crustaceans. These include crayfish ("crawfish" or "crawdads" to southerners), cress bugs, scuds, sow bugs, and freshwater shrimp. Of these, the crawfish, scuds, and sow bugs are most important to tailwater anglers.

The scud is the most plentiful regionwide. These tiny, hard-shelled relatives of the shrimp often thrive in water that has some aquatic vegetation. Where they are present, they are generally quite small. Dead-drifting flies in sizes 18 to 22 under a strike indicator is the standard tactic when the trout are keying on scuds.

Sow bugs tend to be similar to scuds in the eastern part of the region, but larger and more important in the western. Anglers headed to the rivers of Arkansas are advised to stock their fly boxes with some sow bug imitators in sizes 12 to 16.

Although crawfish are eaten by trout, and spin-fishers take the fish on crawfish imitations, the critters go largely ignored by fly-casters. Working a weighted crawfish pattern along rocky bottoms will improve the chances of tangling with the larger trout present.

Another form of trout food worth mentioning with regard to fly-fishing is worms. In this case, "garden hackle" or common earthworms are not the topic. Rather, at certain times inchworms fall into the rivers in large numbers; some flows are inhabited by aquatic red worms as well. A light green worm pattern in hook size 12 or 14 works well when inchworms are present, while the San Juan Worms in the same sizes are good patterns to imitate the aquatic worms.

The final denizens of the tailwaters to be mentioned that trout use for food are minnows. As explained earlier, besides healthy swimming minnows, the area just below the tailrace of the rivers is sometimes littered with injured ones that were sucked through the turbines. Casting streamers such as the Woolly Bugger, Muddler Minnow, or Matuka in sizes that approximate the baitfish's length can produce some big trout.

BAIT-FISHING

For the bait-fisher, the baits that prove productive on tailwaters are the same as those that serve in mountain streams across the region. Crickets, earthworms, and salmon eggs adorn the hooks of those inclined to use natural baits, while cheese concoctions and kernel corn are also popular. The bulk of tailwater bank-fishers use bait, but bait-anglers will also take to the water in boats. For whatever reason, bait-fishers rarely wade in tailwater rivers.

SPIN-FISHING

Spin-fishers who prefer to toss artificial lures at the trout often employ in-line spinners, such as those produced by Blue Fox, Mepps,

Panther Martin, and Rooster Tail. These all have a spinning blade up front, followed by a weighted metal body, then by either a single or a treble hook. The hook may or may not be covered by a hair skirt. In-line spinners come in a wide variety of color schemes and body shapes, and have long been staples in the tackle boxes of southern anglers, regardless of the size or type of water they tackle. The lures range in weight from ⅟₃₂ ounce up to 2 ounces. Tailwater anglers are more likely to use ½-ounce-or-larger sizes, which are rarely employed by small-stream fishers in this region.

Two more types of artificial offerings that spin-fishers present to tailwater trout are the crankbaits and jerkbaits ordinarily used for bass fishing. The crankbaits may be ultralight versions—often as small as ⅟₁₀ ounce—of the original lure patterns. On the other hand, some fishers cast the originals—bass-sized models of up to ½ ounce. Either way, crankbaits imitate baitfish or crawfish, and are retrieved with a steady "cranking" of the reel handle.

Jerkbaits float on the water's surface and get their name from the fact that they are twitched or "jerked" to simulate injured baitfish struggling to swim. In tailwaters, jerkbaits have proven very effective when fished around shoreline logjams and brush piles, or in the tailrace just below the turbine outlets. They usually account for the magnum-sized trout taken in the larger rivers.

Spin-fishers are just as likely to wade the river as to fish from a boat or float ring. It is not unusual to encounter such anglers even casting from the shore.

The rods and reels used to present baits or lures range from ultralight models on up to heavy bait-casting rigs. This variety results in part from the differences in weight of the lures being cast, but also from individual anglers' preferences. The only requirement is that the gear be suitable to get the chosen lure out to where the fish are.

2
Tackling Tailwaters

Trout fishing traditionally has been thought of as a sport practiced afoot. In Europe, where it began, it was thought of as a shorebound endeavor as well. Even today, it is considered bad form to wade into the water on English chalk streams. While some angling from boats was practiced on lakes, the flowing waters were the bank-fisher's territory.

As with many other customs, however, we Americans took a more tolerant view. From the first days of pursuing trout on this continent, anglers used whatever means were needed to get to the fish. Very early on, trout fishers were wading streams as well as fishing from the shore, and they took to the water to float-fish from boats when necessary.

This utilitarian approach to angling has carried over nicely to modern-day tailwater trout fishing in the Southeast. In fact, one is hard-pressed to make a definitive statement on which of the three methods—bank-fishing, wading, or floating—is most prevalent in the region. On an individual stream there may be a clear winner, but in total the distinction would be difficult.

REACHING THE FISH

Fishing from shore has been popular since the gates were closed on the first hydroelectric dam in Dixie. This is particularly true among bait-fishers. Shore-fishing was a natural carryover from river-fishing for warm-water species or from pursuing trout in smaller streams of the mountains.

Much of the early bank-fishing with bait was concentrated in the tailrace area, where concrete fishing platforms are located. Another factor was that trout were generally stocked at the foot of the dams. There was almost always roadside access to the water at these points, allowing the hatchery trucks to deposit their fish easily. Naturally,

*Whether you call it a float ring, a belly boat, or a float tube,
it is an ideal craft from which to fish southern tailwaters.*

where the fish are known to be is where the anglers congregated.

Of course, in the ensuing years, anywhere that permitted shore-bound anglers easy access to the tailwater became a popular fishing hole. Some spin-fishers tossing artificial lures from shore also practiced their art at these access points, but the need for mobility in order to cover more water limited this type of bank-fishing. Repetitive casting of a lure into a single area lacked appeal for these fishers, as well as rarely being very productive.

The next progression was taking to the water in boats. This step was taken by both bait-anglers and spin-fishers. The use of smaller, flat-bottomed johnboats came first, but as better access to the water in the form of gravel or paved boat ramps evolved, anglers used larger boats where practical. Again, this fishing was at first concentrated around the dam tailraces, giving the anglers better access to the water they were already fishing. Later, it developed into float-fishing from one access point to another.

Eventually, johnboats were joined on the tailwaters by canoes, V-hulled crafts, and inflatable rafts. Particularly in cases of rafts and canoes, anglers traveled farther and farther downstream. Both of these crafts made good vehicles for float-fishing from access point to access point.

More recently, float tubes have shown up in increasing numbers on the South's deeper tailwater rivers. These devices, which were originally adapted from automobile inner tubes, have now become quite sophisticated. Today's float ring comes complete with a fabric seat inside the tube, suspenders to raise it out of the water when wading shallow areas, a variety of zippered or Velcro-closure pockets, and fins that fit onto the feet for locomotion through the water. The modern float tube allows anglers—regardless of their preferred fishing method—to cover the whole river conveniently and with limited expense.

Another innovation seen more often on southern rivers is the use of MacKenzie drift boats by some guide services. These river dories, pointed at both ends, have belatedly made their way from western and Pacific waters to our eastern tailwaters. Such crafts, in the hands of skilled oarsmen, are more maneuverable than johnboats and more stable than canoes, making them ideal for fishing. Since drift boats do, however, require one person always to be at the oars, they have always been more of a guide's boat. Now that tailwater fishing guides are more common on southern waters, the MacKenzie boat has appeared as well.

The final method used in fishing tailwaters in the South is wading into shoals. While this has always been common for fishing smaller streams, it is relatively new to tailwaters. It is also limited on many such flows due to their lack of shallow shoals. On other streams, however—particularly at low water levels—virtually the whole river is conducive to this type of approach. In the case of several area rivers it is also possible to find some wadable areas even at higher water levels.

Wading has always been more popular with spin- and fly-casters than with bait-anglers. Still, one major drawback has been that shore access is needed to get into the water. Most tailwater rivers are considered navigable and are, therefore, open to unrestricted boating and floating. Land along the shore that is in private hands may be posted, however, preventing easy access. This is, unfortunately, an all-too-common problem on these waters.

TAILWATER SAFETY

The single greatest safety concern on tailwater rivers is the water surge that occurs during power generation at the dam. While this is the major distinguishing characteristic of this type of trout water, it is also the major threat to life and limb for the anglers utilizing these fisheries.

On some of the region's smaller tailwaters, such releases may raise the water only a couple of feet, while streams like Arkansas's White River, Kentucky's Cumberland, and Georgia's Chattahoochee can rise by as much as 6 to 8 feet very quickly. Even a 2-foot rise, however, is enough to be life-threatening.

On most tailwaters, fishing activity is virtually nil during high-water periods. These streams have a tendency to turn into violent torrents of muddy water, making angling difficult—if not impossible. As with any rule, however, there are exceptions. The White and Cumberland Rivers mentioned earlier, as well as the Nantahala in North Carolina, are noted for providing fishing opportunities at all water levels.

Probably the most dangerous aspect of water releases on tailwaters is their unpredictability. One of the major purposes of most reservoirs is the generation of electric power. During the spring and summer in the Southeast, a driving force of power demands is the use of air conditioners. The resulting peak demands tend to fall during the time of the year when interest in fishing these waters is also at its height.

Although efforts are made to establish water-release schedules and to make them public, if power demands require additional hours of

Many tailwater rivers are large enough that you can fish for trout by boat.

generation, unscheduled water surges do occur. This, of course, creates very dangerous conditions for the unwary wader or boater downstream. All dams have published phone numbers that provide recordings of the scheduled power-generation hours. These also include a disclaimer stating that the plans are tentative, and unscheduled releases are possible.

Other safety precautions include powerhouse sirens, which are sounded several minutes prior to the opening of the turbine gates. These are usually powerful enough to be heard several hundred yards downstream. Needless to say, when they do sound, any sane bank- or wade-angler heads for the high-water mark. Boaters also need either to get off the flow or to be prepared for the rapidly rising water.

In some instances, low-power radio transmitters have been used at the dams to broadcast release schedules, including any sudden changes of plans. Signs are posted along the river instructing visitors to tune their radios to a specific AM setting to hear the recorded messages. While these broadcasts can be received up to several miles down the river, few anglers tend to take a radio on the water with them. For this reason, such broadcasts have not been particularly effective.

Naturally, the area of most serious concern on any tailwater is the portion of the river immediately below the dam. From the tailrace to a couple hundred yards downstream, the surge is violent and immediate when water is released. Some special rules thus apply to fishing these areas.

A number of the streams forbid wading or even fishing from the shore below the high-water mark within a safety zone immediately downstream of the dams. Also, boaters on the water in the tailrace area are mandated to wear Coast Guard–approved life jackets at all times. In some instances, such as on the Savannah River below Hartwell Lake on the Georgia–South Carolina border, the safety zone is completely closed to wading and boating.

The best rule of thumb for fishing tailrace areas on any river is to find out what regulations apply and follow all of them to the letter, while remaining aware of your surroundings. There is always the chance that you will not hear the siren announcing an imminent release. Anytime, however, that you see other anglers scurrying for shore, it is wise to follow them. It could be that they are just in a hurry to get ashore for a snack or cold drink; but they may have heard something you did not. Tailrace areas are great places to err on the side of caution!

Due to the fact that most anglers are so aware of the potential for

Fast-rising water is a safety concern on all southern tailwaters.

trouble near dams, these areas actually end up being responsible for fewer problems than portions of the river farther downstream. On most flows, it is the part of the stream a couple miles downriver that accounts for most rescue situations or drownings. In these areas, dam sirens are out of anglers' hearing range, so water releases can take them by surprise.

The best defense against trouble here is to always pay attention to the water level. Since a surge has to travel several miles from the dam, the water will not rise instantly. By mentally marking the water level on a rock, log, or other feature on shore and monitoring it constantly while fishing, it can be seen when the level begins to rise and anglers will have several minutes to get to shore. It is lack of attention or procrastination that leads to life-threatening situations.

It is impossible to put too much emphasis on the fact that anglers should obey all the posted or published safety rules applying to the various rivers. These are not designed simply as nuisances or to rain on one's parade. People have lost their lives on tailwater rivers because of foolhardiness or just bad luck. The regulations were developed to make fishing these waters safe!

One other safety concern on tailwaters is water temperature. On the bulk of these waters, year-round temperatures are in the 45- to

60-degree range. These levels are conducive to hypothermia for the individual exposed to them for very long. If an unexpected dunking occurs while boating or wading, get out of the water as quickly as possible and take appropriate measures to restore body heat immediately. One of the dangers of hypothermia is that a person suffering from it can become disoriented and often be incapable of helping him- or herself. Thus it is always wise to have a fishing buddy along to offer aid in the event of trouble.

One final bit of safety technology is worth mentioning in regard to wading tailwaters. A number of manufacturers now have on the market either fishing vests or wader suspenders that have built-in flotation devices. These use a carbon dioxide cartridge to inflate built-in compartments by pulling an activation ring. Although such devices are not Coast Guard approved as personal flotation devices, they do add a margin of safety for the wade-angler. In the event that you get caught in rising water, or simply wade into a deep hole, the price of this additional equipment can seem very reasonable.

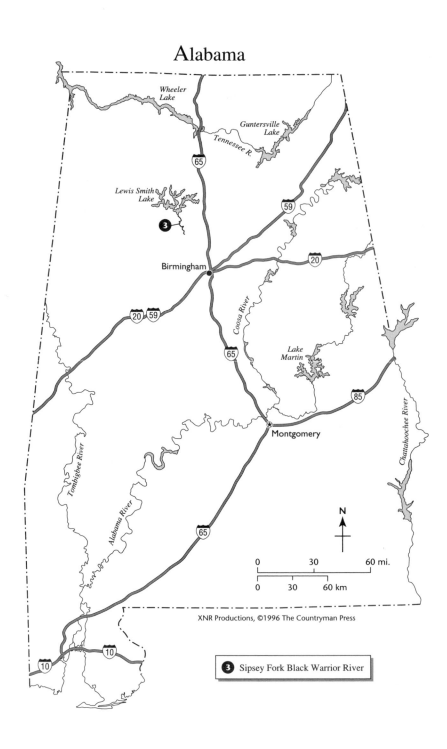

Alabama

Wheeler Lake

Guntersville Lake

Tennessee R.

65

Lewis Smith Lake

59

3

20

Birmingham

20 59

Coosa River

65

Lake Martin

85

Montgomery

Chattahoochee River

Tombigbee River

Alabama River

65

N

0   30   60 mi.

0   30   60 km

65

10   10

XNR Productions, ©1996 The Countryman Press

3 Sipsey Fork Black Warrior River

SECTION ONE

ALABAMA

When discussing trout water, there are few places in the United States less likely to pop into most folks' heads than the state of Alabama. Nestled between Mississippi on the west and Georgia to the east, this state stretches from the Gulf of Mexico to just north of the Tennessee River valley. The bulk of the land in the southern and central portions of Alabama is on the coastal plain. It then fades into the southernmost foothills of the Blue Ridge mountain chain in the northern edge of the state. Alabama is known as the Cotton State for its close association with that agricultural commodity, which was once king in Dixie. It is, however, not a plant that is synonymous with trout country.

Alabama had no natural trout populations within its borders when the first Europeans entered the area. Indeed, the highlands in the northeastern corner of the state are composed of sandstone ridges separated by limestone valleys, which make for poor cool-water habitat, particularly at the Cotton State's latitude.

Alabama's fisheries managers have experimented with introducing trout to the state—with mixed results. Some seasonal trout fishing exists in Madison County Lake, a state-operated pond north of Huntsville, as well as in the streams of Tannehill State Park near Birmingham. The former is a fall and winter fishery; Tannehill offers strictly spring put-and-take fishing.

On the other hand, attempts to establish brown trout in the streams of the Talladega National Forest in the northeast of the state proved unsuccessful. One oddity is that Alabama's state record for rainbow trout (there is no official record for any other species of trout) was caught in Weiss Lake, a Coosa River impoundment that straddles the Georgia border. The 7-pound, 2-ounce fish was caught by a crappie fisherman in 1991 and is reportedly the only trout ever taken from the lake. It undoubtedly found its way downstream from a stocking done on a fork of the Little River in northwestern Georgia.

On a more positive note, a successful and growing trout fishery has been established on the tailwaters of the Sipsey Fork of the Black Warrior River below Lewis Smith Lake in the hill country of northwestern Alabama. This is also the only tailwater trout stream found in the Cotton State.

To fish for trout in Alabama requires only a regular resident or nonresident fishing license. There is no closed season for trout fishing in Alabama; the creel limit is 5 fish per day, regardless of species of trout. No minimum or maximum size limits apply to trout taken from tailwaters in the Cotton State.

3
Sipsey Fork Black Warrior River

USGS Cold Springs

Located in the northwest portion of the state near the town of Jasper, the Sipsey Fork of the Black Warrior River is Alabama's only tailwater trout fishery. The tailwater begins at the base of the dam at 21,200-acre Lewis Smith Lake, and flows in a southeasterly direction for about 15 miles before dumping into the Mulberry Fork of the Black Warrior River. Along this course the river forms the border between Cullman and Walker Counties. The dam and powerhouse at the lake are operated by the Alabama Power Company.

With no real competition, the Sipsey tailwater is the Cotton State's premier trout water. For a number of years this would have been a misleading statement, indicating simply that the Sipsey was the *only* site of regular put-and-take stocking in Alabama. Fortunately, new meaning has been attached to the claim in recent years due to the efforts of the Birmingham Fly Fishing Club. By bringing pressure on Alabama Power to improve the fishery below Lewis Smith, as well as rolling up their collective sleeves and pitching in on manual labor, the local angling club has made this tailwater a promising resource.

The Sipsey Fork begins as a warm-water flow. When it exits Lewis Smith Lake it is a 50- to 60-foot-wide river, carrying waters from the bottom of the reservoir that are well within the temperature range needed by trout. The first rainbows were stocked in the river back in the early 1960s, but the fishing was lackluster then. Any carryover of fish from year to year appeared to be minimal, and—particularly in the upper stretch of water near the dam—the river was quite infertile. Very little food was present for the fish even if they did manage to avoid anglers' hooks. This lack of aquatic insect life continues to plague the area immediately below the dam.

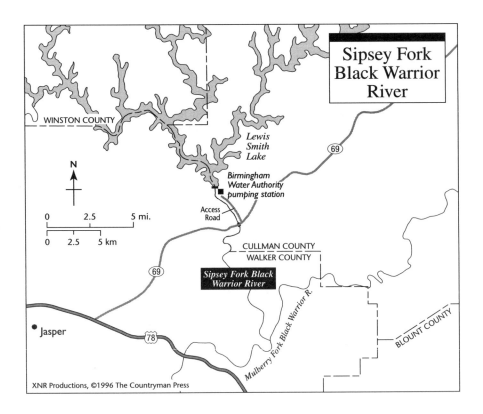

Turning over rocks on the streambed through here will reveal virtu-ally no bug life.

From the dam downstream to the Birmingham Water Authority pumping station on the eastern shore, the river is very shallow, crys-tal clear, and extremely cold during low-water periods. This roughly ½-mile stretch is quite popular with anglers, since it is almost all wadable. Below this point the river broadens to about 70 or 80 feet, and becomes deeper as well. This lower portion appears more suited to floating in a canoe or float ring, but a gravel-and-mud shelf ex-tends out from the accessible east bank. This shelf allows anglers to get out to the main channel during low water, providing limited ac-cess for wading much of this area. When water releases are taking place, the river is virtually unfishable.

Today the tailwaters of the Sipsey are stocked with up to 40,000 catchable-sized rainbow trout annually. These fish come from the US Fish and Wildlife Service hatchery at Dale Hollow in Tennessee, since Alabama's Department of Conservation and Natural Resources has no trout-hatching or -rearing facilities. These fish are most common in the river for about 6 miles downstream from the dam. They have, however, turned up as far downstream as the Tuscaloosa area on the Black Warrior River. Nearly all of the fish here are recent stockers of 8 to 12 inches, but a rare holdover fish can be found in the downstream areas that will go 20 inches.

Some promising experimentation is under way on the Sipsey tailwater to add variety to the trout fishery and the insect life that supports it. Again, this is a result of efforts of the local angling community. Elizabeth and John Eisenbarth are active members of the Birmingham Fly Fishing Club, as well as the owners of Riverside Fly & Tackle. Their shop is located on AL 69 on the Sipsey Fork and has been the site of efforts to introduce brown trout eggs to the river, thus adding a dimension of wild trout to the stream. By the spring of 1995, browns in the 8-inch range were being reported in the tailwater—fruits of the first plantings of eggs.

In conjunction with this effort, some new forage for the fish is being transplanted to the river. Sow bugs taken from the Elk River in Tennessee have been moved to the Sipsey. It is hoped that these small crustaceans will provide more nutrition for the browns and give them the opportunity to thrive in this otherwise fairly barren habitat. At present, the jury is still out on the ultimate success of both of these efforts.

In the meantime, the most dependable source of insect life for the trout continues to be the midge hatches that are common year-round in the deeper downstream areas of the river. When fishing these hatches, matching the size of the insects with very tiny flies seems to be more important than color on most days.

Nearer the dam, a streamer known locally as a Big-Eye (a Woolly Bugger pattern tied with bead eyes) is reported to work well, with green being a favorite color to take the stocked rainbows.

Access to the tailwater below Lewis Smith Lake begins with a catwalk above the tailrace at the foot of the dam. This concrete fishing platform can be reached on the west side of the dam via Smith Lake Dam Road. It is located high above the water level and is only practical for use by bait-fishers. Even if you could get down to the water here, it would be an extremely dangerous place to be during power generation.

The next downstream access is at the Birmingham Water Authority facility on the east shore. A paved road runs north along the

Low water and morning mists make the Sipsey Fork of the
Warrior River an ideal stream for fly-fishing.

Cullman County side of the stream. There is presently no sign at the intersection identifying the road, but it begins at the east end of the AL 69 bridge over the river. This road dead-ends at the pump station, where parking and easy entry to the river are available. Although a dirt path continues upstream of the pumping station as an extension of the road, it is easier during fishable water levels to simply walk upstream on the rocky shore. Although all of this water up to the tailrace is shallow enough for wading, this is also the area of greatest concern during releases; the water level rises quickly. Listen for the warning siren when fishing here.

Between the pumping station and AL 69 there are three other points of river access at dirt spurs off the paved road. All are obvious from the road and provide a couple of parking spots, plus a trail down to the water. This is along the portion of the stream with the shelf that extends out from the shore.

The Alabama Power Company provides a toll-free number that gives the tentative release schedules for all of its dams in the state, including the one at Smith Lake. To use this service, you must have a touch-tone phone. One unique feature of the recordings is that they generally cover a 3-day period, rather than the single-day information given for many other tailwaters in the region. The number to call is 1-800-525-3711.

Arkansas

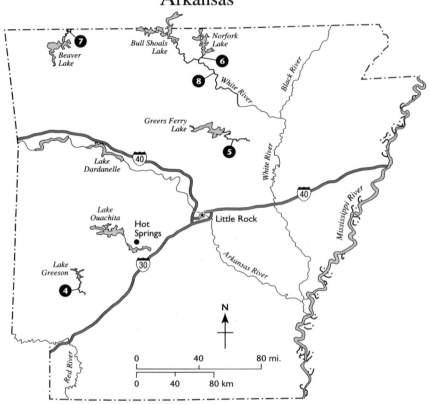

XNR Productions, ©1996 The Countryman Press

4 Little Missouri River
5 Little Red River
6 North Fork River
7 White River—Beaver Tailwater
8 White River—Bull Shoals Tailwater

SECTION TWO

ARKANSAS

Of all the states covered in this book, Arkansas is the best testament to the angling variety, quantity, and quality that can be achieved in tailwater trout fisheries. The Natural State historically had no native trout populations, yet today the Ozark Mountain region in the north-western part of the state has arguably the best cold-water fisheries in the world. The two most recent all-tackle world-record brown trout were caught in Arkansas, and the number of magnum-sized trout taken from the state's rivers each year is astounding. Oddly enough, this situation came about more as an "apology" than as any planned program.

The story of trout fishing in Arkansas can properly be traced to 1898, when the first of several major floods struck the White River drainage. From then until 1927, the valuable farmlands along this river system were inundated a total of four times. The desire to con-trol these natural disasters lay at the heart of the Flood Control Act of 1938, which was pushed through Congress by the Roosevelt ad-ministration. The fact that the resulting dam construction would employ a large number of Ozark folks during these Depression years was another selling point of the plan.

An unforeseen consequence of the dam-building projects, which began in earnest in 1941, was the eventual destruction of a world-class smallmouth bass fishery. The White River and its feeder streams had for years been noted for the quality of the fishing available for this species, and had drawn anglers from around the country. A tra-dition of float-fishing was long-established in the area, and some of the local families had been guiding anglers on the rivers for several decades.

Once the dams began to come on-line, the cold water released into the river system from the depths of the lakes made the habitat too cold for smallmouths; the fishery soon collapsed. Beginning in 1948, the Arkansas Game and Fish Commission (AGFC) released small numbers of brown trout into the tailwaters below Norfork Dam on the North Fork (or Norfork) River. This was followed by larger plantings of browns and rainbows in the Bull Shoals tailwater on the White River in 1952. Additionally, the AGFC transplanted aquatic vegetation from Ozark springs into the Norfork River during the early 1950s.

All of these plantings proved very successful, prompting the US Fish and Wildlife Service to get into the act in 1955. That year, Congress authorized the construction of the Norfork National Fish Hatchery as compensation for the loss of the smallmouth bass fishery in the region. By the late 1950s, the White River system was already becoming renowned for producing trout weighing in double digits, and many of the smallmouth bass guides of the Ozarks switched over to guiding these newcomers on the rivers.

Today, the White River system in the Ozark Mountains provides the bulk of Arkansas's trout fishing. Beginning at the foot of the Beaver Dam, the White River's trout water runs through a short stretch of Missouri below Table Rock Lake before reentering Arkansas. It then passes through the dam at Bull Shoals Lake and continues southeasterly. Along this route it picks up the cold flows of two tributary rivers that have trout-bearing tailwaters: the North Fork and the Little Red River. All told, the White River system contains 168 miles of trout-supporting tailwaters. All but 22 of those miles are located in Arkansas.

While the White River basin gets most of the publicity, the Natural State has experimented with trout in other areas as well. A number of free-flowing streams, most notably the Spring River, have been stocked and are now quality trout waters. Also, the establishment of two other tailwater fisheries has been attempted in southwestern Arkansas. The one on the Little Missouri River has produced some interesting fishing results and continues to be managed for trout. On the other hand, the tailwaters on the Ouachita River have been a failure.

For a number of years, the waters on the Ouachita below the Remmel Dam at Lake Catherine in Garland County were stocked with trout during the winter months. It was hoped that a fishery for the species could be developed for at least a portion of the year along this stream in the vicinity of the town of Hot Springs. The results, however, were never very successful, and in the early 1990s stocking was discontinued. Presently, there are no trout planted in the Ouachita River.

Unlike the tailwaters of some of the other southern states, Arkansas's rivers tend to run clear and cold, whether or not the hydroelectric generators at the dams are in operation. As a result, local anglers have developed tactics for fishing these rivers at all water levels. These tactics are discussed in later chapters.

The fish these anglers target are a bit different from those in other Dixie tailwaters as well. While browns and rainbows constitute the backbone of the trout fishing, brook trout are also stocked. Additionally, some of Arkansas's tailwaters have received plantings of cutthroat trout, which have also thrived.

To fish for trout in Arkansas both a regular fishing license and a trout permit are required. The only exceptions to this rule are for persons under 16 years of age or holders of lifetime fishing licenses. Anglers under 16 do not need either the license or the trout permit, while lifetime license holders are not required to have a trout permit.

The trout permit is required in order to *keep* trout caught from any waters in the Natural State, but is mandatory simply to fish in the tailwaters of the White River below Beaver or Bull Shoals Dams, as well as the tailwaters of the Norfork and Little Red Rivers.

Fishing licenses and trout permits can be purchased from many sporting goods stores, discount chain stores, bait shops, or trout docks throughout Arkansas, as is normal in most states. Additionally, in Arkansas it is possible to purchase the license and permit by phone using a MasterCard or Visa. Have your credit card and driver's license numbers ready and simply call 1-800-364-GAME (1-800-364-4263). Upon placing the order, a confirmation number is issued and fishing privileges begin immediately. The actual license and permit will arrive a few days later by mail.

An individual can use no more than two rods to fish for trout in Arkansas, and these must be attended at all times. The creel limit for trout is 6 per day in any combination of brook, brown, cutthroat, and rainbow. No more than 2 of that number may be brown trout, nor can more than 2 be cutthroats. There is no minimum size for brook or rainbow trout, but browns and cutthroats must be 16 inches long to be harvested. There are exceptions to these regulations in effect on some of the tailwaters; these are covered in the individual stream descriptions.

One other regulation unique to Arkansas merits mention. It is illegal to drive, harass, rally, or pursue trout with noise, objects, or boats, or by wading, to concentrate or congregate them. The wording of this rule was prompted by some anglers' discovery that large trout could be driven into pods in the clear tailwaters. These fish would become excited and were susceptible to either baited hooks or illegal snagging. The regulation was enacted to put an end to this practice and to make the policing of it easier on the rivers.

4

Little Missouri River

USGS Narrows Dam, Murfreesboro • FIA 107

There are a couple of circumstances that set the Little Missouri River apart from the other tailwater trout fisheries of Arkansas. The first of these is its location. The Little Missouri is the only trout-stocked tailwater in the Natural State that is not located in the Ozark Mountain region.

The Little Missouri River rises in the Ouachita National Forest of southwestern Arkansas. Descending from the Caddo Mountains in Montgomery County, the upper portion of the river above Lake Greeson is a small, free-flowing stream that is stocked with rainbow trout in the winter months, especially around the forest service's Albert Pike Campground. After the river crosses into Pike County, running into and emerging from Lake Greeson, it is a larger stream, but still rates as only moderate in size when compared to Arkansas's other tailwater rivers.

The second of the factors making the Little Missouri tailwater an oddity is that the stream is stocked with trout only from November through early April each year. Due to its southerly location, and the relatively small size of Lake Greeson, the releases of water from the Narrows Dam do not maintain water temperatures low enough for trout during the summer and early fall. During the summer, virtually no trout are present. This lack of carryover fish makes the Little Missouri a put-and-take fishery.

The history of the Little Missouri tailwaters closely parallels that of Ozark rivers in that it was a noted smallmouth bass stream prior to the building of the Narrows Dam in the early 1950s. When it was realized that the dam had adversely impacted that fishery, the AGFC first tried restocking smallmouths. This proved impractical because the water temperatures in winter and spring were too low to support these fish. Next, year-round stocking of rainbow trout was attempted.

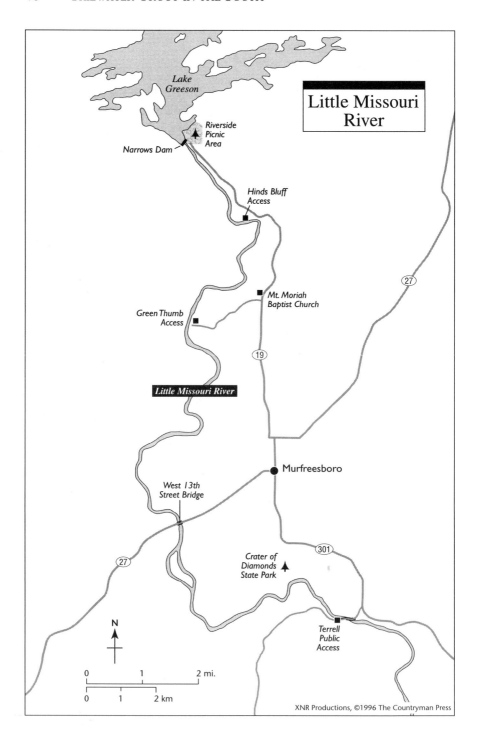

Little Missouri River

XNR Productions, ©1996 The Countryman Press

This also did not work out, because summer and fall water temperatures could soar to over 75 degrees when no generation was taking place at the Narrows Dam. Finally, the present program of a winter-through-spring trout fishery was accepted as the only practical alternative.

In 1992, the US Army Corps of Engineers and the AGFC cooperated on a plan that made structural changes in the Narrows Dam to improve the amount of dissolved oxygen in the water released into the river. Additionally, boulders and several rock weirs were placed in the riverbed to create more turbulence, which also aids in improving the dissolved oxygen levels.

All of the trout stocked in the Little Missouri below the Narrows Dam are rainbows. Fish of 12 to 14 inches in length are most often planted, but some trout of up to 2 pounds are also released periodically. On this tailwater, most of the angling pressure comes from bait-fishers using corn and wax worms. In-line spinners and small spoons are the choices of spin-casters, but heavier marabou jigs or small diving crankbaits are called for during higher water levels. Fly-fishers are most often found on the river during low water levels; at these times, much of the river is wadable. Many of the anglers taking advantage of the trout fishing on the Little Missouri are from southwestern Arkansas, but this fishery also draws folks from northwestern Louisiana and northeastern Texas.

There is public access to the Little Missouri at the foot of the Narrows Dam at Lake Greeson, about 6 miles north of the town of Murfreesboro on AR 19. The Riverside Picnic Area has ¼ mile of the eastern shore within its boundaries. This park has picnic tables, a playground, and rest rooms. Although there is no boat ramp, the sloping grassy bank does permit the launching of canoes. A bridge on AR 19 crosses the river just below the power plant at the dam, but there is no fishing access here.

The river is roughly 150 feet wide through the park. There are both concrete and wooden piers that permit even handicapped anglers to fish this portion of the river. Just upstream of the piers is a shelf running out from the shore that permits some wading, even during high water.

The next downstream access is found 2½ miles south of the dam on AR 19. The Hinds Bluff Access has a parking lot and canoe launch, as well as walk-in access to the river. There is a deep run here, with a long, bending, and wadable shoal downstream.

A concrete fishing pier in the picnic area at the foot of the Narrows Dam offers access even to handicapped anglers.

At 5 miles south of the dam is an access point that, while still open to the public, appears to have been abandoned. It is located at the end of the first gravel road running west, just south of the Mt. Moriah Baptist Church on AR 19, but there is no sign to indicate its presence. The access point is 1½ miles down this road. An old, overgrown, county-owned picnic ground called Green Thumb Access is at stream-side. There is ¼ mile of access, with some possible canoe-launch sites.

Another point of access is located at the West 13th Street Bridge over the river, 1½ miles west of AR 27 in Murfreesboro. Both shores of the river can be reached at this point, which is sometimes referred to as the Old Factory Site. The parking area is on the eastern shore, and a canoe-launch site is provided. The river upstream of the bridge features a long, deep pool, then narrows considerably into a shoal under the highway crossing.

The final access to the trout water on the Little Missouri is found in a day-use-only area at the Terrell Public Access. This site is at the lower end of practical trout water on the river, and provides a parking area and boat ramp. To reach Terrell Public Access, go 3½ miles south of Murfreesboro on AR 301. Take a right at the intersection located here, onto the unmarked, paved road running west. This road crosses the river at ¼ mile; another ¼ mile beyond the bridge is a small sign reading ACCESS AREA on the right. A gravel spur leads down to the parking area and boat ramp.

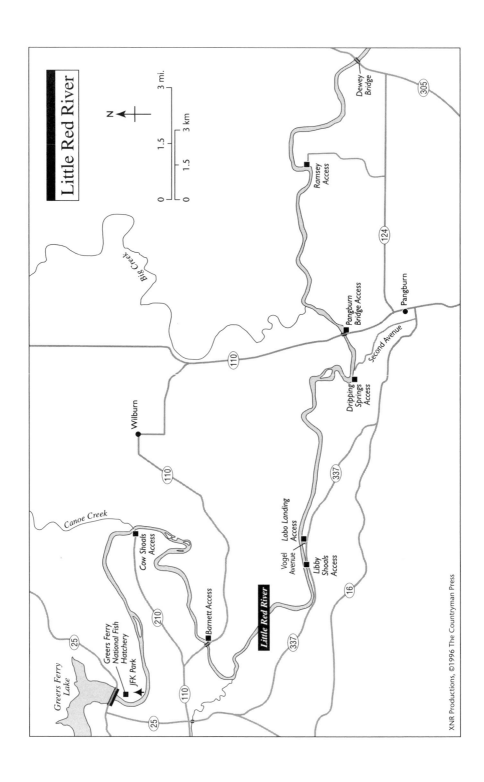

Little Red River

5

Little Red River

USGS Greers Ferry Dam, West Pangburn, Pangburn,
Step Rock • FIA 24, 142

If you want to start an argument among anglers in Arkansas these days, just try gaining a consensus on which is the best tailwater trout fishery in the Natural State. It is fairly easy to find supporters for three heavyweight contenders in this field. All can make some strong arguments in favor of their pet waters, whether they choose the Little Red, Norfork, or White River below Bull Shoals Dam. All three rivers can lay claim to producing vast numbers of trout for anglers, plus some truly gargantuan catches.

Though reputations can change quickly on all of these fantastic Arkansas waters, at the moment it would be hard to produce better credentials than those owned by the Little Red River below 31,500-acre Greers Ferry Lake. Located in Cleburne and White Counties, the Little Red is a feeder stream of the White River, but these two formidable trout streams do not join their flows until they merge at the eastern edge of White County, long after both have ceased to carry water cold enough to support trout.

Although a shorter, smaller, and less heavily stocked river than the White, the Little Red makes up in quality what it gives away in quantity. Receiving over 300,000 stocked rainbow trout each year along its 32-mile course from Greers Ferry Dam to the Dewey Bridge over AR 305, it obviously contains plenty of fish. It is the presence, however, of a wild, reproducing population of brown trout and an abundance of aquatic plant life that gives the Little Red its edge. Not only does the river yield wild browns, but they run very large. The best evidence of this is Rip Collins's May 1992 catch of the present world-record brown from this river. His fish tipped the scales at 40 pounds, 4 ounces, swiping the record previously held by a Norfork River trout.

Collins's behemoth is not the only recent brute of a brown that has been wrestled from the flow of the Little Red tailwater. Back in 1988, Melvin Hallmark hauled a 27-pound, 8-ounce brown from the river just below Greers Ferry Dam. Additionally, in August 1993, Dee Warren took a 28-pound, 14-ounce brown from the Little Red, while Ricky Hunt got in the act a week later with a 24-pound, 10-ounce catch.

While these gigantic fish are the main evidence for giving the Little Red the nod as the best tailwater fishery in the state, it is the presence of abundant moss beds that make the reputation possible. Soon after rainbow trout were first stocked in this tailwater in 1966—2 years after the completion of the Greers Ferry Dam—a program of sprigging aquatic mosses was begun in the river. Both the newly introduced fish and the plant life did well. Soon infesting these new moss beds were tiny crustaceans called sow bugs. These aquatic relatives of the land-bound "roly-poly" bugs most of us remember finding under rocks and playing with as children are present in astounding numbers in the Little Red. One study on the Little Red River at John F. Kennedy Park at the foot of Greers Ferry Dam found 500 of these critters for each square foot of area checked!

While the sow bug is found in all of the Arkansas tailwaters, it is most abundant and important in the Little Red. A major reason for this is the river's lack of sculpins and crayfish. These two forms of aquatic life are food staples of the big trout in the White and Norfork Rivers, yet absent from the Little Red. This void in the food chain is filled by the sow bug. While the sow bug is unable to swim and spends its life crawling and scavenging along the bottom, it is easily swept loose and into the river's flow by changing water levels or simply by strong, localized currents. At these times, the ¼-inch morsels become the targets of every trout in the river, regardless of the fish's size. The result is that almost every fly-caster on every Natural State tailwater has some sow bug imitations in his or her fly box.

There is another interesting facet to the Little Red's saga: The presence of brown trout in this tailwater is an unusual tale in itself. Neither the AGFC nor the US Fish and Wildlife Service has ever stocked any of these European immigrants into the flow. Rather, the browns got into the Little Red beginning in the mid-1970s due to the efforts of a couple of local fly-fishing clubs. Those introductions were done with the complete blessing of the AGFC.

In 1975, the Arkansas Fly Fishers of Little Rock placed Vibert boxes containing 10,000 eggs in Cow Shoals. These fertilized eggs were protected until they hatched, thus releasing brown trout fry to the river. In 1979 the Arkansas Fly Fishers teamed up with the Mid-South Fly Fishers club of Memphis, Tennessee, to plant an additional 5000 Montana fingerling browns in the Little Red.

The infant brown trout fishery took hold quickly and no stockings of browns have taken place in the Little Red River since 1983. The population of these wily fish has continued to grow in the ensuing years, with the trout steadily increasing the number of shoals that they use for spawning. Heavy spawning runs are recorded as beginning in mid-October each year, with peak activity occurring during the first half of November. In 1988 the two fly-fishing clubs mentioned above raised the money to purchase land adjacent to Cow Shoals on the Little Red. They then donated this property to the AGFC for use as a low-impact, walk-in access point, thus providing protection to this valuable spawning area.

Beginning in 1990, special size and creel limits for brown trout were enacted on all Arkansas tailwaters. They were patterned after rules that had been in effect on the Beaver tailwater of the White River since 1988, and were designed to enhance the brown trout fishery. The creel limit was reduced from 6 browns per day to only 2. Additionally, only brown trout of 16 inches or longer were legal to harvest.

The results of these regulations again provided proof that catch-and-release angling is a good fisheries management tool, but one that cannot successfully be applied indiscriminately. Within a couple of years the large population of browns in the Little Red became unbalanced. Samplings of the fish found that some areas of this tailwater had densities of up to 12,000 brown trout per mile, and average populations of over 6700 per mile! Of these, the vast majority were under 16 inches, indicating that most browns were being harvested soon after reaching minimum size. On the other hand, angler surveys revealed that even prior to the change of regulations, 88 percent of brown trout being caught were released. Meanwhile, the numbers of subminimum trout were exploding.

These conditions actually came as no surprise to the AGFC biologists. When the regulations had been extended to all Arkansas tailwaters in 1990, they had recommended that the Little Red be exempted. Due to the problem of enforcement, however, the rules were applied to this river as well. Now—since January 1995—the Little Red River tailwater has its own set of special regulations governing brown trout. The daily creel limit has been increased to 4 fish, only 1 of which may be larger than 21 inches. There is also a slot limit in effect, requiring anglers to release all brown trout between 16 and 21 inches. It is hoped that this new approach will get the population back in balance.

It is obvious that despite the imbalance, large trout have been in the Little Red all along. This was highlighted by Rip Collins's world-record brown taken on May 9, 1992. Collins, a longtime Little Red River angler from the nearby town of Heber Springs, ordinarily fishes the river with fly tackle, but on that fateful day was using ultralight spinning gear. He was fishing with angling buddy Van Cooper of Forrest City, who was having a better day than Collins: The tally showed Cooper with four trout to Collins's none.

Then, about a mile upriver from the Barnett Access near the Swinging Bridge Resort, Collins switched lures, tying on a ⅟₃₂-ounce olive marabou jig. Three casts later he hung something he described as feeling "like a log." When the log began to run, the world-record battle was on. Collins finally brought the fish to the boat, but neither man had thought to bring a landing net along. They flagged down a passing boat, but the anglers there only had a small, trout-sized net. The next boat flagged did have a boat net and the monster trout was brought aboard.

Collins managed to keep the record trout alive in a cage in the river until it could be taken by a US Fish and Wildlife Service hatchery truck to be weighed on a certified scales. His plan was to release the fish back into the river after documenting it. Unfortunately, the 40¼-inch female, with a girth of 28½ inches, died before the release could be made. Collins's catch has since been recognized as the all-tackle world record by both the National Fresh Water Fishing Hall of Fame and the International Game Fish Association.

Another result of that day's fishing was that a new spark of interest in the Little Red's angling was ignited in Rip Collins. He joined with other local anglers to form the Friends of the Little Red River, whose mission is to preserve and enhance the tailwater's position as one of the nation's best trophy-trout streams. With more than 500 members as of early 1994, the organization encourages the use of fiberglass replica mounts of trophy trout, thus allowing the fish to be released. By taking measurements of the fish, along with a photo or witness's account, such catches can be substantiated for creating accurate mounts without killing the larger trout. To encourage this ef-

Wading is possible at Libby Shoals even when the
Little Red River is running high.

fort, the group offers a free Live Trophy Release Kit, available at a number of trout docks on the river. For more information on the group, write to Rip Collins, Executive Director, Friends of the Little Red River, PO Box 1003, Heber Springs, AR 72543.

Despite all the attention garnered by the brown trout fishery on the Little Red, the fact remains that the bulk of the action is provided by rainbow trout, which are heavily stocked here. Each year, more than a quarter-million rainbows are released in the tailwater, which has a constant year-round temperature of 40 to 55 degrees. While most of these fish are in the 9- to 12-inch range, carryover rainbows of 5 to 12 pounds are common. Growth rates for the released rainbows of up to 1 inch per month have been documented on this tailwater, so a day of fishing here will generally yield at least a couple of fish in the 1- to 3-pound range. Back in 1968 a 15-pound, 8-ounce Little Red River rainbow taken by David Kitchens of Conway held the Arkansas state record for the species for a period of more than 2 years. There is negligible rainbow trout reproduction in the Little Red, and no minimum size limit for harvest of the species.

Another facet of the stocking program is the annual release of roughly 50,000 cutthroat trout into the flow. This program began in 1990 with the introduction of 25,000 of the 6-inch fish and has grown to its present level. Only 2 cutthroats may be creeled per day, with a minimum 16-inch size limit.

With abundant fish, the Little Red River attracts its share of Arkansas's anglers. You will rarely have a stretch entirely to yourself when fishing here, and the stream can become downright crowded on long holiday weekends. Still, with more than 30 miles of water, fishing is easily had on the tailwater, and under usual conditions there is enough elbow room for a quality experience.

The factor governing fishing conditions on the Little Red—as on any tailwater—is the volume of water being released into the river. There are two power generators at Greers Ferry Dam. When one of these is in use, the level of the river will rise 4 feet above the minimum flow, but when both are on-line the level rises from 8 to 9½ feet. During the spring and summer months, the turbines ordinarily are quiet up until about noon.

Conditions on the Little Red tailwaters are a bit different from those on the White and Norfork Rivers. This stream is, as mentioned earlier, smaller; it tends to run less clear, especially at high water levels; and, due to its more abundant vegetation, drift-fishing is less popular and a bit more difficult on the Little Red. Whereas bait-anglers tend to drift the larger rivers, fishing upstream behind the boat, on this tailwater anchoring and fishing to specific bits of in-stream cover—such as weed beds, deep holes, or downed trees—is more common. Be aware, however, that when two generators are running, anchoring in the current can be dangerous. The force of the moving water is sufficient to swamp most boats, which puts the dunked anglers at risk of hypothermia during any season of the year. Some fatalities have been recorded on the Little Red due to just this kind of situation. Despite the drawbacks of the vegetation, drift-fishing during high water is still the most practical and safest alternative.

On the other hand, during low-water periods the Little Red becomes a series of long pools separated by shallow, swift runs. Expect to find a lot of the trout concentrated near the heads of the pools where the shoals empty into deeper water. It is easy to wade many of the riffles and some of the pools during low water. The shallower waters, naturally, are particularly popular with fly-casters.

Aficionados of the long rod find the Little Red River gives up its trout to dry flies, streamers, or nymphs, depending on the season of the year and the conditions of the water. In the spring, up through the month of June, caddis fly hatches will occur on the river, since the Little Red contains both case-building and burrowing varieties of these aquatic insects. Elk Hair Caddis in standard tan hues and size 16 are popular imitations for this fishing. At times local casters add some life to these flies, rather than simply dead-drifting them on the current. Indeed, twitching or skittering the fly on the water can be effective in provoking strikes, since this imitates the action of actual adult bugs on the surface.

Beginning in June and becoming more prevalent into July and August, hatches of midge-sized blue-winged olives are frequently seen on the Little Red. The fly-fishing during this time can be tough, however. All types of food are most abundant at this season, giving the trout plenty of choices. Also, fishing pressure will be at its peak, making the fish a bit more skittish. Finally, when no water is being released from Greers Ferry, the water temperature can get warm enough to make the trout sluggish.

In the summer, midge-imitating flies fished in the surface film on extremely fine tippets (7X to 8X) are often needed to fool the trout. Hook sizes of 18 to 24 dressed in gray or olive will usually do the trick. Look for trout that are steadily rising and actually breaking the water's surface. These are usually fish taking the emergers from the film, rather than taking the adult bugs on the surface. A common mistake novice midge fishers make is to set the hook too quickly when fishing to this type of action. The tiny flies are usually quite difficult to see when floating either on the surface or in the film, so when a rise occurs in the vicinity of where you think your fly is, wait an extended count—to give the trout a chance to turn with the fly—before striking. If the hook is set as soon as the fish breaks the water, it will either just barely strike the trout in the lip or miss it altogether.

For subsurface fishing, local anglers turn to such patterns as the Squirrel Tail, Pheasant Tail, or Tellico Nymph fished beneath a strike indicator. The most common fly, however, is a sow bug imitation.

Some local experts suggest that up to 90 percent of the trout's staple diet year-round on the Little Red is made up of these crustaceans. Again, suspending a size 12 to 18 sow bug pattern beneath a strike indicator and fishing it around rocks or moss is a surefire tactic.

When the waters are on the rise in the Little Red, streamer fishing is another option. Big patterns such as the Zonker or Woolly Bugger in hook sizes up to 4 are excellent choices for taking larger brown trout. White or olive are favored colors for the flies, as is either of these hues in combination with yellow. The technique most often employed is to drift the river, casting to rocks, timber, or backwater eddies along the shore. The key is to make those casts extremely close to the bank, where the trout tend to hold. The fishing for browns is at its best during the fall and winter months.

One final fly-casting tip merits mentioning. When the brown trout are making their autumn spawning runs into the various shoals on the Little Red, an egg-pattern fly can be deadly. Rainbow trout congregate at the foot of the shoals to feed on any brown trout eggs that drift downstream and will readily take imitations.

Anglers who prefer to tackle the Little Red with spinning gear use a number of lures successfully. Mepps, Rooster Tail, Cordell, and Panther Martin in-line spinners in small sizes all attract the rainbow trout in this tailwater. The Little Cleo Spoon, the Rebel Wee Crawdad crankbait, and the No. 7 Rapala top-water minnow imitation are also favorites of many Little Red anglers.

Probably the most often used spinning lures on this river, however, are marabou jigs in sizes ranging from 1/16 ounce down to micro sizes of 1/32 to 1/64 ounce; at times, local anglers add a wax worm to the tip of the hook on these jigs to further entice the fish. (The wax worm is the larval form of the bee moth, which lays its eggs in beehives. When the eggs hatch, the larvae feed on the wax found there. The worms are off-white in color, about 1/4 inch long, and dry to the touch. They are sold at some of the trout docks along the Little Red River tailwater.) The marabou jigs are fished either on the bottom or suspended 3 to 4 feet beneath a float, although most of the largest trout taken on these lures come from bottom-fishing. Black, brown, green, yellow, and orange are all colors that produce fish on the jigs, but black and brown are the two most often used by local anglers. It is worth noting, though, that Rip Collins was using a 1/32-ounce version in olive when he boated the world-record brown.

The jigs are generally cast to the edges of weed beds or submerged structure in the river during periods of low water. If the stream is running high, drifting near the shore and casting onto the submerged weed beds is a favored tactic. Rainbow trout tend to hold close to the bank at these times, to escape the heavy current.

One other spin-fishing technique is employed on the Little Red during high water levels: Some anglers use rigs with line of up to 14-pound test and cast big "stickbait"-type bass lures. These are fished on the surface around shoreline structure in a series of jerks in the fashion used on lakes for largemouth bass. This method targets large brown trout, which show less caution when feeding during high water.

In the case of bait-fishers, corn, salmon eggs, earthworms, and wax worms are good choices. Ordinarily these are bumped along the bottom with the current, or slowly hopped along the streambed in eddy areas. Just as fly-casters use egg-pattern flies to catch rainbows below shoals where the brown trout are spawning in the fall, bait-fishers can effectively use the real salmon eggs at the same time and places. These are drifted downstream to the hungry trout waiting at the foot of the riffle areas.

Another technique employed by bait-anglers is placing a split shot or other tiny weight about 18 to 20 inches above their hook to get the rig down to the bottom. Then, a tiny marshmallow is threaded over the eye of the hook, with one of the standard baits added on the bend. The marshmallow adds enough buoyance to raise the baited hook just off the bottom and, hopefully, entice a strike from a trout.

Public access to the Little Red River tailwater is provided at eight points, plus about a half-dozen trout docks along the flow. All of these are found from Greers Ferry Dam down to Dewey Bridge on AR 305. Between these access points, float-fishing is the only way to reach the water.

At the dam, John F. Kennedy Park provides access to the river on the east side. It is interesting to note that the park received its name in honor of President Kennedy, who made his last dedication ceremony appearance at the opening of Greers Ferry Dam in October 1963, just prior to his assassination in Dallas. This park contains a campground, parking area, and boat ramp, and is the site of the Greers Ferry National Fish Hatchery. Located just off AR 25, which crosses the dam, JFK Park is the only access point on the river controlled by the Army Corps of Engineers.

Just downstream of the dam the park contains some shoal water, then a deep-water bend at the boat ramp. The west bank of this bend has some large boulders that generally hold trout, but this area is heavily hit by bait-fishers. A trail down the eastern shore leads to what is called the Power Line Pool (which obviously lies beneath a power line crossing the river). This is a favorite with fly-casters during low water. As mentioned earlier, the Little Red in JFK Park gave up a 27-pound, 8-ounce brown trout to Melvin Hallmark back in 1988.

The next public access point is downstream at Cow Shoals, which was the first site on the Little Red River where brown trout were confirmed to have spawned. It quickly acquired a reputation as a good fly-fishing destination and continues to attract long-rodders. Fishing is possible here for 1½ to 2 hours after releases at Greers Ferry Dam; then the water begins to rise.

Cow Shoals is a walk-in area. As noted earlier, it was purchased by local fly-fishing clubs and donated to the AGFC. It is located at the end of AR 210 on the west side of the river and to the east of the AR 210/AR 110 junction. A parking area is provided. The last ½ mile of AR 210 as it nears the river is gravel. Foot access to the river is easy during low-water levels, as is wading, due to a ½-mile-long gravel bar located on the western shore.

As of 1995, seasonal catch-and-release regulations are in effect from the head of Cow Shoals down to the mouth of Canoe Creek. From October 1 through December 31, only single barbless hooks with artificial lures may be used, and all fish must be immediately released unharmed. The purpose of the rules is to protect the brown trout during their fall spawning run.

Farther downstream at the AR 110 bridge is the Barnett Access. This is another of the AGFC properties and is located on the southeastern side of the river. Upstream of the highway bridge is a deep pool with a boat ramp. Under and downstream of the bridge is Winkley Shoals, which provides good wading access, but attracts a lot of anglers on weekends. Collins's world-record brown trout was taken roughly a mile upstream of this point, and Ricky Hart caught his 24-pound, 10-ounce brown in this area as well.

Water releases from the dam take 3½ to 5 hours to reach the Barnett Access.

Another walk-in access point is located at Libby Shoals, on the south side of the river, off AR 337. Through here the tailwaters flow in the shadow of Libby Bluff, which lines the north shore and is a very scenic part of the Little Red's course. It is a steep 100-yard walk from the gravel parking area at the road to the river. This is another popular fishing area, especially since it is possible to wade portions of it even during high water. It takes the rising waters 6 to 7 hours to reach this point from Greers Ferry Dam.

The next two downstream accesses are at Lobo Landing and Dripping Springs. Both of these have AGFC boat ramps and parking lots. Neither, however, offers much in the way of wading access. On the other hand, Dunham Shoals and Mossy Shoals are located between these two landings. The waters from Dunham down to Mossy are designated for catch-and-release angling. Only artificial lures with single barbless hooks are legal, and all fish must be released. These restrictions are enforced at all times of the year. Float trips from Lobo Landing down to Dripping Springs are popular with fly-casters, who stop off in the shoals to wade.

To reach Lobo Landing, on the south side of the river, a ¹⁄₁₀-mile drive on Vogel Avenue off AR 337 is required. Dripping Springs Access is at the end of Second Avenue, which runs north off AR 16 in the town of Pangburn. There is a sign for the access point at the intersection in town; from there, the point is 1½ miles.

The Pangburn Access, where AR 110 again crosses the Little Red River, offers even handicapped anglers an approach to the water. An old bridge downstream of the present highway span has been left standing, with only the middle segment removed. This creates fishing piers on both shores, and parking areas are provided on either side of the river as well. Additionally, Pangburn Shoals are located just downstream, and can be reached from the south side of the tailwater.

Although the official end of trout water on the Little Red River is at the Dewey Bridge on AR 305, the Ramsey Access is the last practical approach to the water for anglers. Located 3 miles upstream of the Dewey Bridge, Ramsey has a parking area and a boat ramp at the end of a paved road running north off AR 124. Although there is no sign identifying the road, there is a directional sign for the Ramsey Access at the intersection. A wadable shoal is just downstream of the boat ramp.

To obtain current information on water conditions on the Little Red River tailwater, call 501-362-5150 for a recorded message, courtesy of the Army Corps of Engineers.

6

North Fork River

USGS Norfork Dam South, Norfork • FIA 6, 7

Although the North Fork River is the shortest tailwater fishery in Arkansas that holds trout, it is also arguably the best trophy-trout water in the world. Better known by its shortened name, the Norfork River, this flow is only 4⅘⁄10 miles in length. It originates at the foot of Norfork Dam in the north-central part of the state and runs to the southwest through Baxter County to empty into the White River. Norfork Dam impounds 22,000 acres of water in Norfork Lake, which extends across the state line into southern Missouri.

While often identified as the North Fork of the White River, or the abovementioned Norfork, the officially correct name of this stream is simply the North Fork River. Part of the confusion over its moniker results from it flowing through Norfork Lake, which is actually named for the nearby town of Norfork. In the interests of brevity, "Norfork" is the term that will be used to discuss this flow.

While the Little Red River tailwater has recently attracted most of the attention for trophy-quality brown trout, and over the long haul the Bull Shoals tailwater on the White River has been Arkansas's most consistent producer of big trout, the Norfork has also yielded some very impressive fish. To date, this short tailwater has given up the Arkansas state-record brook trout, a 3-pound, 10-ounce specimen taken by Tony Salamon of St. Louis, Missouri, back on October 27, 1984.

Additionally, a former Arkansas- and world-record brown trout was pulled from these waters by Mike "Huey" Manley of North Little Rock on August 7, 1988. That huge 41-inch trout tipped the scales at 38 pounds, 9 ounces and stood as a disputed world record for 2 years.

The controversy surrounding Manley's fish centered on the fact that his ultralight gear, which used 6-pound-test line, ended in a baited

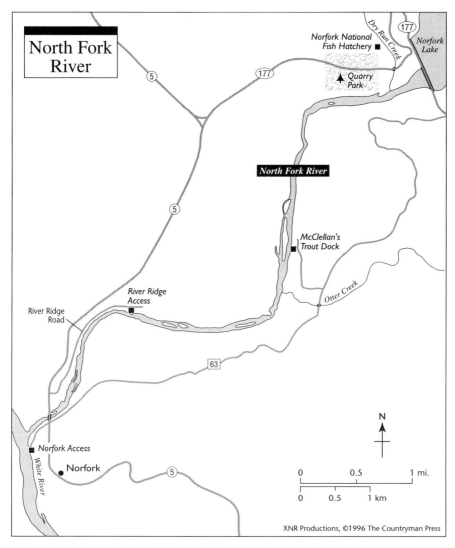

North Fork River

Norfork National Fish Hatchery ■

Norfork Lake

Dry Run Creek

177

5

177

▲ Quarry Park

North Fork River

McClellan's Trout Dock ■

Otter Creek

5

River Ridge Access ■

River Ridge Road

63

Norfork Access ■

White River

● Norfork

5

N

0   0.5   1 mi.

0   0.5   1 km

XNR Productions, ©1996 The Countryman Press

treble hook. While perfectly legal in Arkansas, the use of treble hooks with bait is not recognized as a sportfishing technique by the International Game Fish Association; thus the IGFA never accepted his catch. On the other hand, the AGFC recognized it as the official state record, as did the National Fresh Water Fishing Hall of Fame. The Manley trout was finally displaced from both record books by Rip Collins's 40-pound, 4-ounce brown, taken from the Little Red River in 1992.

Manley's trout, however, still reigns as the Hall of Fame's 8-pound-test line-class rod and reel record. Another line-class world record on this list that came from the Norfork is held by Tony Salamon (also the owner of the Arkansas-record brook trout catch) in the 6-pound-test category for a 30-pound, 8-ounce brown taken on August 31, 1986. In the 17-pound-test class, a 34-pound monster caught by David Wooten on August 13, 1988, stands as the benchmark for browns.

Often overlooked in this flurry of brown trout records are two former Arkansas record rainbow trout that the Norfork also produced. Back on June 14, 1970, Frank Mandernach of St. Louis, Missouri, boated a 16-pound, 2-ounce rainbow he caught while tossing a Mepps spinner. Just over 2 years later, on July 1, 1972, his record was broken by Raymond Sullivan of Des Moines, Iowa, with the 16-pound, 12-ounce fish he took from the Norfork. That catch stood as the state record for the next 4 years.

While it is abundantly clear that the Norfork River is capable of producing record fish, what makes it outstanding among tailwaters is the consistency with which it produces big fish within its very limited length. Brown trout of 4 to 6 pounds are common, and browns of 10 to 15 pounds are so often caught that they go almost unnoticed. In the earlier years of this tailwater, rainbows of 2 to 6 pounds were also the norm, but fishing pressure has greatly reduced this fishery recently. Cutthroat trout have been stocked in the Norfork since 1982 and thrive here. In fact, Arkansas's first state-record cutthroat came from the Norfork on March 13, 1985, when Thomas Else of St. Louis, Missouri, caught a 3-pounder. That fish has since been bested by several from the White River. Some brook trout continue to be planted in the North Fork River as well.

With such a varied and high-quality fishery, it is hardly surprising that the Norfork is a very popular fishing destination. A survey released back in 1990 revealed that this 4⁸⁄₁₀-mile stretch of water was the site of 16 percent of all the trout fishing in Arkansas the previous year. Particularly during low water, when neither of the dam's generators is active, the fishing on the Norfork tailwater can get crowded. This is especially true from spring through fall, when the bulk of the stocking takes place. Planted fish are released year-round, however, and anglers looking to beat the crowds will find February and March to be the times of lowest usage. Fishing pressure also is lower at other times of the year when one or both of the turbines at Norfork Dam are active.

The North Fork was the first of the streams in the White River system to be dammed by the Corps of Engineers. Norfork Dam was begun in 1941, and its two power generators came on-line in 1944. With the release of 600 fingerling rainbow trout in July 1948, the Norfork also became the first Arkansas tailwater to receive stocked trout.

As with other stockings in tailwaters of the Natural State, these were intended to compensate for the loss of smallmouth bass fishing in the river. The first trout released into the Norfork were an experiment—to see if the new tailwater would be able to support the cold-water species. Within a year of the first planting of 4- to 6-inch trout, rainbows of 2 to 3 pounds were being caught, and in the second year 4- to 6-pounders were showing up. The productivity of the river was astounding and the program a success by any standard.

An appeal to the US Congress resulted in funds being allotted for the US Fish and Wildlife Service to build a trout hatchery on the Norfork. In 1957 the Norfork National Fish Hatchery was opened on Dry Run Creek, a feeder of the river that enters it just below Norfork Dam. Just 5 years later this hatchery was supplying 1.8 million trout annually for planting in the Norfork and White Rivers.

Recently the Norfork has received up to 85,000 rainbows of 9 to 12 inches, 25,000 cutthroats, and 20,000 brookies from stockings each year. Since the river has very few spawning shoals in comparison to the Little Red or White Rivers, 10,000 brown trout have also been released in the flow. All of the brook, brown, and cutthroat trout are in the 6- to 8-inch range.

The environment into which these hatchery fish are released is referred to by some experts as the most productive trout stream in the world. Growth rates in the fish have been documented at as much as 7½ inches per year—in some cases, ¾ inch a month. Add to this the fact that the growing season for trout on the Norfork is year-round, and the numbers of huge trout it has produced are easily explained.

The fluctuating water levels of the tailwater are not conducive to high populations of mayflies or stone flies, but the fact that Norfork Dam has only two power generators mitigates the problem. Water surges are not as pronounced here as those found on the White River below Bull Shoals Dam, so aquatic vegetation has an easier time hanging onto the riverbed.

Of course, the sensational growth rates mentioned above need a tremendous forage base to sustain them. For a number of reasons, the Norfork has the most substantial and dependable such food chain in the White River system. To begin with, fish of up to 20 inches gorge themselves on the abundant freshwater shrimp, sow bugs, and scuds found in the flow. These tiny critters are quite at home in the Norfork's weed beds.

Once the trout, particularly the browns, get past the 20-inch plateau, they become quite carnivorous in their feeding habits. They can still find plenty to eat, though, thanks to the river's large population of sculpins. These small bottom-dwelling fish, which are sometimes referred to locally as mountain minnows, are a favored food of the browns. It is during the winter months, however—when cold weather causes shad die-offs in Norfork Lake—that the brown trout in the tailwater attain their greatest growth spurts of the year. The dead and dying shad are sucked through the turbines at the dam and the trout binge on the minnows. Additionally, many of the large number of small trout stocked into the river yearly end up being feed for the huge browns.

Because of the short length of trout water and the scarcity of spawning shoals on the Norfork, there is thought to be a close and unique connection between this tailwater and that below Bull Shoals Dam on the White River. Some of the association is obvious. By the time the two rivers join, the White has already flowed more than 60 miles as a cold-water trout river and is beginning to warm. The infusion of the Norfork's chilly waters renews the White, allowing it more than 40 more miles of life as a cold-water fishery.

Less obvious, but strongly suspected, is the movement of brown trout from one river to the other. Some big browns in both the Bull Shoals and Norfork tailwaters were tagged with radio transmitters during the 1992 spawning season; one result was the discovery that these fish traveled up to 24 miles in a day. Movements of 18 miles were recorded in several instances, and all of the tagged fish traveled at least 8 to 10 miles every 24 hours during the spawn. With the abundance of big browns in the Norfork, it is almost certain that some would have to move into the White to spawn. On the other hand, the survey also found that after spawning, all of the fish returned to virtually the same location where they had lived when first tagged.

As on all tailwaters, the amount of water being released at Norfork Dam dictates the fishing conditions downstream. The least appealing conditions occur during high water when both generators are in use. At these times virtually the entire tailwater is unwadable, leaving float- or bank-fishing as the only options. Since almost all of the shoreline of the Norfork is privately owned, bank-fishing is quite limited. Fortunately, it is such a short river that float-fishing all of it in a single day is feasible during high water.

High water was traditionally thought to make fly-casting impossible on the Norfork, but some local anglers developed fishing pat-

Johnboats, such as this one on the Norfork River, are popular for float-fishing on all of the Ozarks' tailwaters.

terns to beat the conditions. The key, they discovered, was to imitate bait-fishers. By using heavier gear (often in the 6- to 10-weight range) with sink-tip lines, egg- or San Juan Worm–pattern flies can be fished very near the bottom and catch fish even during the highest water flows. Zonkers, Squirrel-Tailed Nymphs, and streamers that mimic small trout or shad will also attract some fish. Naturally, fishing these imitations in eddies, backwaters, and calmer runs will produce the most action.

Another key to fishing high water is boat handling. Guides who take johnboats into this tailwater during maximum generation must run their outboard motors continuously to hold the boats into the current at either the head or the foot of shoal areas. For the most part, anchoring is an iffy, and quite possibly dangerous, idea on high water. At one time anglers dragged heavy chains along the bottom to slow the drift of their boats, but this tactic has been outlawed on the Norfork because of the damage it did to the aquatic weed beds.

Anglers with spinning equipment during high water use all of the popular in-line spinners, plus Shad Raps, Countdown Rapalas, and Rebel Fastracs; they also use a host of other ultralight bass-type lures. Silver hues that imitate shad, or colors that mimic juvenile brown and rainbow trout, are popular.

For the bait-fisher, all of the usual tailwater baits will produce:

corn, cheese balls, marshmallow rigs, night crawlers, or salmon eggs. Anglers targeting larger browns cover their hooks with crawfish or spring lizards, but their number one choice is a sculpin. Surprisingly, these minnows are best fished dead. Live sculpins have the annoying habit of burrowing down between streambed rocks where trout cannot get to them.

When only one generator is in use at Norfork Dam, the tailwater develops a split personality. While floating is still practical, many areas become wadable as well. One good way to fish the stream at this time is to float from shoal to shoal, then getting out to wade each shallow area.

It is, however, during low water—when no power generation is taking place—that the Norfork is at its best. Virtually the entire flow is wadable; the river is so low that floating is practically impossible. Bait- and spin-fishers will continue to attack the fishing with the same methods they used during higher water, but for fly-casters the river becomes very different.

Almost all of the North Fork's insect hatches occur during low water, and the midge hatches of spring and summer can be abundant (although they are often overlooked by anglers). When a lot of gentle rises are taking place on the more placid water, tossing a size 20 to 22 midge pattern can produce some exciting fishing.

Although fish can be found throughout the river during low water, many will congregate in the remaining deeper pools. Fishing these locations with 5- to 6-weight fly-rods using Matukas in black or olive, Woolly Buggers, or Muddler Minnows usually provokes some strikes. Subsurface fishing with sow bug or scud imitations also works, as do Squirrel-Tailed Nymphs, Woolly Worms, or Gold-Ribbed Hare's Ears.

Along the Norfork's course, there are only three sites that offer public access to the fishing, but there are five privately operated trout docks. Still, considering there are less than 5 miles of water, access is good.

At the foot of Norfork Dam and on the northern side of the river is Quarry Park, which is managed by the Corps of Engineers. This access contains a paved boat ramp, parking lots, and a campground. Near the park is the Norfork National Fish Hatchery on Dry Run Creek. The creek itself is open to fishing only by anglers who are disabled or under 16 years of age. (Fishing piers over the water are provided for the handicapped anglers.) Only artificial lures with single barbless hooks are allowed, and all fish must be released.

Just below the boat ramp and the mouth of Dry Run is a small shoal that is quite a popular fishing destination. The 22,000 gallons of water emptying out of Dry Run and into this shoal every minute are high in dissolved oxygen and carry plenty of excess fish food from the hatchery. Such a combination attracts both trout and anglers to the shoal. Of course, when you are fishing here so close to the dam, it is imperative to keep an ear peeled for the whistle that sounds when water releases are about to occur. Since there is plenty of time after the horn sounds to exit the river, it is not necessary to run for the shore, but it is a good idea to immediately begin wading back to your access point.

In all, Quarry Park offers roughly ¾ mile of bank access to the North Fork. Foot trails run along the north shore from the boat ramp to the downstream areas. Quarry Park is just off AR 177 where it crosses Norfork Dam.

Moving downstream, and before the next public access point, there is a designated year-round catch-and-release area. As of January 1, 1995, the stretch of river from the mouth of Otter Creek (which enters the Norfork from the east at about the midpoint of the river's journey to the White) to about a mile downstream, 100 yards above the River Ridge Access, is under these fishing restrictions. Only artificial lures with single barbless hooks are legal and all trout must be returned to the river. The only practical access to this part of the river for wade-anglers is through McClellan's Trout Dock. For a small fee, anglers can park their cars in the pasture just above Otter Creek and walk down to Ace In The Hole and other shoals on this part of the river.

The River Ridge Access is managed by the AGFC and is the next point of public access to the North Fork. It is located at the end of River Ridge Road to the east of its junction with AR 5. A boat ramp, handicapped fishing pier, and walk-in area are provided here. At low water levels, a long gravel bar is exposed on the near shore.

The final access point to the North Fork is the Norfork Access just off AR 5 at the town of Norfork. This access is at the junction of the Norfork and White Rivers and features a parking area, a gravel bar (where boats can be launched), and bank access. These are located on the southeastern side of the river. The opposite shore—from the railroad bridge visible upstream, down to the junction of the rivers—is lined with downed trees and is noted for holding plenty of trout.

To obtain water-release information on the Norfork tailwaters, call the Corps of Engineers recorded message at 501-431-5311. This automated system is located at Bull Shoals Dam on the White River and provides schedules for both rivers.

7
White River—Beaver Tailwater

USGS Beaver • FIA 16

When tailwater trout fishing in the Ozarks is mentioned, most southern anglers immediately think of the White River below Bull Shoals Dam. That reaction is understandable in light of the river's 100-plus-mile length and the spectacular quality of the trout it produces. Competing for second billing with regard to trout fishing in the region are the Table Rock tailwaters of the White in Missouri and Arkansas's Little Red and Norfork Rivers. The tailwater below 28,000-acre Beaver Lake on the upper White River in northwestern Arkansas is relegated to the status of the "red-headed stepchild" of the White River system.

There are several reasons for the relative obscurity of this part of the White River. Located entirely in Carroll County between the towns of Rogers and Eureka Springs and flowing northward to the Missouri border, the Beaver tailwater is only about 8 miles in length, depending on the water level in Table Rock Lake downstream. The stream is also quite narrow by Arkansas tailwater standards—only a "cast" wide at some places during low water. The trout fishery was created by the last of the dams built by the Corps of Engineers in the White River basin, completed in 1966. Being such a youngster in a region of spectacular trout tailwaters is not an ideal way to gain notoriety—even though the Beaver tailwater fishing would be considered terrific if it were located elsewhere. Although it does draw anglers from the northwestern corner of Arkansas, as well as from southwestern Missouri and adjoining portions of Kansas, the area below Beaver Lake still accounts for only 8 percent of all trout angling taking place in the state.

While this may give the impression that the Beaver tailwater is deserted, that is not a true picture of the situation. Since there are only three public access points between the dam and the end of trout

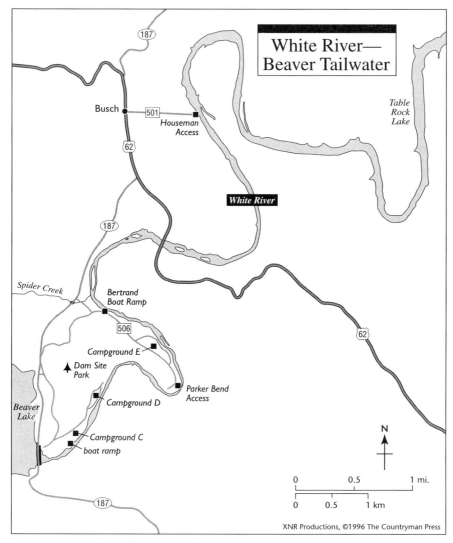

water at County Road (CR) 501, anglers will often be thick at these sites. On weekends, evenings, and holidays when the weather is fair, bank-anglers spread their lawn chairs and two legal fishing rods apiece all along the shores. At times it becomes difficult to wade some portions of the flow without getting tangled in these staked-out bait rigs.

The fishery in the Beaver tailwater is supported by the stocking of up to 80,000 catchable-sized rainbow trout per year; the releases take place at all three access points from spring to fall. The first planting of trout in this portion of the river took place immediately after the dam was completed back in the 1960s. Brown trout have also been stocked in the river since 1985, when an initial release of 7600 browns that were 7 inches long occurred. At present about 10,000 brown trout are added to the fishery each year, with the planting taking place on a one-time basis in the fall. Finally, since April 1990, roughly 25,000 cutthroat trout have been released into the Beaver tailwater annually.

Among Arkansas's tailwater trout rivers, the White below Beaver Lake was traditionally a classic put-and-take fishery. An electroshock survey conducted on the river in 1988 provided some interesting specifics. To begin with, AGFC biologists discovered a rainbow trout density of close to 1200 fish per river mile, with over 40 percent of those being trout of 12 inches or larger. Of particular interest was the fact that the shocking had been carried out in September, after the tailwater had been subjected to heavy fishing pressure through the spring and summer. It was estimated at the time that the rainbow population fluctuates between 300 and 1500 fish per mile at all times. A later check of the river in March 1991 found 429 rainbows per mile, even though no stocking had occurred since the previous September. Most of these fish were 12 to 14 inches long, but 2-pounders were present, as well as the rare rainbow of up to 8 pounds.

On the other hand, the brown trout population found in the 1988 survey indicated that up to 94 percent of these less heavily stocked fish were harvested within a year of stocking. The survey also revealed the fact that the browns that did avoid being caught grew at the astounding rate of 1 inch per month here. Even before the survey, such growth rates had been suspected. One tagged brown that was stocked in 1985 at 8 inches long was caught in August 1988 and tipped the scales at 10 pounds, 3 ounces. Its growth rate topped 3 pounds per year!

It was just such unrealized trophy potential that led to the Beaver tailwater becoming Arkansas's "laboratory" for trout management. Beginning in 1988, a 2-fish creel limit with a 16-inch minimum size was established for brown trout on the White River between Beaver Dam and Table Rock Lake. Very quickly the population of browns in the tailwater rose from 40 or 50 per mile to 340. Within 2 years that figure reached 2000 per mile.

The success of the brown trout regulations led to them being applied to other tailwaters in Arkansas; they became the state norm in January 1990. Additionally, the excellent results of the brown trout rules led to a 2-fish, 16-inch minimum being applied to cutthroat trout as well. These fish had also shown a growth potential in the Beaver tailwater of 7/10 inch per year. Cutthroats are particularly popular because they do not become as carnivorous or as nocturnal as brown trout when they attain trophy size. It is possible to catch them on flies and baits regardless of the time of day, or whether they have attained trophy proportions.

Today, the waters below Beaver Dam continue to be a classroom for trout biologists. An electroshock survey in the fall of 1991 discovered that the brown trout population had plummeted to only 340 fish per mile. The two suspected causes of this collapse are the record rainfall in the spring of 1990 and an outbreak of disease among rainbow trout in federal hatcheries that year.

On the one hand, the record rains spawned flood conditions on the upper White River, prompting the Corps of Engineers to leave the Beaver Dam floodgates open for 10 straight days. Fifty thousand cubic feet of water per second (cfs) poured through the dam—where 10,000 cfs was the normal maximum—and a number of striped and hybrid bass in the 8- to 12-pound range were washed downstream into the tailwater.

These voracious feeders are quite fond of dining on trout. When 400 were subsequently removed back to the lake via electroshocking, stomach samples showed that about a third of them had been eating trout. In the ensuing years, some 20-pound stripers have continued to be taken by surprised anglers in the Beaver tailwater. Fortunately, since no hybrids or stripers are stocked in Table Rock Lake, these odd catches are probably just leftovers from the flooding; they likely spend most of their time in Table Rock and move up into the tailwater only occasionally. Neither of these species spawns in the White River system.

The other possible cause of the decline in trout numbers was a 30 percent cutback in rainbow stocking in 1990 due to disease problems. It is feared that anglers who were used to taking their limit of 6 rainbows with relative ease became frustrated and began poaching undersized browns to fill their creels. Adding to that problem was an apparent unwillingness by local courts to take violations of the brown trout restrictions seriously.

The result of this situation was that local Trout Unlimited chapters began watching the judicial proceedings closely to highlight the problem. Meanwhile, AGFC officers worked to improve enforcement procedures as well.

To counter some of the damage caused by the flooding, and to learn more about how the trout habitat on the Beaver—and thus all tailwaters—functions, the AGFC began a $150,000 research and restoration project on the river in 1993. A consortium of public agencies and Trout Unlimited chapters is repairing the flood damage with in-stream placement of boulders and log shelters to reproduce the deep holes and gravel bars that previously existed and benefited the trout. They have also begun programs to curb bank erosion.

Probably the two streamer patterns most often used by fly-rodders on this portion of the White River are olive or black Woolly Buggers in sizes 4 to 12 and Muddler Minnows with olive or yellow marabou dressings. Pheasant Tail and Hare's Ear nymphs are also standards here, with egg-pattern flies getting some use as well. As with all the other Ozark tailwaters, scud and sow bug imitations are usually found in anglers' fly boxes, too.

Although occasional mayfly hatches take place in the spring, most of the surface action for fly-fishers will be in the form of casting to the midge hatches that come off virtually year-round on the Beaver tailwater. Tiny flies in the size 18 to 24 range are needed for this fishing.

Anglers using spinning gear and artificial lures fish standard in-line spinners on this river, with gray and brown being the most popular colors. On overcast days, however, fluorescent patterns in orange and chartreuse are better choices. Spoons, Countdown Rapalas, and ultralight crankbaits are also good choices. Lines in 4-pound-test or lighter are recommended because of the very clear water below Beaver Dam.

Other popular lures on this tailwater include ultralight to microsized jigs. And we are talking about very small ones here! Sizes of $\frac{1}{32}$ ounce all the way down to $\frac{1}{256}$ ounce are used. These are fished under a tiny float, either with or without a small split shot beneath the float, on 2-pound-test line. In beige or brown, these can be deadly on the river's rainbow trout.

When bait-anglers tackle the trout in the Beaver tailwater, the choice of baits resembles those used on other Ozark rivers: Salmon eggs, wax worms, night crawlers, marshmallows, cheese concoctions, crickets, and corn are all popular. Either live or dead shad work well when shad die-offs take place in Beaver Lake, from January through April. For trophy browns, a lip-hooked sculpin fished in a shoal area after dark is another option. In fact, night-fishing for all sizes of trout seems

The Beaver tailwater as seen from the top of
Beaver Dam on the White River

to have a larger following below Beaver Dam than on the other Arkansas trout rivers, with many anglers preferring to take to the water from midnight to dawn.

During high water, anglers most often target the backwaters and eddies created as either one or two turbines operate at the dam. Of course, float- and bank-fishing are the only options at these times, since wading is not practical on high water.

When the generators at Beaver Dam are silent, the river becomes a series of pools separated by wadable shoals. Floating in a canoe, which makes for a long day of fishing from the dam down to the end of practical trout water at the Houseman Access, is a favorite way for many anglers to tackle this water. Areas just above shoals or the holes washed out below the shoal waters are the best places to look for trout under these low-water conditions.

The Beaver tailwater is noted for having the most public access per stream mile of any of the rivers in the White system. This statement may seem a bit contradictory when matched up with the fact that there are only three access points along this portion of the White

River. However, the Dam Site Park below Beaver Dam stretches for 3²⁄₁₀ miles downstream, contains two of these access areas, and takes in almost half of the stream's trout water on the northwestern shore. Stretching from the tailrace down to the junction with Spider Creek, this park has three campgrounds, two boat ramps, a walk-in area, a couple of shoals, several long gravel bars, and a trophy fishing area.

The trophy area runs from Campsite #13 in Campground C for 1 mile down to the Parker Bend Walk-In Access. Through here only single-barbless-hook artificial lures are legal, and all fish must be released. These rules apply year-round.

The gravel bar extending downstream from the boat ramp and the boulders along the opposite bank from the ramp are very popular angling destinations in this part of the park. Both bank- and wade-fishing can get crowded, in part because of the location of Campgrounds C and D along here.

To attain access to this part of the park, travel ¼ mile north of Beaver Dam via AR 187 (which crosses the dam) and turn right into the paved entrance drive. As with most tailwater fisheries, a horn sounds at Beaver Dam to alert anglers to imminent releases of water.

Between the upper and lower portions of the Dam Site Park lies Crane Roost Bluff, where tall cliffs overlook a sharp bend in the river. Below this spot is Parker Bend Walk-In Access at the end of CR 506, to the east of AR 187. The shoals at this bend of the river are the most popular fishing site for both wade- and bank-fishing on the Beaver tailwater, and are noted for producing big brown trout.

The part of the river along CR 506 is also within the confines of the Dam Site Park and contains Campground E (Parker Bottom Campground), the Bertrand Boat Ramp, and some off-road parking, as well as the walk-in access. Wallace Bluff's sandstone ridge overlooks the river in the walk-in area, adding to the beauty of this portion of the tailwater.

The final 4 miles of trout water down to the Houseman Access can only be reached by boat and contain virtually no wadable water. The Houseman Access has a boat ramp and a parking area, and is the last downstream site that is stocked with trout. To reach this access, take CR 501 east from US 62 at the crossroads of Busch. There is presently no sign at the intersection indicating that the access point is at the end of the road. It is ¾ mile from the intersection to the Houseman Access.

To receive information on water releases at the Beaver Dam, call 417-336-5083 for a recorded message. This service of the Army Corps of Engineers is provided from the Table Rock Dam, farther down the White River in Missouri, and also gives water level data for that dam.

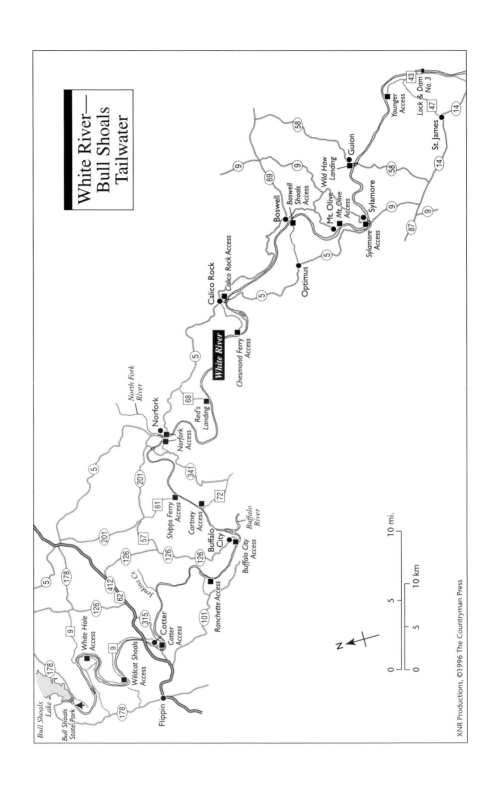

White River—
Bull Shoals
Tailwater

White River

Bull Shoals Lake
Bull Shoals State Park
178
9
White Hole Access
126
62
412
315
5
178
201
Wildcat Shoals Access
9
9
Cotter
Cotter Access
101
Flippin
178
Jenkins Cr.
57
126
126
Ranchette Access
Shipps Ferry Access
61
Cartney Access
72
Buffalo City
Buffalo City Access
Buffalo River
341
201
5
North Fork River
Norfork
Norfork Access
Red's Landing
68
5
Chesmond Ferry Access
Calico Rock
Calico Rock Access
5
Optimus
5
69
9
9
58
Boswell
Boswell Shoals Access
Mt. Olive
Mt. Olive Access
Wild Haw Landing
Guion
Sylamore
Sylamore Access
58
9
87
9
Younger Access
Lock & Dam No. 3
43
47
St. James
14
14

N

0   5   10 mi.
0   5   10 km

XNR Productions, ©1996 The Countryman Press

8
White River—Bull Shoals Tailwater

USGS Cotter, Mountain Home West, Buffalo City, Norfork,
Norfork Dam South, Calico Rock, Boswell, Sylamore,
Guion, Mount Pleasant, Bethesda •
FIA 6, 7, 60, 61, 62, 63, 134, 135

If faced with the problem of coming up with a single word to describe the tailwater trout fishery on the White River below Bull Shoals Dam, one's uncontested choice would be "big." Everything about this resource is outsized. Bull Shoals Lake, from which the tailwater emerges, is the largest reservoir in the White River system, spreading to 45,440 acres at normal level. Bull Shoals Dam contains eight turbines in its powerhouse, and these generators are capable of changing the river from a trickle to a raging, big-water torrent in minutes.

Downriver from the dam, the tailwater continues to merit expansive adjectives. The stream's width is measured in hundreds of yards along its roughly 101-mile course as a trout resource. Its fishing rates with the best in the world as a result of massive stockings—more than a million trout per year. Additionally, the naturally reproducing brown trout found in the flow regularly reach weights measured in double digits; more monster trout of 30-plus pounds are produced here than in any other single stream in the world. Finally, the portion of the river from the dam down to the town of Cotter (self-proclaimed "Trout Capital of the World," but only officially recognized by the Arkansas General Assembly in 1993 as the "Trout Capital of the USA") boasts more than 200 fishing guides and better than two dozen trout docks or resorts.

The tailwater below Bull Shoals accounts for fully 36 percent of all trout fishing in Arkansas. Since it is estimated that each day of angling here generates $123 for the local economy, this river provides a hefty portion of the $150 million that trout fishing produces for the statewide economy. This is a stream that truly invites superlatives.

Beginning at the foot of Bull Shoals Dam near the Arkansas-Missouri border, this tailwater on the White River flows in a southeasterly direction. Fueled by the frigid waters from the 120-foot depths of the impoundment, the river contains excellent trout water for 44 miles down to its junction with the North Fork River at the town of Norfork. Here the infusion of the North Fork waters again lowers the river temperature, keeping it within the tolerance range for trout for an additional 57 miles down to Lock and Dam No. 3, about 9 miles downstream of the village of Guion.

Originating on the border of Marion and Baxter Counties, the White's tailwater cuts a swath down through the north-central portion of the state. Along this route toward the sea, the river forms the border of Stone and Izard Counties before changing to a warm-water flow. The river towns of Cotter, Buffalo City, Norfork, Calico Rock, Boswell, Mount Olive, Sylamore, and Guion are all situated on the White's trout-supporting tailwater. The White River's course is laden not only with trout, but with a heavy dose of history as well.

The Bull Shoals area was described as early as 1819 by Henry Rowe Schoolcraft, who was impressed by the power of the rapids situated on the present site of the dam. Beginning in the 1830s, the White was the scene of a thriving steamboat trade that carried agricultural and other products down to the Mississippi River. The need to ship iron and zinc ore mined along the Buffalo River (a tributary of the White whose mouth is located at Buffalo City) prompted the construction of locks and dams along the river, starting in 1899. Only 3 of 10 planned locks were completed by 1905 when the St. Louis, Iron Mountain and Southern Railroad linked the town of Cotter to Batesville downstream, effectively ending the building program and the riverboat era in the White River basin. In the ensuing years, the White River was used to float rafts of cedar trees out of the Ozark Mountains to be turned into pencils in a factory at Cotter. The stream's waters were also probed by local folks in search of freshwater mussels. These shellfish supplied a thriving button industry, and old-timers report seeing piles of shells as big as houses at buying stations near the old ferries. On rare occasions fine pearls were even found in those White River mussels!

The first bridge on the upper White was completed in 1930, replacing a number of the ferries. This highway bridge near Cotter, with its twin, rounded arches, is still in use on AR 315 and has been placed on the National Register of Historic Places.

Disastrous floods along the White River in 1898, 1915, 1916, and 1927 led to the Army Corps of Engineers' program of building dams on the river system. The Bull Shoals Dam was the second and largest of the projects, beginning power production in 1952 with four generators. An additional four turbines came on-line in 1963.

Once cold water began flowing in the Bull Shoals tailwaters and the smallmouth bass disappeared, the earlier experiment with trout on the North Fork River was extended to the White. That first year saw 16,156 rainbows and 1800 brown trout stocked in the tailwater. These fish were all 6 to 8 inches long. By 1959, when Arkansas began keeping statistics on trout catches, the state record for rainbows fell four times in a single year, increasing from 11 pounds, 3 ounces to 15 pounds, 3 ounces. All of these trout were taken from the Bull Shoals section of the White. In 1994, trout stockings on the White River had grown to 1,225,000 rainbows, 100,000 browns, and 150,000 cutthroat trout.

From the very beginning, the White River's potential for producing lunker-sized fish was apparent. In the early years of the fishery, it was the rainbow trout population that produced the impressive catches. The combination of the 48- to 54-degree water released through the dam, the forage base of sculpins in the river and stunned shad coming through the turbines from Bull Shoals Lake, and a year-round growing season was ideal for trout growth.

In the mid-1950s, the release of browns into the White was discontinued. It was feared that the difficult-to-catch browns would feed too heavily on the freshly stocked rainbows, diminishing the quality of the fishery. Thus, for 25 years the rainbows did not face competition and thrived. Unfortunately, the rapidly shifting water levels in the tailwater are not conducive to rainbow spawning, so almost no reproduction takes place. With estimated yearly carryovers of 10 to 15 percent of the fish, however, rainbows of 2 to 6 pounds became quite common, with some trout of more than 10 pounds showing up as well.

Eventually a total of six Arkansas state-record rainbow trout were taken from the Bull Shoals tailwaters; the final one remains the standard bearer. On March 4, 1981, Jim Miller of Memphis, Tennessee, was fishing a Rooster Tail spinner tipped with a worm near Sylamore when he boated a 19-pound, 1-ounce rainbow.

In the ensuing years, the fishing pressure on the White has grown so heavy that the chances of catching such a monster rainbow have diminished greatly. The estimates of AGFC biologists suggest that up to 97 percent of stocked rainbows are harvested within a year of release in the best trout water from Bull Shoals down to Cotter. Such figures greatly reduce the possibility of anyone tangling with a trophy-sized rainbow. Still, since White River trout grow from ⅓ to ⅞ inch monthly, and since harvest rates for rainbows drop to 72 to 82 percent on the portion of the flow below Norfork, some good fish are still possible.

Much the same story can be told of the cutthroat trout that were introduced into the Bull Shoals tailwater in 1982. By 1985, a steady stream of new state records for the species had pushed the mark to 9 pounds, 9.76 ounces. That fish was caught on a combination bait of worm and crawfish by Scott Rudolph of Ozark, Arkansas, on October 6. Since then, overfishing has been a problem for cutthroats as well, and the state eventually mandated a 2-fish creel limit and a 16-inch minimum size limit on the species.

Despite the good fishing for the staple rainbows and the exotic cutthroats, the true calling card drawing fishers to the White River is the presence of wild, naturally reproducing, and often huge brown trout. As mentioned earlier, after the initial stockings in the 1950s, the practice was discontinued for more than two decades out of concern for the rainbow fishery. Plantings of browns were not resumed until the 1980s, long after the rainbow trout population had stabi-

PHOTO BY BOB BORGWAT © 1994 BOB BORGWAT OUTDOORS

Casting into the morning mist rising over the White River

lized and then begun to decline due to heavy fishing pressure. At about this time it also was discovered that browns were spawning in the river. Eventually, the first mile downstream of Bull Shoals Dam was identified as the major spawning ground, but spawning was also seen below Wildcat Shoals, 12 miles downriver, as well as at Rim Shoals, some 25 miles below the dam.

Although the Norfork and the Little Red Rivers have claimed much of the attention in recent years, due to each having produced world-record brown trout, the river that has most consistently yielded monster fish has been the Bull Shoals tailwater. From the beginning of record keeping in 1959, seven different Bull Shoals browns kept the Arkansas state record on the White River until 1988. The size of the top fish increased from the 10-pound, 13-ounce specimen taken by Frank Tilley of Norfork on a crawfish tail on June 27, 1959, up to the 33-pound, 8-ounce brute hooked on a worm-and-crawfish-tail combination bait on March 17, 1977, by Leon Waggoner of Flippin. This latter fish—which was taken from the White Hole, about 4 miles below the dam—held the state record for more than 11 years.

To put the White River brown trout production in perspective, also consider that the stream has produced an average of more than one fish a year of better than 30 pounds since the early 1970s! Additionally, a brown brought to the surface and later released during an electroshock survey in 1990 measured slightly longer than the 39 inches of Huey Manley's 38-pound, 9-ounce former-world-record fish from the Norfork River. One of the more amazing feats of angling on the White River occurred on September 19, 1987, when fishing guide Carl Jones of Flippin boated a 20-pound, 12-ounce brown trout on 2-pound-test line. The fish was subsequently recognized as a line-class world record by the International Game Fish Association.

While the truly huge trout in the Bull Shoals tailwater are the attention grabbers, the sheer numbers of fish that most folks would think of as trophies is even more astounding. A 1986 survey found an average of 266 browns of more than 20 inches for each river mile. Nine of these fish per mile were in excess of 30 inches.

Unfortunately, fishing pressure on these trout was on the increase in the late 1980s as well. Particularly during the spawning season, when the fish congregated in shoal areas, they became susceptible to legal angling methods—but also to unscrupulous snaggers. A technique was even developed for low-water periods of using several boats to "herd" the browns into schools that produced the same fishing conditions as spawning runs. This herding technique has now been made illegal on Arkansas trout waters. Before it was, however, a 1988 survey showed that the number of trout of more than 20 inches had fallen to 192 per river mile.

At that point the AGFC stepped in to implement the present state-wide regulations mandating a 16-inch minimum size and 2-fish creel limit for brown trout. These rules took effect on January 1, 1990. Eventually, even more stringent catch-and-release rules were put into effect on certain portions of the river.

A survey in August 1991 revealed an astounding 700 browns of 20 or better inches per river mile! Such a rebound was logical, however, after the trout were offered some added protection. To begin with, each spawning female lays 10,000 to 12,000 eggs. Given some time to grow and experience fishing pressure, it is easy for mature browns to avoid a hook. The White River is so large that there are plenty of places to hide from even the heavy fishing pressure exerted on the waterway. As the fish mature they become more nocturnal, feeding mostly at night when the fewest anglers are fishing. Finally, the shrimp, scuds, sow bugs, sculpins, and shad in the river provide plenty of forage to fatten the browns. The bottom line is that the White River is the best place in the world to seek a brown trout of trophy proportions.

Such a reputation does not go unnoticed. From spring through fall, angling pressure on the Bull Shoals tailwater is heavy. There are places and seasons, however, that allow the enterprising angler to beat the crowds. Though the fish continue to bite during the winter months, the number of anglers falls dramatically. The same can be said for after-dark angling. Yet, due to the habits of browns, either of these periods is an excellent time to challenge the fish.

Where you fish on the White River also comes into play in avoiding the crowds. The portion of the river from the dam down to Cotter is noted for being the best fishing stretch; therefore, it receives the lion's share of the pressure. The portion of the tailwater from Buffalo City down to Calico Rock, on the other hand, is its least-fished stretch. The pressure then picks up slightly from Calico Rock to the end of trout water on the White.

As with any resource, not all the story is pleasant. The Bull Shoals tailwater has suffered from some water-quality problems as a result of low water and oxygen levels in the stream. One cause of such conditions is the too-low minimum water flow coming through Bull Shoals

Dam, which resulted in a major fish kill in the fall of 1990. An additional cause of the low oxygen levels is periods of extremely high rainfall. These will wash a lot of nutrients into Bull Shoals Lake, promoting the bacterial growth that depletes the oxygen. These oxygen-starved waters then are drawn from the depths of the lake and released into the tailwater. In other words, too much or too little water tends to be the problem in the White River.

Starting in 1991, the Corps of Engineers and Southwest Power Administration began venting the turbines to add oxygen to the water during critical periods. Unfortunately, this limited the amount of power generated, thus costing money. More recently, hub deflectors have been added to the turbines, which accomplishes the same end without sacrificing electrical production.

When it comes to catching the trout, the Bull Shoals tailwater on the White River is where float-fishing was developed and refined. The standard rig for this angling is a 20-foot johnboat with captain's chairs for the anglers, a cooler for drinks in the middle of the boat, and a 10- to 20-horsepower outboard motor at the rear. Nearly every guide on the river has this type of setup, with only slight variations. Needless to say, many of the local anglers copy the setup for their own use. Expect to see plenty of boats on the White during the prime fishing months of spring through fall.

During high water on the Bull Shoals tailwater (when five to eight turbines are running at the dam), float-fishing is virtually the only option. Practically all of the shoals will be far too deep and swift for wading—the river can rise by as much as 12 feet. Also, trying to anchor a boat in this powerful current is foolhardy. Such an effort can lead to the rushing water capsizing the boat, depositing everyone aboard into sub-50-degree water. Poor boat handling and hypothermia have cost the lives of a number of anglers on this river. As a general rule—but *not* one on which to bet your life—the lowest water levels occur during the morning hours, from dawn to about 11. As with most tailwaters, Bull Shoals Dam has a siren that announces imminent releases, but it is only useful to anglers immediately downstream of the powerhouse.

The proper way to attack the high-water bait-fishing on the White is to drift downstream, employing what the local folks call "drag fishing." Hooks with standard baits are "dragged" along the bottom as they are fished off the upstream side of the boat. In some cases the guides use the outboard to slow the boats' descent, or even employ drag chains. As noted earlier, these chains have been outlawed on the North Fork River because they destroy the aquatic vegetation. Due to the power-generation surges in the White, aquatic weeds and mosses are extremely rare, so chains are allowed here.

When the turbines are running full bore at Bull Shoals Dam, the trout are not bunched up in deeper holes but are dispersed throughout the river. This is a good time to concentrate on areas nearer the bank of the stream, especially around logs or rock piles. The best portion is generally the corridor between the low-water mark and the present shoreline.

For the caster using spinning lures, high-water periods can also yield fish. Artificial baits should be cast into the same areas that the bait-fishers concentrate on. It is usually necessary to slow the boat's drift to provide enough time to properly present a lure. The most popular lures are Rooster Tail spinners, Little Cleo spoons, and Countdown Rapalas. Colors that mimic juvenile rainbow or brown trout are usually successful. These lures are used on all water levels on the White.

When only one to four generators are active at the dam, the tactics employed on the White change a bit. While drift-fishing is still the best choice, much of the action will take place in the middle of the river. The currents at these water levels are not great enough to push the trout out of their feeding lanes, so they hang in midstream eddies and current breaks.

When only one turbine is turning at the dam, or none at all, the White is but a shadow of its former self. The raging lion turns into a meandering pussycat that can be waded in many areas. For the float-fisher, this is the time to cast out the anchor and begin tight-lining into the deeper holes where the fish are concentrated. The water is ordinarily so clear that some guides cruise the river sight-fishing to the larger brown trout. Some locals, including guides, claim that the very best fishing on the White occurs when the river has been low for periods of 2 to 3 days.

These low-water periods are also the time that fly-fishers own the river. Although in the early years of the tailwater it was commonly thought that White River trout could not be taken on flies, this has since been very emphatically disproved. Some of the shoal areas produce mayfly hatches in the spring that call for size 16 Sulfur Duns, and hatches of light Cahills come off in the late summer in the same sizes. During the winter months the Bull Shoals tailwater is noted for its hatches of midges in the size 18 to 22 range; these take place predominantly on the long, slow pools.

Despite these hatches, most of the fly-casting action on the White is composed of tossing Gold-Ribbed Hare's Ears, Squirrel-Tailed Nymphs, Woolly Buggers, or Woolly Worms. Brown, black, and olive are the most popular colors for these latter two flies. Sow bug and scud imitations are staples of subsurface angling as well. For the fly-caster targeting big brown trout, a sculpin imitation tied with marabou is a good bet, regardless of the water level.

As to the best time of the year to fish the Bull Shoals tailwater, opinions differ. As a rule of thumb, however, a lot of anglers mention that the fishing picks up beginning in mid-May and continues on through June, July, and August, especially during low-water periods. If big brown trout are your quarry, the winter months are probably just as good. But remember to dress appropriately in the fall and winter. The water is always bitterly cold, and the air can be as well.

Access to the White River tailwater is quite good, with more than 30 commercial trout docks and 17 public access points along the 101 miles of trout water. A large number of these points, of course, are located in the first 25 miles from the dam down to Rim Shoals—the portion of the river that is noted for the best fishing. Still, with the number of boat ramps and low-water-wadable shoals along the stream, anglers can find room to practice their craft regardless of their tackle preference.

The first access point below the dam is in 725-acre Bull Shoals State Park. Located on Corps of Engineers land, the park contains bank access, wadable shoals, a boat ramp, a campground, parking areas, and a state-owned trout dock. All of these are arrayed on the eastern side of the river. The shore access to the river is via the park campground and the Big Bluff Hiking Trail. At the lower end of the park is a major shoal known as Dew Eddy Shoals.

Additionally, the park is the site of the Ozarks' largest spawning ground for brown trout. Each winter big browns move upriver to this point with procreation on their collective minds. To protect these fish, beginning in 1990 a catch-and-release regulation for brown trout went into effect for the winter months on the portions of the river from the dam to the downstream boundary of the state park. Only artificial lures or flies having single barbless hooks may be used. These regulations apply from November 1 to January 31.

Additionally, beginning on the first day of 1995 a new year-round catch-and-release area was established within the park. From Bull

Shoals Dam downstream to a point 100 feet above the Rivercliffe Trout Dock (located across the river from the park), only artificial lures with single barbless hooks are legal, and trout of all species must be immediately returned to the river. The regulated area is marked by signs in the park.

Access to Bull Shoals State Park is via AR 178, which crosses the dam. The entrance to the park is at the southeastern end of the dam.

The next downstream public access point to the tailwater is at White Hole Access. Located on the western shore of the river, the site contains a boat ramp and a parking area. A steep, scenic stone cliff lines the opposite shore at this point, while the near shore features a long gravel bar that is exposed at low water. At medium water levels it provides some wading possibilities around the boat ramp. A 5-mile paved road runs from the ramp westward to AR 178. A sign at this intersection indicates the direction to White Hole Access.

At 12 miles downstream of Bull Shoals Dam is Wildcat Shoals Access on the eastern bank of the river. Approach to this access is via Denton Ferry Road, which has signs that identify it as both County Road (CR) 1 and CR 9. It is paved coming in from the east, and gravel to the north of the access.

A paved boat ramp is available at this AGFC site, as are parking spaces. There is a wadable section of water at the ramp, but Wildcat Shoals is actually located around the bend downstream. This is one of the most popular shoals with fly-casters on the White River. There is a spur road just east of the access point that leads to a path providing wading access to the main shoal. For boaters, the shoal can be quite difficult to negotiate during low water.

The Cotter Access is the next point of public use on the Bull Shoals tailwater. It is just off AR 315, south of the town of Cotter. At 18 miles below the dam, this AGFC facility is one of the busiest on the White River. Located just upstream of a railroad bridge and the historic AR 315 bridge, the access's paved boat ramp is next to Cotter Springs, which forms a natural swimming hole before flowing down into the river.

An unnamed island splits the river to the two bridges, and the nearside channel and island are accessible to waders on low water. The fishing is good on the far channel as well, but even slight increases in the water level can leave an unwary angler stranded on the island.

Although Rim Shoals does not have a public access site, it is still worth noting in any description of the White River trout waters. Two small islands, sometimes referred to as Upper Rim and Lower Rim, are found in this shoal. Rim Shoals is one of the areas of the Bull Shoals tailwater most frequented by fly-fishers, and has also been identified as a brown trout spawning area. Since January 1, 1995, the portion of the river from the mouth of Jenkins Creek above Redbud Shoals down to the power line that crosses below Rim Shoals has been designated catch-and-release only, with artificial lures having single barbless hooks mandated. Access to Rim Shoals is available to wade-fishers through the Rim Shoals Resort for a daily fee.

The AGFC maintains Ranchette Access as the next downriver point of public entry. This site is located 28½ miles below Bull Shoals and provides a jump-off point for Rough Hole, which lies just downstream. There is also some low-water wading available near the paved boat ramp.

The road that approaches the access runs from AR 101, which is 2 miles to the west. At this writing, the approach road does not have a sign identifying it, but the junction with AR 101 has a directional sign for the access point.

Buffalo City Access has dual paved boat ramps at the end of AR 126 on the northeast side of the White River. These are located 4 miles downstream of Ranchette, and just above the junction of the White and Buffalo Rivers. There is some wadable water here, and the far shore of the river is dominated by high, sheer sandstone bluffs.

The boat ramps at Buffalo City are good spots to launch for a short run upriver to Buffalo Shoals. This shoal is considered by many to be the most scenic on the entire tailwater, and it provides a long stretch of wadable water. For the hardy trekker, it is possible to reach the shoals by hiking from Buffalo City up the railroad tracks that parallel the river.

At 36 river miles below Bull Shoals Dam, the AGFC provides the Cartney Access. There is a boat ramp located at the end of a 3-mile drive on CR 72, which is gravel as it approaches the river from AR 341. The ramp is on the southeastern side of the flow.

The next public access to the Bull Shoals tailwater is found at Shipps Ferry Access. On the southeastern side of the river the old ferry-boat landing is still visible, but the access point itself is on the northwestern shore. The approach is via CR 61, but the last ¼ mile of the road is gravel. Besides the ramp and parking area, there is some good fishing around in-stream boulders and ledges on the near side of the river.

The last 6 miles of the White above its junction with the Norfork is the least appealing trout water on the upper river. Through here the stream gets rather warm in the summer months, and trout do not fare well. Fortunately, when the Norfork's cold waters enter the White, the main river is again rejuvenated as a cold-water fishery.

At the town of Norfork, boat ramps are available on either shore in the Norfork Access. The AGFC ramp on the eastern shore is gravel, while the western ramp is paved. This is a popular site for both bank-fishing and boat launching, so usage is heavy. Both ramps are immediately below the confluence of the two rivers. Access to the western ramp is from AR 341, while the eastern ramp is reached from AR 5.

The next two access points are found at Red's Landing and Chesmond Ferry Accesses. Both of these AGFC facilities have boat ramps. Red's Landing Access is at the end of a 3-mile drive on gravel CR 68 and lies on the northeastern side of the river. You can reach Chesmond Ferry Access via a spur road to the west of the town of Calico Rock. The access is on the northeastern side, and the old ferry landing is visible across the river. Almost the entire western bank from Norfork to Calico Rock lies within the Ozark National Forest.

At 18 miles downriver from the mouth of the Norfork, the AR 5 bridge spans the White in Calico Rock. The town sits on a high bluff on the northeastern shore of the river and derives its name from the rocky cliff on which it perches. Calico Rock Access is located under the highway bridge at the foot of the cliff below the town. A boat ramp, parking lot, and rest rooms are located here. Wading is impractical through this stretch of water, but bank-fishing is available.

Finding the access at Calico Rock is no easy matter unless you are familiar with the town. Driving south on AR 5 through Calico Rock, you need to turn left on the last street before reaching the river bridge. Next, take the first right turn over the railroad spur track. Once over this spur, the road goes through an underpass beneath the main rail line. From there the road descends steeply to the right approaching the parking area and boat ramp. There are no directional signs at any of these turns.

The next public entry point on the White River tailwater is located near the town of Optimus. Although occasionally referred to as the Optimus Access, the actual name is Boswell Shoals Access. This access is unique in that it is managed by the US Fish and Wildlife Service, due to its location on the western shore, within the Ozark National Forest. Also setting it apart from most other accesses is its status as a walk-in area. There is no boat ramp, although it is possible to carry canoes and small boats down to the water from the parking area.

The village of Boswell is located directly across the river from this access and lends its name to Boswell Shoals, which are just downstream. These are the last shoals located on the Bull Shoals' trout water. You can reach them by foot from Boswell Shoals Access on the western bank.

To reach Boswell Shoals Access, travel east on the road that runs from the village of Optimus (the village is on AR 5) to the parking area at the end of this gravel track. There is a directional sign for the access at the intersection in Optimus.

The next three access points to White River's trout water are found in the villages of Mount Olive, Sylamore, and Guion (pronounced *Guy-on*). All of these contain boat ramps for accessing this slower portion of the tailwater, which is characterized by sweeping turns through bottomland.

At both Sylamore and Guion, access is available on both shores of the river via the old ferry landings. In the case of Guion, the access on the eastern shore is also known as the Wild Haw Landing, taking its name from both an early pioneer family and the 19th-century steamboat landing at the site. All three of these access points are managed by the AGFC.

The final point at which the public can reach the trout water is at the AGFC's Younger Access, 98½ miles downstream of Bull Shoals Dam. The access is located on a spur off CR 47 on the southwestern side of the river, to the northeast of the village of St. James. Where the spur runs to the Younger Access, a right turn onto CR 43 to the south leads to Lock and Dam No. 3. This marks the official end of trout water on the White, 101 miles below Bull Shoals. There is no access at this dam, which is marked with warning buoys. Care is needed to approach the old facility in a boat, and a portage is necessary to get around it.

For up-to-date water-release information for Bull Shoals Dam, the Corps of Engineers maintains a recorded message at the powerhouse. Call 501-431-5311.

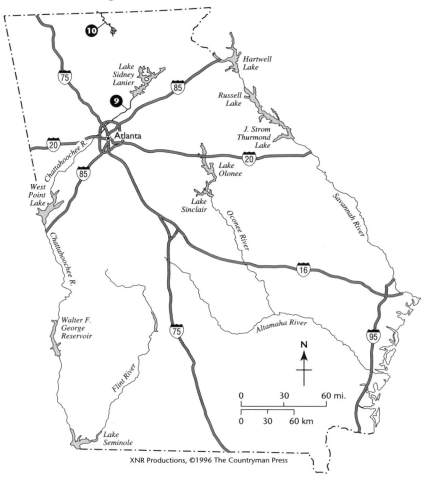

Georgia

75

10

Lake
Sidney
Lanier

Hartwell
Lake

85

Russell
Lake

9

J. Strom
Thurmond
Lake

20

Chattahoochee R.

Atlanta

20

85

Lake
Olonee

West
Point
Lake

Lake
Sinclair

Oconee River

Savannah River

Chattahoochee R.

16

Walter F.
George
Reservoir

75

Altamaha River

95

Flint River

N

0   30   60 mi.

0   30   60 km

Lake
Seminole

XNR Productions, ©1996 The Countryman Press

9 Chattahoochee River
10 Toccoa River

SECTION THREE

GEORGIA

Among the states that have traditionally been called the "Deep South," Georgia is unique in that it is the only one that contains natural trout habitat. A band of mountain counties stretching from the Blue Ridge Mountains in the northeastern corner of the Peach State, across to the Cohutta Mountains of the northwest, has always been home to native southern Appalachian brook trout. Over the years, through the introduction of brown and rainbow trout, that range has increased to most of the northern third of Georgia. Today, trout are stocked on a seasonal basis well down into the Piedmont region of the state, south of Atlanta.

As a result of these efforts, Georgia vies with North Carolina for the most total trout-stream miles of any southern state, with both claiming around 4200. Additionally, with 1500 miles of Class 1 or natural trout waters, the Peach State places third in the region (behind North Carolina and Virginia) in this category. The state's cold-water resources are quite extensive for a providence not usually associated with trout angling!

Georgia does not possess a great many tailwater streams. Two of the three that are located in the state, however, are of exceptional quality. The Chattahoochee River carries cold water from Lake Sidney Lanier down into the heart of metropolitan Atlanta on the northern rim of the Piedmont, creating an unusual urban fishery. In the northwestern corner of the state, water releases from Blue Ridge Lake add about 16 miles of excellent trout waters to the Toccoa River. Finally, in the northeastern corner of the state, the tailwaters of Hartwell Lake, on the Savannah River, support a small trout fishery as well. This last stream is shared with South Carolina—it forms the border between the two states. For this reason, a description of the Savannah River will be found in section 7 of this book, which covers South Carolina.

Although Georgia has a general trout season that lasts from the last Saturday of March through the final day of October, this season does not apply to any of the state's tailwaters. All of these tailwaters are managed instead as year-round trout fisheries. A Georgia Trout Stamp is required, along with a regular fishing license, for all resident and nonresident anglers between the ages of 16 and 64. The creel limit for trout in Georgia is any combination of 8 fish per day, regardless of species. There are no minimum or maximum size limits enforced on the tailwaters of the state.

9

Chattahoochee River

USGS Buford Dam, Suwanee, Duluth, Norcross, Chamblee, Sandy Springs, Northwest Atlanta

The Chattahoochee River is one of Georgia's best-known waterways. It rises in the Mark Trail Wilderness Area in the north-central portion of the state. From there it courses down to Lake Sidney Lanier, which is the most heavily used Corps of Engineers reservoir in the United States, with between 15 and 20 million visitors per year. After exiting the lake, the Chattahoochee runs through metropolitan Atlanta, then goes on to form the boundary between Georgia and Alabama. Eventually—in Lake Seminole at the Florida border—its waters become part of the Apalachicola River.

The Hooch, as it is referred to by many local anglers, begins its journey to the Gulf of Mexico as a natural trout stream in the mountains above Lake Lanier. By the time it reaches that 38,000-acre impoundment, it is already becoming a warm-water stream. The water drawn through Buford Dam from the 200-foot depths of Lake Lanier, however, revitalize the river as trout habitat. In fact, the Chattahoochee tailwater becomes the Peach State's premier trout water for the next 47 miles.

The story behind the conversion of the Chattahoochee tailwater to a trout fishery is a bit unusual in that the state fisheries managers played no role in the original endeavor. When Buford Dam was closed in 1957, there were no plans to introduce trout into the river. At the time, a program of stocking and stream renovations was in progress in the mountainous northern portion of the state, and the old Georgia Game and Fish Commission was trying to draw anglers to those northern counties. At that time, it had no interest in creating a competing trout fishery closer to the center of population in metro Atlanta.

In 1959 the local chapter of the Izaak Walton League obtained

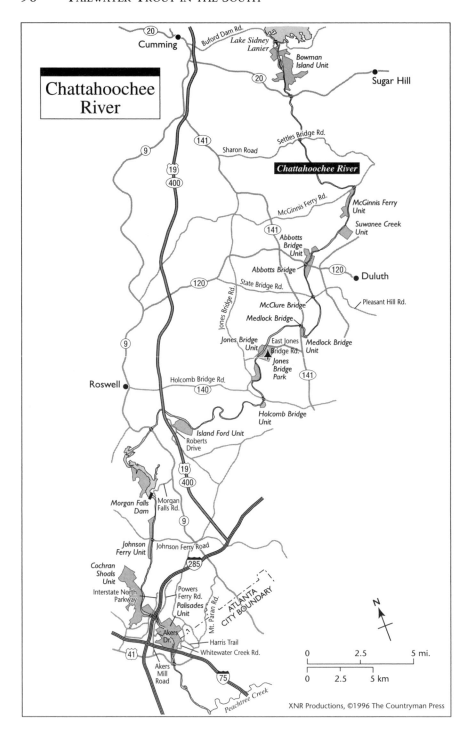

Chattahoochee
River

XNR Productions, ©1996 The Countryman Press

about 5000 rainbow trout fingerlings and surreptitiously released them into the tailwater below the dam. Once the fish had grown to catchable size, club members invited the state biologists to join them for a day of fishing on the new trout water. Needless to say, such actions today with regard to amateur stocking projects would be illegal, but the state fisheries managers quickly climbed aboard this bandwagon when the river's trout potential was demonstrated.

From this unique beginning, the stocking program expanded. It now releases about 250,000 catchable-sized 9- to 10-inch rainbow, brown, and brook trout per year into the Chattahoochee. The lower portions of this tailwater receive an additional 100,000 to 125,000 fingerling browns and rainbows annually.

The Chattahoochee is one of Georgia's most heavily fished trout streams; fortunately, with over 45 miles of big water, it is also by far the state's largest. The river is about 100 feet wide at Buford Dam and stretches to 200 to 300 feet by the time it reaches Atlanta. Also, beginning in July 1995 the entire tailwater was opened to year-round fishing, providing more opportunities for anglers. Previously, only the portion of the trout water downstream of the town of Roswell had been open to year-round fishing. On the downside, the Chattahoochee is strictly a low-water fishery. When generation is taking place at Buford Dam, the river runs very high and muddy, making angling impractical.

Access to the entire Hooch tailwater is very good due to the location of the Chattahoochee River National Recreation Area (CRNRA) along its shores. This "string of pearls" consists of a number of tracts of public land on the river bank from Buford Dam down to Atlanta. In all, park land totals roughly 4000 acres.

There are actually four distinct sections of the Chattahoochee between Buford Dam and the end of trout habitat at the mouth of Peachtree Creek in Atlanta. Such variety is a result of the very long tailwater on the Hooch. This distance serves to moderate the surges of water released downriver, allowing for a more diverse habitat in the lower portions of the run.

The first of these sections extends from Buford Dam down to the GA 20 bridge between the towns of Cumming on the west and Sugar Hill to the east. This bridge is roughly 2½ miles downstream of the dam.

Through here the riverbed is subject to the harshest scouring by the rushing waters released during power generation. It is composed of rock, gravel, and sand that is quite barren of aquatic insect life.

*This stocked brook trout fell for a Woolly Bugger
on the upper portion of the "Hooch."*

While the extremely cold water from the lake provides good year-round temperatures for trout, the forage base for the fish is small. This section of the stream is strictly a put-and-take fishery, with only a few carryover trout turning up. Of course, with plenty of fish stocked, the competition for meals is fierce, so the fish are usually hungry and bite readily.

This portion of the Hooch receives regular stockings of brown, rainbow, and some brook trout. These fish are supplied by the Chattahoochee State Fish Hatchery located just upstream of the GA 20 bridge. The staple of the fishery is the recent stocker, but occasional browns of 20 inches or better will turn up. The area closer to the GA 20 bridge is best for larger fish.

Much of the fishing pressure in this section is from bait-anglers (the only restriction is that no minnows may be used for bait upstream of Morgan Falls Dam); spin-fishers tossing in-line spinners or Little Cleo spoons place second. This is not the best fly-fishing water on the river, but Woolly Buggers, adult caddis imitations, and attractor dry-fly patterns will take some fish.

There is one easily wadable shoal on this part of the river, at Bowmans Island, within sight of the dam. It is, however, a location that calls for extreme caution. Water releases can turn it into a raging torrent in a hurry. In fact, a 1995 regulation requires that anyone boating, in a float tube, or even wading in the river between the dam and GA 20 must wear a Coast Guard–approved Personal Flotation Device (PFD, or life jacket to most of us laypeople) at all times. This dangerous water has claimed the lives of several anglers over the years.

The next section of the tailwater runs from GA 20 downstream to GA 141 at Medlock Bridge. This 14½-mile segment of the river is managed under "artificial-lure-only" fishing regulations and is the most heavily fished section of the river. It is also a primarily float-fishing stretch of water.

Fish Weir Shoals, just downstream of GA 20, is the only shoal area on this run, but farther downstream midriver sandbars offer some wading opportunities. Many anglers combine floating with wading by anchoring their boats on the bars, then wading in and casting back toward shore. Most of the trout through here—stockers of all three trout species—are found around the brush piles and blown-down trees along the shoreline. Although water-release scouring is less intense here, the forage base is still small. More fish hold over here than upstream, with some bruisers in the 5- to 8-pound range taken each year. Brown trout make up the bulk of these larger fish.

The most popular fishing tactic is tossing Rapala topwater minnows or in-line spinners, but you will also encounter anglers trolling the Countdown version of the Rapala minnow through the deeper portions of the flow. Some anglers use imitation salmon eggs as well, but be aware that the ones permeated with organic oils are not legal on this part of the river. Nymphs, streamers, and dry flies in attractor patterns are used by fly-casters. In years when Japanese beetles are present, their imitations can be deadly; grasshopper patterns will also work during the summer months.

Access to this part of the tailwater is available at the McGinnis Ferry, Suwanee Creek, Abbotts Bridge, and Medlock Bridge Units of the CRNRA. Improved boat ramps are located at Abbotts and Medlock Bridges, providing good put-in and take-out points for a

4½-mile float. Other limited access through here is found at Settles Bridge and at McClure Bridge.

The third segment of the Chattahoochee tailwater runs from GA 141 down to the GA 9 bridge at the town of Roswell. On this stretch the river is again open to angling by any method, and is noted as the best area to catch a truly big trout. Browns of 14 to 16 pounds have been taken, while rainbows of up to 14 pounds have also been reported. The extremes of the water surges abate on this 12-mile stretch of water, and the first aquatic weeds begin to appear.

There are two wadable sections on this run: Jones Bridge Shoals and Island Ford Shoals. Jones Bridge is just over a mile downriver from Medlock Bridge and boasts some hatches of caddis flies during spring and summer. Be aware also that this is the single most heavily fished location on the river, and most of its anglers are bait-casters. With the exception of caddis imitations and natural baits, the fishing tactics used on section two of the tailwater apply through here as well.

Access points for this run are at Medlock Bridge, Jones Bridge, Holcomb Bridge, and Island Ford Units of the CRNRA. Although Jones Bridge is no longer serviceable, there are boat ramps on both sides of the river in the park.

One note of concern regarding sections two and three of the Hooch's tailwater needs to be mentioned. The portion from the mouth of Suwanee Creek, near the midpoint of section two, down to Morgan Falls Dam has had a fish consumption advisory in effect since the spring of 1995. Rainbow trout tested here contained above-normal levels of PCBs. It is recommended that no more than one meal of these fish be eaten per week. Oddly enough, brown trout from this stretch did not show PCB contamination and are not covered by the advisory.

The final section of trout water on the Hooch extends 18 miles, from GA 9 down to the mouth of Peachtree Creek in northwestern Atlanta. While not the best fishing area of the tailwater, in some ways it is the most interesting.

The first 5 miles of water through here is impounded behind Morgan Falls Dam, a small hydroelectric installation operated by the Georgia Power Company. Although the lake contains trout, it is not considered part of the tailwater fishery.

Though the water rises and falls below Morgan Falls, the surges from Buford Dam have been all but eliminated. As a result, aquatic weeds and insects are plentiful. Add to this the presence of four distinct wadable shoals and the result is the best fly-fishing area of the tailwater. This is not to say, however, that bait- and spin-fishers do not also utilize this portion of the stream. And as mentioned earlier, in this run below Morgan Falls the use of minnows for bait is legal. Fishing pressure is not as heavy here as it is on other portions of the river, although fly-fishers are much more prevalent.

Only fingerling trout are stocked below Morgan Falls Dam, with half being browns and the rest rainbows. This fishery has been on the upswing since the winter of 1992, when rainbows were stocked for the first time in 15 years. This followed several seasons of drought and some silting problems, caused by construction upriver, that had affected the fishing on this part of the tailwater.

A more recent concern for the trout fishery through here is the appearance of striped bass in the river. These fish apparently moved upriver from West Point Lake, about 60 miles downstream of Atlanta. It is feared that these large fish will prey heavily upon the rainbows stocked here. Due to this concern, the Georgia Department of Natural Resources has ended the stocking of stripers in West Point Lake.

Today, rainbows and browns of 8 to 14 inches can be found in the Cochran Shoals Unit, as well as Devils Race Course, Thornton, and Long Island Shoals in the Palisades Unit; the occasional fish of over 18 inches may show up, too. All of these shoals are accessible from portions of the CRNRA lands and host springtime hatches of light Cahills, plus midges throughout the summer. Woolly Buggers are another good fly pattern for the deeper pools, while nymphs such as the Tellico and the Gold-Ribbed Hare's Ear also produce fish.

The last couple of miles of river down to the Atlanta City Water Works at the mouth of Peachtree Creek are not generally fished, although they do contain trout. The shore through here is all privately owned, and there are no take-out facilities at Peachtree Creek for float-fishers.

Another factor to keep in mind when planning a fishing trip below Morgan Falls is that it is one of the most popular rafting destinations in the Southeast. Particularly on weekends, from 10 AM to around 6 PM, the river will be virtually covered with rafts, canoes, kayaks, and tubes. The most heavily used portion of the stream is from the Johnson Ferry Road Bridge down to the Cobb Parkway (US 41) Bridge. While this armada of floaters may detract from the quality of the fishing experience, it does not usually affect the fishing itself. Even rising trout are only put down when a raft passes directly over them, and they will start feeding again almost immediately. Apparently, the fish get used to the heavy traffic pretty quickly.

The first access point to the tailwater below Morgan Falls is via Morgan Falls Road on the eastern side of the river at the foot of the dam. Other access points are at the Johnson Ferry Unit of the CRNRA on Johnson Ferry Road and the Cochran Shoals Unit off Interstate North Parkway. Additionally, both Devils Race Course and Thornton Shoals can be reached from the parking lot at the CRNRA headquarters off Akers Drive—although this does require a ½-mile hike down to the river. Long Island Shoals can be reached from Whitewater Creek Road through the Palisades Unit of the CRNRA, while the final access point is at the Paces Mill take-out point for rafting at the US 41 Bridge.

The National Park Service distributes a free brochure with an excellent map showing all the access points and public properties along the Chattahoochee's tailwater. For ordering information, see the Map Sources appendix at the end of this book.

The Corps of Engineers' tentative water-release schedule for Buford Dam is available by calling 770-945-1466. For the generation schedule for Morgan Falls Dam, call the Georgia Power Company at 404-329-1455.

10

Toccoa River

USGS Mineral Bluff

Georgia's other major tailwater trout fishery is found on the Toccoa River below Blue Ridge Lake in the northwestern corner of the state. Beginning at the Tennessee Valley Authority's (TVA) Blue Ridge Dam just east of the town of Blue Ridge, the Toccoa's tailwater flows northwesterly for 16 miles to the twin towns of McCaysville, Georgia, and Copperhill, Tennessee, at the state boundary. As the river crosses the state line its name changes to the Ocoee, which is a well-known rafting and kayaking destination, but not a trout stream. The practical range of trout does not extend into Tennessee. Along this course through Georgia, the Toccoa is located entirely in Fannin County.

The tailwater on the Toccoa River is only about 60 to 80 feet wide along its entire length—not a particularly large river. Although it is possible to catch trout from the Toccoa at all water levels, most of the fishing pressure occurs when the water level is falling after power generation ends. Once the water level has bottomed out, the fish become difficult to find and catch.

Presently the Toccoa is stocked only with rainbow trout, with a total in excess of 20,000 fish released annually. These stockings of 7- to 9-inch fish take place every 2 weeks from April through Labor Day. State biologists describe the Toccoa as a put-and-take fishery with very low holdover potential. It is quite rare to find rainbows of even a foot long in this river.

There are, however, also some browns present. These are wild, naturally reproducing fish that drop down into the river from feeder streams. (Almost no reproduction is thought to take place in the Toccoa tailwater itself.) A few of the browns reach weights of 3 to 5 pounds, but even these fish are probably not year-round residents of the tailwater. One oddity concerning big trout in the Toccoa is that a former state-record brook trout of just under 5 pounds was taken

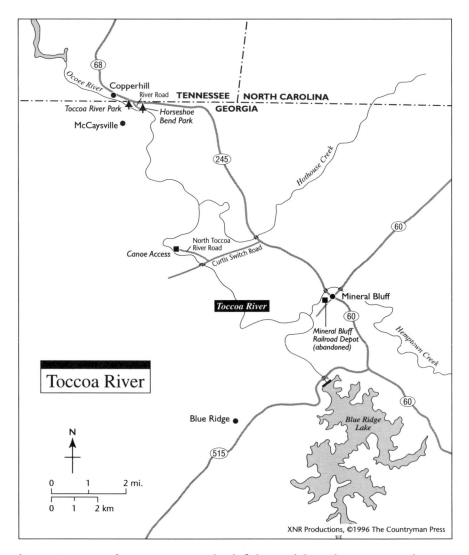

here. It was, of course, a stocked fish, and brookies are no longer stocked in the tailwater.

The Toccoa's trout fishery suffers from a trio of limiting factors. To begin with, water temperatures will often reach the high 60s to low 70s in August and September of particularly warm years. This sends the brown trout back up the feeder streams and makes the surviving rainbows sluggish.

The other two problems are low dissolved-oxygen levels in the water during power-generation periods, and the scouring of the bottom that also takes place at these times. The low oxygen levels are a direct threat to the trout, while the surges destroy the aquatic weeds and insects that make up their food chain. The TVA is looking at the idea of installing a second turbine at Blue Ridge Dam, which should solve the oxygen problem, while the Wildlife Resources Division of the Georgia Department of Natural Resources is considering constructing a weir dam downstream of Blue Ridge Lake to regulate the surges.

The Toccoa's tailwater is made up of long, deep pools broken by occasional shallower runs. It is better suited to float-fishing than to wading, particularly while the water is still falling and fishing is at its best. Since bank access is not abundant on the river, this also adds to the appeal of floating in a belly boat, canoe, or johnboat.

Hatches of dark-hued caddis flies in the size 14 to 16 range are seen each spring and summer on the Toccoa, especially in the areas of shallow shoals. These are sporadic and difficult to predict accurately. Another insect to look for is the Japanese beetle. These do not appear every summer in this region, but when they do the trout gorge on those that fall in the water. As on most large streams in the southeastern states, Woolly Buggers in black or olive are good choices for probing the river when no surface activity is visible. With spinning gear, in-line spinners are the most popular offering on this tailwater. Bait-fishers, who are most numerous in the immediate vicinity of the tailrace at Blue Ridge Dam, comprise the largest percentage of anglers. Their favorite baits are corn, worms, crickets, and salmon eggs.

As mentioned, a lack of public access to the water along the Toccoa is the biggest drawback to fishing it. The most popular angling location and launch site for float-fishing is the TVA park at the foot of the dam on the eastern side of the river. There is a concrete catwalk at the tailrace, which is very popular for bait-fishing. At lower levels the water is clear enough to sight-fish the trout holding along the wall beneath the fishing pier. It is also worth noting that the overall fishing pressure on the river is light, with more than two-thirds of the anglers being local residents.

The portion of the river immediately downstream of the dam on the TVA property is shallow enough to wade easily across the river during low water levels. This is also an area in which to keep a sharp ear peeled for the siren announcing water releases.

This park at the dam is accessible from GA 515 (also marked as the Appalachian Scenic Highway or Zell Miller Parkway) by turning

Blue Ridge Dam on the Toccoa has a distinctive
single-turbine powerhouse.

south onto the paved (but unmarked) road at the east end of the GA 515 bridge over the river.

The first downstream access is near the town of Mineral Bluff. When traveling north, an unmarked paved road runs west from GA 60 just before it crosses Hemptown Creek. This is one block north of the town's main intersection. The road passes the abandoned Mineral Bluff railroad depot and at ¼ mile changes to gravel; the last few hundred yards of this approach road is quite rough and prone to washouts. At just over ¾ mile the road dead-ends at a closed bridge on the river. Here there is a short, wadable shoal beginning under the abandoned bridge and running to the abandoned railway bridge just downstream.

The next access points are found off Curtis Switch Road (CR 195) to the north of Mineral Bluff. This paved road runs west off GA 245, but presently has no road markers at the intersection. The intersection is, however, just south of the GA 245 bridge over Hothouse Creek, which does have a sign identifying it. There is limited access to the river where Curtis Switch Road crosses the flow. Additionally, North Toccoa River Road (gravel) runs to the north off Curtis Switch just before the bridge. By traveling ½ mile on this road, you will encounter a small TVA canoe-launch park on the river's eastern bank. The park is marked with a very small, inconspicuous sign, and there is no directional sign for it back at the intersection of Curtis Switch and North Toccoa River Roads.

Finally, there are two parks in McCaysville proper that offer access to the river, as well as some wadable water. To the southeast of town, 1³⁄₁₀ miles to the southeast of GA 245 on River Road, is Horseshoe Bend Park. This playground and softball complex has over ¼ mile of river frontage and easy access to the water. Farther downstream, practically in downtown McCaysville, Toccoa River Park offers easy access to the river and a section of wadable shoals just upstream. There are some old Cherokee fish weirs in the river between these two parks.

To obtain details on the water-release schedule at Blue Ridge Dam, call the TVA's automated information line at 615-632-2264 and punch in the appropriate code for the Toccoa by following the instructions provided. A Touch-Tone phone is needed to use this service.

Kentucky

11 Barren River
12 Carr Fork
13 Cumberland River
14 Dix River
15 Johns Creek
16 Licking Creek
17 Licking River

18 Little Sandy River
19 Martins Fork
20 Middle Fork Kentucky River
21 Nolin River
22 Paint Creek
23 Rough River

Ohio River

Licking River

Kentucky R.

Louisville

Lexington

Rough River Lake

Barren Lake

Cumberland Lake

Ohio River

Lake Barkley

Kentucky Lake

XNR Productions, ©1996 The Countryman Press

N

0   30   60 mi.

0   30   60 km

SECTION FOUR

KENTUCKY

A cursory glance at the atlas would lead one to believe that the Blue-grass State of Kentucky would be a prime location for trout in the South. It shares with Missouri and Virginia the distinction of having the most northerly position among the states of the region. This location, with its resulting colder climate and a mountainous eastern half, would seem to make Kentucky an ideal spot to find cold-water streams.

As is sometimes the case, however, simple geography is not enough to explain the whole story. One must delve into geology as well to understand Kentucky's cold-water fisheries. While much of the eastern end of the state is composed of highlands, only a very slender rib of truly mountainous land runs down the edge of the state. To the west of this Appalachian Mountain terrain are the Cumberland Plateau and its associated river valleys. Although the land rises to heights of 1300 to 1500 feet above sea level, these peaks have little in common with the igneous and metamorphic, hard-rock mountains of the Appalachian chain. The basic building blocks of the Cumberland Plateau are sedimentary rocks formed on the bottom of the ancient inland sea that covered the central United States in prehistoric times.

These sedimentary rocks are much softer than the stone of the true mountain ranges of the South, and less resistant to weathering. As a result, stream water does not tumble over them, but rather cuts through them. Thus, most of the creeks and rivers of the Cumberland Plateau have long since sliced down to form deep valley courses. The result is low-altitude streams that meander sluggishly around the higher ground. Many of the creeks are seasonal, going dry during the summer and fall because they descend into subterranean channels. As for those streams that remain aboveground, the only ones that can support trout year-round are fed by cooler waters from the limestone springs and caverns of the region. The number of such streams is small.

In fact, fisheries biologists do not unanimously support the idea that Kentucky ever supported natural trout populations. (Some creeks along the extreme eastern border are now managed as wild brook trout waters, but the fish had to be introduced into these streams.) Some speculate that trout once inhabited the area but were wiped out by mining and timber cutting; it is equally plausible, however, that they never ranged this far west in the Appalachian foothills.

Due to this topography and geology, the Bluegrass State's modern trout waters are artificial and extensively managed. Most streams support put-and-take, seasonal fisheries. Included among these is the most extensive system of tailwater streams in any state of the Southeast. The Kentucky Department of Fish and Wildlife Resources (KDFWR) manages 14 rivers and creeks as tailwater trout resources. These run the gamut from mighty rivers with scores of miles of water to small streams with only a mile of cold-water habitat. Some are true tailwaters, while others are tailwaters in name only.

The best example of such a stream—listed as a tailwater, yet falling short of what most anglers expect of one—is Wood Creek. Located below the dam on Wood Creek Lake in Laurel County, some 6 miles northwest of the town of London, the lake is impounded behind the highway fill embankment for I-75. While the 627-acre lake is 127 feet deep at its maximum depth point, it has no hydroelectric power facility.

Below the dam, Wood Creek is but a small stream—in places, barely 20 feet wide—and is stocked with rainbow trout. A total of 1500 fish are released in monthly increments, in every month except October and November. Most of the land below Wood Creek Lake is privately owned, offering little access as well. Due to its small size, the small number of trout available, and the difficult access, this stream is covered only briefly.

There is no closed season for trout in Kentucky. Besides a valid Kentucky fishing license, all anglers aged 16 to 64 must possess a Kentucky Trout Stamp to fish for the species in the state. The general regulations mandate a creel limit of 8 trout per angler per day, regardless of species. Only 3 of these may be brown trout, and no more than 2 brook trout. There is no minimum size limit for browns or rainbows, but all brookies harvested in Kentucky must be 10 inches or longer. There are exceptions to these regulations that apply on some of the tailwaters, but these are discussed in covering the specific streams.

11

Barren River

USGS Meador

The Barren River tailwater is located below Barren Lake in south-central Kentucky, near the Tennessee border. The river below the 10,000-acre lake forms the extreme northern border of Allen County with Barren County at the dam, and then with Warren County farther downstream. The river runs in a northwesterly direction from the dam, eventually flowing through the city of Bowling Green.

Although the Barren vies with the Nolin River for the title of Kentucky's second most heavily stocked tailwater trout stream, it is only a minor tailwater by southeastern standards. The river is roughly 100 feet wide where it emerges from the dam at Barren Lake, and it broadens only to a couple hundred feet along its course. Barren Lake Dam is just 80 feet high and contains no powerhouse, since this is a Corps of Engineers flood-control project. While the flow of water through the dam varies, its rise and fall is not as drastic as that associated with power surges at hydroelectric facilities. Of course, caution is still necessary when fishing during low water levels. When releases do occur, they raise the river level enough in a short period to merit caution. Even during high water levels, the Barren's flow tends to be rather sluggish below the tailrace.

In all, the KDFWR presently stocks the Barren tailwaters with 18,600 trout each year. These are all rainbows of standard 9- to 12-inch stocking size, released monthly in varying numbers from April through November. Carryover fish are relatively rare, and no natural reproduction takes place in this river. The Barren's location—close to the major population center of Bowling Green—dictates that it receive moderate to heavy fishing pressure year-round. This pressure is heaviest for the first 3 days after each month's stocking. Many of the anglers fish from the several gravel bars that jut into the river from the southern shore just below the dam.

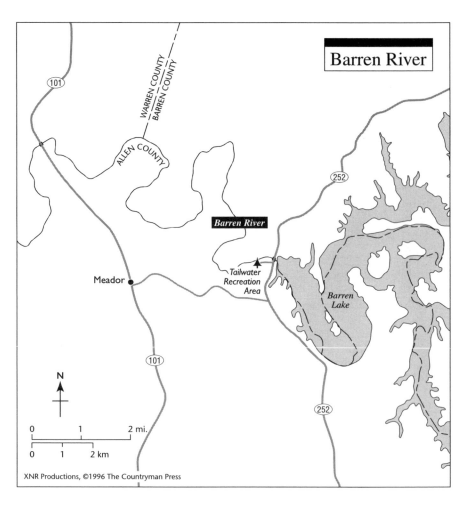

Most of the anglers on the Barren are bait-fishers casting from the bank, with a few tossing spinners from shore as well. Although fly-casting is possible, it is unusual here. The public access portion of the tailwater is not good wading territory. Anglers accustomed to the big waters of hydropower rivers will undoubtedly be rather disappointed with the Barren. It is, however, representative of the smaller tailwater flows of Kentucky flood-control reservoirs. While not world-class fisheries, these rivers provide local anglers with trout fishing where it would not otherwise exist.

The prime trout water on the Barren is short, extending only a mile or two downriver. Through this section, public access is quite limited. The river shore can be reached via the Tailwater Recreation

*At low water levels, the Barren River is a gentle flow
whose gravel bars are favorites with bait-fishers.*

Area from the southern end of Barren Lake Dam on KY 252 (which crosses the dam). A paved drive leads down to a parking area on the river's southern shore. Downstream of the parking area is a Corps of Engineers campground that provides both tent and RV sites, as well as a paved boat ramp. The campground is open from spring through fall. In all, there is ½ mile of river bank in the Corps' land. The river then runs through private farmland, crossed only by the KY 101 bridge before it reaches Bowling Green.

12

Carr Fork

USGS Vicco

Carr Fork is located only a mile or so from the coal-mining town of Hazard. Lying in the mountainous southeastern corner of Kentucky, the creek eventually adds its waters to the Kentucky River via that stream's North Fork. The dam on Carr Fork forms a reservoir of the same name that was completed in 1976 mainly to control flooding. It has no hydroelectric powerhouse.

As noted above, Carr Fork is only a creek downstream of the lake. Immediately below the dam is a large pool with riprap walls; this constitutes the major fishing location on the tailwater. Although there is roughly a mile of suitable trout habitat on Carr Fork, only ¼ mile of it has any appreciable public access. This is no handicap to local anglers, however, since almost all of the fishing pressure occurs at the foot of the dam.

Sassafrass Road crosses a bridge over the stream just below the big pool at the dam. According to one local angler I encountered at stream-side, the fishing here can be summed up succinctly.

"When they stock them, they just dump the fish off the bridge," he observed. "Everybody crowds around the pool underneath and takes them right back out."

Indeed they do. Biologists for the KDFWR consider the Carr Fork one of the most popular trout fisheries in the commonwealth. A total of 12,600 rainbow trout are released into the stream each year, with plantings taking place monthly from April to November. When the stocking truck leaves the Carr Fork, expect to find hordes of anglers there for the next couple of days. The shore of the pool just above the Sassafrass Road bridge will be lined with folks, nearly all of them bait-fishers.

After Sassafrass Road crosses the creek, it comes to a parking area with rest rooms and a playground on the stream's northwestern side.

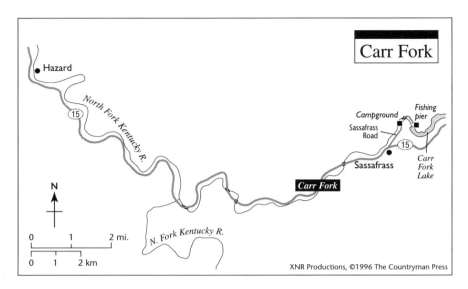

From there a set of concrete stairs descends to a paved fishing pier that runs several hundred feet along the shore of the big pool. There is also a walkway and stairs leading over the tailrace gate to a similar, but shorter, pier on the other shore.

Once the stream exits the dam pool, it flows under Sassafrass Road and past the pilings of an old bridge immediately downstream of the present structure. Through the rest of the public access area the creek is only about 30 to 40 feet wide. This downstream access area consists of a Corps of Engineers park containing picnic and playgrounds, as well as more rest rooms. It is a seasonal park, however, and closed in the winter months.

Although the stream is shallow enough for wading and has some small shoals and gravel bars through the park area, the crowds from the dam pool spill over into this portion of the creek during stocking periods. These crowds make wading and fly- or spin-casting chancy propositions.

Downstream of the Corps of Engineers land, the creek parallels Sassafrass Road for ¾ mile to where the road intersects with KY 15 (at the crossroads in the town of Sassafrass). Along this stretch of road are a couple of turnouts that offer parking and access to the stream. Below the KY 15 bridge there are no more access points, but the end of trout water is imminent anyway.

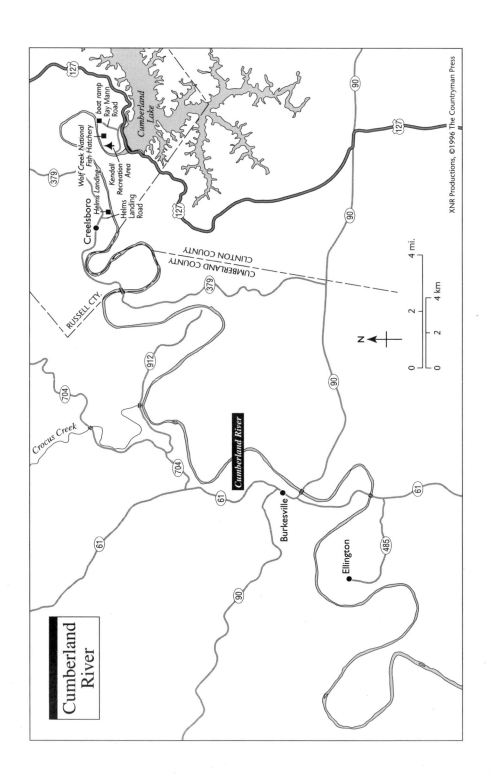

Cumberland River

Cumberland Lake

boat ramp
Ray Mann Road
Wolf Creek National Fish Hatchery
Helms Landing
Kendall Recreation Area
Helms Landing Road
Creelsboro

RUSSELL CTY.

CUMBERLAND COUNTY
CLINTON COUNTY

Crocus Creek

Cumberland River

Burkesville

Ellington

N

4 mi.

4 km

XNR Productions, ©1996 The Countryman Press

13

Cumberland River

USGS Creelsboro, Wolf Creek Dam, Amandaville,
Burkesville, Waterview, Blacks Ferry, Dubre, Vernon

There can be no doubt that the Cumberland River below Cumberland Lake in south-central Kentucky is the commonwealth's premier trout water. Beginning in Russell County, the river rushes from outlets of Wolf Creek Dam's hydroelectric turbines to create a cold-water fishery that can support trout as far downstream as the Tennessee border, almost 80 river miles away. Although trout will show up on the lower end of this tailwater, the best fishing runs only for about 50 miles down into Cumberland County. Still, this makes the river below the 50,250-acre reservoir Kentucky's longest and biggest trout stream.

Unlike many other tailwaters stocked by the KDFWR, the Cumberland is very large, often stretching to widths of several hundred yards. Along its course it can be a raging torrent or a gentle flow, depending upon the amount of water released from the powerhouse at Wolf Creek Dam. When all six turbines are turning, the river rises 6 to 7 feet above minimum flow; it becomes difficult to navigate in a small boat and downright dangerous to unwary waders.

Of particular note is the fact that the releases from Wolf Creek Dam are controlled by computer from the Corps of Engineers' office in Nashville, Tennessee. Although a siren is supposed to warn of impending releases, local anglers have reported that it is undependable, either not sounding or giving false alarms. Obviously, such a record leads to complacency that can end disastrously. If you choose to wade in the ½ mile of park water immediately below the dam, use extreme caution. Pay close attention to water levels and heed the siren every time it sounds. This is a good place to wear one of the newer inflatable fishing vests as an insurance policy.

The turbulence created when the turbines begin turning at Wolf Creek Dam is so great, and the current so strong, that the Corps of

Engineers requires all boaters on the tailwater within ²/₁₀ mile to wear a personal flotation device (life jacket) at all times. This rule has been in effect since 1990.

The first rainbow trout were stocked in the Cumberland River tailwater in 1952, soon after the dam was completed. These fish thrived over the years, making up most of the cold-water fishing in the river. Presently, the KDFWR stocks 82,500 catchable-sized rainbows in the river annually. The fish are obtained from the Wolf Creek National Fish Hatchery, which is just below the dam. Stocking takes place once a month from April through November; fish are released at the foot of the dam and downstream at Helms Landing. The number of fish involved in these monthly releases varies but is announced in advance. Stockings draw plenty of anglers.

Though the large numbers of fish released is the main attraction of the rainbow trout fishery, bigger specimens do turn up. Rainbows of 3 to 4 pounds are commonly caught, along with the occasional lunker. In fact, the Cumberland has laid claim to the Kentucky state record for rainbow trout since September 10, 1972, when Jim Mattingly of Somerset landed a 14-pound, 6-ounce monster from the tailwater.

In 1982 the KDFWR began releasing subadult brown trout into the river as well, adding a new dimension to the fishing. It was this addition to the program, in fact, that turned the Cumberland into a true delight for trophy anglers. Most recently, 30,000 fingerling browns have been added to the flow yearly; stockings take place in the colder months. Since these fish are not of catchable size, the plantings are not announced. They usually occur at up to five locations along the tailwater.

Boasting growth rates of up to 3 pounds per year, the Cumberland fishery produced a state-record brown of more than 11 pounds in 1987. That fish was taken by Randal (Randy) Gibson of Bakerton in the Wetstone Creek area of the tailwater, about 25 miles below Wolf Creek Dam. Apparently not one to rest on his laurels, Gibson later boated browns of 17 pounds, 14 ounces and 18 pounds during 1987 and 1988. Finally, on June 11, 1988, Gibson—one of the few fishing guides working the tailwater of the Cumberland—caught the present Kentucky state-record brown trout. This fish tipped the scales at 18 pounds, 8 ounces.

As Gibson has proven, some big browns exist in the Cumberland. Biologists and anglers alike expect the river eventually to produce a fish of more than 20 pounds. If you are looking for such a trophy brown, surveys have shown that the best places to begin your search are from the area several miles downstream of the dam and extending as far as 50 miles downriver. This water probably holds more of the larger trout because it gets less fishing pressure than do the accessible areas near the dam. The most effective fishing method is tossing crankbaits such as the Rapala Shad Rap or Countdown (crawfish, black-and-gold, or silver are productive finishes) near shoreline log-jams, submerged tree trunks, or root tangles. The browns tend to hold tight to this cover during the day. Rock outcroppings, which are abundant along the tailwater, are secondary locations for casting. Blue Fox spinners and Rebel crawfish-pattern lures are also popular. Although fly-fishing is not common on the Cumberland, big, weighted streamer patterns would be an obvious choice for this water.

The best fishing for the bigger browns occurs when three or fewer turbines are running at the dam, and particularly as the water is first rising when power generation begins. This is probably due to increased amounts of food being washed downstream by the rising waters, which provoke feeding binges by the trout. Overcast days are another good time to fish.

The most-targeted times of year on the Cumberland are from late spring (after the runoff from early spring rains has subsided) to late summer, and from September through mid-November. Randy Gibson, however, boated most of his record-breaking trout in June and July. There are clearly no hard-and-fast rules.

Another tactic for hanging some bigger trout is to troll or cast the abovementioned lures in the boiling current just below Wolf Creek Dam during high water. Some anglers run their boats right up to the tailrace of the dam, fish while floating with the current for several hundred yards downstream, then repeat the sequence. Shad and other baitfish are often sucked through the turbines here and easily fall prey to the waiting trout. The presence of these stunned baitfish is evident from the numbers of gulls that circle and dive. Using lures that imitate the struggling minnows can produce plenty of action. This fishing is noted for being at its best in early autumn.

For those trying to catch some rainbows, the first ½ mile of the river below Wolf Creek Dam is the prime area, with populations of these trout found to be highest there. Since the rainbow trout are noted for being less inclined to bite during high water, virtually all of the angling from shore occurs when the turbines are still. During these periods the river is reduced to a series of pools with gravel bars

Anglers run their boats up to the base of the Wolf Creek Dam on the Cumberland River and fish as they float back downriver with the current.

jutting out among them, creating excellent access. This ease of access also means the fishing pressure can be very heavy through here. Ordinarily, low-water periods occur from dawn to about 9 AM during spring and summer, but there are no set rules on water releases.

The standard rainbow stocked into the Cumberland tailwater is 8 to 12 inches long. These fish fall for all of the usual baits to which hatchery-reared trout are susceptible. Kernel corn, red worms, salmon eggs, and cheese balls are all popular baits. Spin-fishers cast ⅟₁₆- to ⅛-ounce Rooster Tail and Mepps spinners, especially in brown colors, or red-and-white Dardevle spoons.

Fly-fishing tends to be a neglected art on the Cumberland. Occasionally, long-rod anglers fish below the dam during low water, or possibly in some of the shoal or riffle areas farther downstream, but these are the exception. Overall, the Cumberland tailwater is not an ideal fly-fishing destination. Late spring and early summer are most popular for fly-casting, with the river hosting hatches of mayflies, caddis, and midges, plus some occasional stone flies. These hatches can be numerous, but are sporadic. Attractor flies and standard nymph patterns are the best choices when no surface activity is visible.

Access to the Cumberland River tailwater at the Kendall Recreation Area is at the eastern end of Wolf Creek Dam. An approach road drops down to the river from US 127, which runs across the dam. The Kendall complex contains an RV campground, parking areas, and a boat ramp.

There is a lot of bank-fishing pressure applied to the stream just below the dam, especially during low water. In all, there is ½ mile of shoreline access on the eastern bank, while high stone bluffs overlook the river from the west. Shallow areas are quite limited near the dam, but there is wadable water near the boat ramp. A small creek enters the river just downstream of the campground. During high water it is possible to fish a short way up into it.

Since most land along the Cumberland is privately owned, float-fishing offers the best alternative. A float from the dam through the prime trout water down to the city of Burkesville requires 2 full days on the water. Fortunately, the Cumberland is such a big river that bass boats and even pontoon boats can navigate it during all but dead-low water levels.

Another access point is via Ray Mann Road, which runs off the approach road to the Kendall Recreation Area. At the end of this ¾-mile road, which changes from pavement to gravel, is an unimproved gravel boat ramp.

Several shoal areas are located along this floating stretch. These offer the drifting angler the opportunity to get out of the boat and do a bit of wading if the water is low enough. At 1½ miles below the dam there is a shoal at the mouth of Little Indian Creek; there is another one at the mouth of Blackfish Creek, at 3 miles downstream.

The first downstream boat ramp is at Helms Landing, off KY 379 in Russell County. This is approximately 10 miles below Wolf Creek Dam. This boat ramp is paved, and is managed by the KDFWR.

Through here the Cumberland is quite wide and deep. In fact, this part of the river was patrolled by federal gunboats in 1863 during the Civil War, and modern anglers will find that floating provides the best access today as well.

Helms Landing is located at the end of Helms Landing Road, 1 mile from its intersection with KY 379. That junction is 2½ miles east of Creelsboro, a historic crossroads on KY 379. Today all of the buildings in Creelsboro are boarded up, making it a modern-day ghost town.

Below Helms Landing, you will encounter several shoal areas before reaching the town of Burkesville. The first is 2 miles below the landing; others are at the mouth of Crocus Creek, both a mile above and a mile below the area known as the Rockhouse. Finally, there is a shoal a couple of miles above Winfreys Landing (16 miles from the dam). The shoal at Crocus Creek is just off KY 912 in Cumberland County, and there is a gravel boat ramp at Winfreys Landing.

The Burkesville Boat Ramp is located in the town of the same name, and is managed by the KDFWR. It lies on Banks Street between the ends of Lower and Upper River Roads, just upstream of the KY 90 bridge over the river. Riverfront Lodge, located between the bridge and the boat ramp, also has a private boat ramp and dock.

Since March 1995 a special slot limit for trout has been in effect on the portion of the Cumberland tailwater from the KY 61 bridge (between Burkesville and Ellington) downstream to the Tennessee state line. Along this last 35 miles of trout water, the daily creel limit is 5 trout; no more than 3 can be browns. Also, 4 trout of less than 12 inches long may be kept, along with 1 of more than 20 inches. All rainbows and browns of 12 to 20 inches must be returned to the river unharmed.

To obtain information on water-release schedules at Wolf Creek Dam, call the Corps of Engineers' recorded message at 502-343-0153.

14

Dix River

USGS Wilmore

The Dix River tailwater forms the boundary between Mercer County on the west and Garrard County to the east. Unlike most of Kentucky's trout waters, the Dix River is located in the Bluegrass Country of the central part of the commonwealth, just south of Lexington. Although the tailwater is only 4 miles in length, before it empties into the Kentucky River near the historic village of High Bridge it is a notable trout fishery.

Originating at the foot of Dix Dam, which impounds 1860-acre Herrington Lake, the Dix River is managed as a trophy brown trout fishery for 2 miles below the dam. Part of the reason for this unusual management scheme is the inaccessibility of the water. Kentucky Utilities, which manages the Dix Dam and the coal-fired electric-generation plant at the location, does not allow any shore access to the tailwater. Farther downstream the shore is lined with massive stone cliffs; this spectacular gorge is on private lands. The result is a total lack of bank access to this fishery. Also, the waters run deep in the Dix River, so fishing from a boat is the only option for trout anglers here.

The first stockings of trout did not occur on the Dix until 1986, when browns were introduced. These first fish—about 3000 per year—exhibited strong survival and growth rates. At the repeated request of the Bluegrass Chapter of Trout Unlimited in Lexington, the KDFWR established the first 2 miles of water below the dam as trophy brown trout water on January 1, 1990. Signs on the river mark the end of this regulated water. Under these regulations, only artificial lures are permitted; the creel limit is 3 brown trout per day, all of which must be at least 15 inches long. This fishery is presently thriving and only an additional 600 browns are added each year.

Since the spring of 1990, some rainbow trout have also been stocked into the tailwater of the Dix. The regular state creel limit of 8 fish per day applies to rainbows taken here.

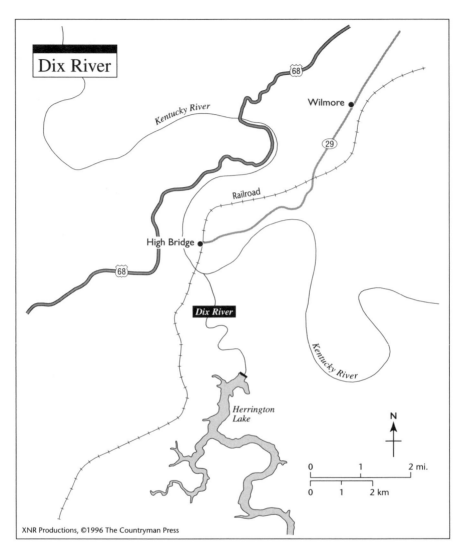

Although some trout have been reported in the Kentucky River below its junction with the Dix during colder months, the portion of the river just below Herrington Lake remains the best fishing area. Most anglers here use jigs or heavy spoons, with fly-anglers opting for streamers or nymphs.

As noted earlier, access is the major problem for fishing the Dix River. The only public access point is located on the Kentucky River at the High Bridge site. This location gets its name from the presence of the highest railroad bridge (308 feet) above a navigable river in the United States. Built in 1876, the span has been updated and is still in use.

*The highest railroad bridge over a navigable river in North America
is just below the mouth of the Dix River. The only access
to this tailwater is just downstream of the bridge.*

Access to the Dix is available by taking KY 29 southwest from the
town of Wilmore to the High Bridge community. The road dead-
ends at the bridge site. Just before reaching the bridge, Dix Drive
descends steeply from the right of the highway down to the river
bank. A park is situated at the site of an old lock and dam at this
location on the Kentucky River, and a public boat ramp has recently
been installed just upstream of the lock. From this point it is roughly
4 miles upstream to the mouth of the Dix River.

15
Johns Creek

USGS Lancer

The Johns Creek tailwater is located in Floyd County in east-central Kentucky, originating at the foot of the dam on Dewey Lake. From there the creek flows to the northwest, then forms an arc as it turns south to empty into the Levisa Fork. The Levisa Fork, in turn, eventually adds its waters to the Ohio River system. Johns Creek is quite small as it exits 1100-acre Dewey Lake, and is a marginal trout fishery.

Dewey Lake is a Corps of Engineers flood-control project and has no hydroelectric facilities. For that reason, there is no true water-release surge in the creek, which flows deep and sluggishly when minimum flows are coming through the dam. When more water is being released, it simply rises and runs a bit faster.

The high concrete walls of the spillway beside the tailrace below Dewey Lake give the tailwater of Johns Creek a distinctive look.

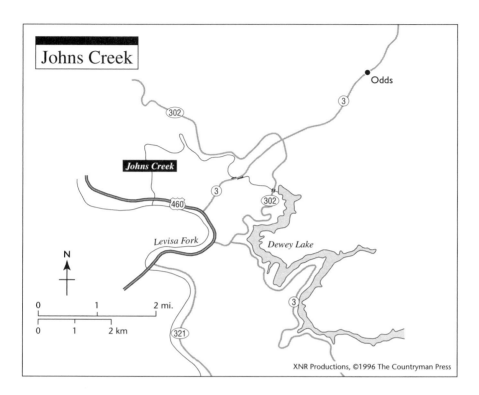

Only 6550 rainbow trout are stocked in Johns Creek each year, with the releases taking place monthly from April to June and September to November. During July and August, Johns Creek is too warm to support the planting of trout. Very little, if any, carryover of fish occurs through the summer. Obviously, this is strictly a put-and-take fishery for catchable-sized stockers of 8 to 12 inches.

Access is available to Johns Creek at the foot of the dam in a Corps of Engineers park that contains playgrounds, a softball field, and rest rooms. In all there is about ¼ mile of shoreline open to the public. All access is on the northern side of the stream. The major features of this tailwater are the huge concrete spillway walls that lie just opposite the park on the southern side of the creek. A large eddy forms where the end of the spillway wall meets the tailrace waters, providing one of the major angling points on this short trout water.

Bait-fishing for the rainbow trout is the predominant angling activity here, although some anglers undoubtedly use artificial lures as well. A fly-caster on Johns Creek would be a very unusual sight.

To reach the dam at Dewey Lake, take KY 302 southwest from its junction with KY 3 south of the hamlet of Odds. An access drive to the creekside park is located off the northern side of the highway just before KY 302 crosses the dam.

16
Licking Creek

USGS Millard

The tailwater on Licking Creek originates below Fishtrap Lake in Pike County. This impoundment is Kentucky's easternmost major lake, and covers 1130 surface acres. Another of the Army Corps of Engineers' flood-control structures, the dam at Fishtrap does not have hydroelectric facilities. Licking Creek flows for roughly 3 miles below the dam before emptying into the Russell Fork. Its water eventually makes its way through the Russell Fork, into the Levisa Fork, then into the Big Sandy River, to end up in the Ohio.

Rainbow trout only are stocked in Licking Creek. The plantings are made monthly from April through November, with 14,250 fish stocked per year. Licking Creek is a medium-width stream in this tailwater section, and provides only marginal trout habitat. Virtually no carryover of fish from season to season occurs.

A footbridge provides access to both shores of Licking Creek at the tailrace below Fishtrap Lake.

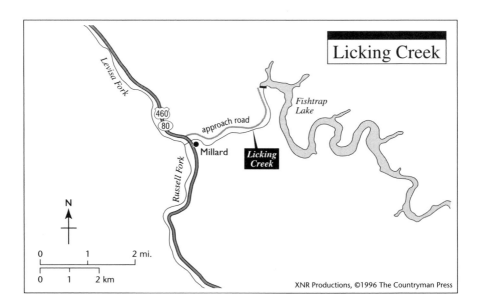

The tailrace area of the creek has riprap along both shores as it exits a tunnel beneath the dam. Immediately below the tunnel are concrete fishing piers along both shores. A bit farther downstream, a footbridge crosses the creek. Once the creek exits the roughly 100-yard-long tailrace, it empties into a couple of short, wadable shoals.

There is a parking area at the foot of the dam, along with rest rooms and a Little League baseball field. Parking can be a problem when ball games are being played in the spring and summer.

The Corps of Engineers land runs along both banks just below Fishtrap Dam and continues downstream for about 1¼ miles on the western shore, providing good access for bank-fishing. Bait-fishing for the fresh stockers makes up almost all of the angling on this stream. Once below the shoals mentioned above, the creek deepens and flows at a sluggish pace.

At ½ mile downstream, there is a picnic area on the western side of the creek. Downstream of this site there is ¾ mile of public access on the corps land, but you can reach the stream only via foot travel. Although the approach road runs along this stretch, there is no place to park along it. Once below the corps land, Licking Creek flows through private property and is rather trashy. At best, this is a marginal tailwater fishing destination.

To reach Fishtrap Dam and the Licking Creek tailwater, travel 3 miles east from the crossroads of Millard at the junction of the approach road (unmarked) with US 460. The approach road is at the northern end of the US 460 bridge across the Licking Creek.

17
Licking River

USGS Louisa, Prichard

The tailwater on the Licking River below Cave Run Lake is located in northeastern Kentucky and forms the boundary between Bath County to the west and Rowan County to the east. Positioned just on the northern edge of the Daniel Boone National Forest, Cave Run covers 8300 acres but is not very deep. It is also one of the state's newer reservoirs, having been completed in 1969. As with most Kentucky lakes that create trout-supporting tailwaters, Cave Run is a Corps of Engineers flood-control impoundment and does not have a powerhouse for energy production.

By Kentucky standards, however, the Licking River tailwater is fairly large, although it does not come close to either the Cumberland

The point jutting between the Cave Run tailrace and the backwater provides anglers good access just below the dam.

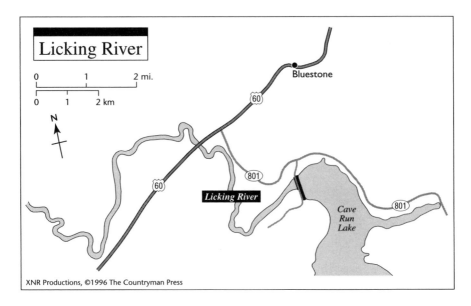

XNR Productions, ©1996 The Countryman Press

or Dix River tailwaters in size. At 75 to 80 yards wide at the end of the dam's tailrace, the stream is large enough to support some float-fishing.

This tailwater receives a total of 7500 catchable-sized rainbow trout annually, but due to its low elevation near the edge of the Ohio River Valley, conditions become marginal for the fish in the summer. No trout are released into this stream from July through September each year.

Bait-fishing is the staple method of anglers targeting trout below Cave Run, but casting or trolling spoons, Rebel Teeny Crawfish, or Rooster Tail spinners (particularly in brown colors) produces fish as well. About the only "hatch" that would interest fly-casters here is the dead and stunned shad that come through the dam when water is released from the lake. These baitfish attract gulls from the lake proper, as well as the attention of the trout. Tossing a minnow-imitating streamer is an option for these occasions. Although the shores are clear enough for casting in the park below the dam, none of the ac-cessible part of the river is wadable.

The tailrace of the Licking, which is lined on both sides with riprap, is a couple hundred yards long. The flow then spreads into a backwa-ter on the eastern side where a small stream enters the river. A point jutting out between the tailrace and the backwater is a popular spot with local anglers.

Access to the Licking River tailwater is available only in the park at the foot of Cave Run Dam. The park provides ¼ mile of shoreline on both sides of the river. A picnic area, rest rooms, parking lot, and boat ramp are on the park's western shore. A paved walkway leads over the mouth of the tailrace on the dam, providing an easy walk to the abovementioned point between tailrace and backwater.

The boat ramp in the park is an excellent paved one, allowing the launch of anything from a canoe to a bass boat. Due to the river's width, it is possible to float-fish downstream of the park, but the trout-supporting portion of the river is only about a mile long, especially in warmer months.

Access to the park below Cave Run Lake is via a drive originating from KY 801 (this road appears as KY 826 on some maps) at the north end of the dam. This is just to the south of the crossroads of Bluestone on US 60 in Rowan County.

18
Little Sandy River

USGS Grayson

The most northerly of Kentucky's tailwater trout fisheries, the Little Sandy River lies below Grayson Lake in Carter County. Nestled in the northeastern corner of the state near Ohio and West Virginia, Grayson Lake was completed in 1969 and covers 1500 acres. This is another of the commonwealth's flood-control reservoirs managed by the Army Corps of Engineers.

Very similar to the tailwater found below Cave Run Lake to the west, the Little Sandy is stocked with 7500 catchable-sized rainbow trout each year, but none are planted in July, August, or September. The river is actually quite a small stream below Grayson Lake and probably has no carryover of fish from year to year. The suitable

The backwater eddy at the end of the tailrace leading from Grayson Dam is a favorite holding site for rainbows.

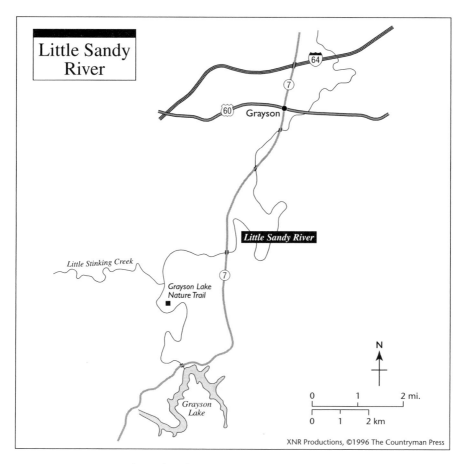

Little Sandy
River

Little Sandy River

Little Stinking Creek

Grayson

Grayson Lake
Nature Trail

*Grayson
Lake*

N

0   1   2 mi.

0   1   2 km

XNR Productions, ©1996 The Countryman Press

trout water extends only about ½ mile downstream to where a major feeder stream, Big Stinking Creek, enters from the west. All of the angling pressure on this tailwater appears to come from bait-fishers—not surprising in light of its marginal habitat.

Where the stream emerges from the dam, a curved tailrace lined with riprap empties over a shallow shoal to form the main creek channel. A small feeder creek enters from the eastern side at the end of the tailrace, forming a little backwater eddy.

A Corps of Engineers park extends down the western shore, while steep rock walls jut out over the water on the eastern. These rocky cliffs, which drop right into the creek channel, run for about ½ mile downstream to the junction with Big Stinking Creek. Access to the lower portion of the tailwater is available via the Grayson Lake Nature Trail, which originates in the park on the eastern shore. This trail forms a loop, with one leg running right along the shore of the Little Sandy.

The park below the Grayson Dam contains parking areas, rest rooms, and a playground. It can be reached via an approach drive from KY 7, which crosses the dam. The drive is at the eastern end of the dam. It is located 7 miles south of the town of Grayson, which is situated near I-64 in Carter County.

19

Martins Fork

USGS Rose Hill, Harlan

Among Kentucky's tailwater streams, Martins Fork is unique in that it supports trout both above and below the reservoir through which it flows. Rising in the northeastern corner of Bell County on the edge of the Cumberland Gap National Historical Park, Martins Fork is a major headwater of the Cumberland River. Flowing northeastward through Harlan County, this stream eventually meets the Poor Fork and the Glover Fork near the town of Harlan to form the Cumberland River. Along this entire route, however, Martins Fork qualifies as only a small to medium-sized stream.

Above Martins Fork Lake, the stream is home to the only population of Coosa red-eye bass in the commonwealth, along with brook

*High water turns the calm pool at the foot of the dam
into a cauldron of churning water.*

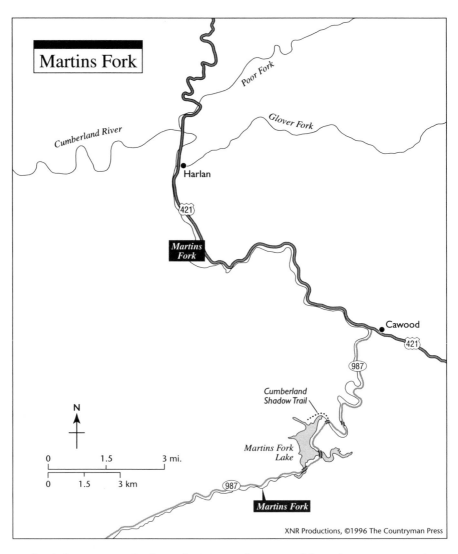

and rainbow trout. In fact, the Kentucky-record brook trout was taken from this creek on August 21, 1982. R. James Augustus of Louisville caught the 1-pound, 15-ounce brookie to claim the record. This upper part of the stream is a rough-and-tumble wilderness flow with a 160-foot-per-mile gradient along its course. It is also difficult to reach, requiring a hike in from KY 987, which parallels the stream.

Below the lake, unfortunately, Martins Fork is a less intriguing trout fishing destination. It remains small in size, but its ability to support trout is not much helped by passing through the reservoir (a

Corps of Engineers flood-control structure). At best, it is marginal trout water.

Martins Fork receives 5900 catchable-sized rainbow trout each year, with fish released below the lake every month from April to November, except August and September. When minimum flows of water are coming through the dam, the large pool at the tailrace is quite clear. Trout are visible mixing with bass and bream in the low waters from the dam to the KY 987 bridge just downstream. During higher flows, Martins Fork is turbulent, murky, and churning. Only bank-fishing is practical at those times.

Wading is possible during minimum water levels from the lower half of the tailrace pool on down to the highway bridge. Below the bridge, the creek deepens and flows sluggishly away toward its junction with the other headwater forks of the Cumberland. Trout undoubtedly move downstream during colder months, but virtually no carryover of fish occurs here. During low water in the summer the stream gets quite warm.

Access to Martins Fork tailwater is provided by a gravel parking lot at the foot of the dam on the eastern shore. A steep riprap incline descends to the water on this bank. At the western end of the KY 987 bridge there is a parking area for the Cumberland Shadow Trail. In all there is about ½ mile of access along the stream below the dam on Corps of Engineers lands. Only foot access is possible below the highway bridge. Downstream of that point, Martins Fork flows on private lands and is not suited to floating.

To reach Martins Fork, travel southeast on US 421 from Harlan to the village of Cawood. Turn right (southeast) onto KY 987 and follow this road until it crosses Martins Fork at the dam.

20
Middle Fork Kentucky River

USGS Buckhorn

The tailwater of the Middle Fork of the Kentucky River, which lies below 1250-acre Buckhorn Lake in east-central Kentucky, is another of the Army Corps of Engineers' flood-control projects that support some trout fishing. As with most of these water-control projects, however, the Buckhorn Dam's tailwater provides only marginal trout habitat.

Situated in Perry County near the village of Buckhorn, the Middle Fork of the Kentucky is a small stream as it flows to the north below Buckhorn Lake. Eventually it joins the North and South Forks at the town of Beattieville to form the main stem of the Kentucky River.

Mature rainbow trout of 8 to 12 inches are planted in the Middle

The tailwater below Buckhorn Lake is a narrow,
turbulent flow when water is being released.

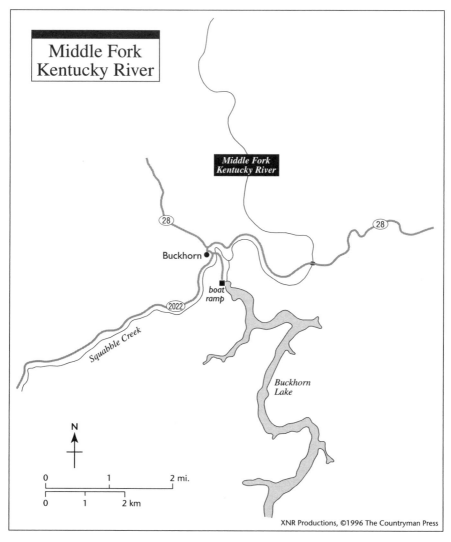

Fork monthly from April to November. A total of 6100 fish is released into the stream annually. It is unlikely that any appreciable carryover of trout from year to year occurs. As with all of the similar small tailwaters in the Bluegrass State, bank-fishing with bait is the method of choice for most anglers. During periods of high water, this tailwater is virtually unfishable. At these times, however, the mouth of Squabble Creek, which enters the Middle Fork from the west ¼ mile downstream of the dam, offers a fishing option. Though the Middle Fork is a murky torrent during high flows, the water backing up into Squabble Creek remains clear. It is accessible from the bank in the Corps of Engineers campground located along its shore.

There is roughly ¼ mile of access to the tailwaters of the Middle Fork on the western shore in the corps park. The park contains a picnic area, a seasonal campground (closed during winter months), and a boat ramp. The campground extends downstream to the mouth of Squabble Creek. Below that point, the Middle Fork flows through private land into the town of Buckhorn.

To reach the park at Buckhorn Dam, travel ¼ mile south of KY 28 in Buckhorn via a paved access road. The road does not have a sign identifying it, but there is a directional sign for Buckhorn Lake at the intersection. The park is directly behind the campus of Buckhorn School, which is visible from KY 28.

21
Nolin River

USGS Nolin Lake, Bee Spring

The Nolin River below Nolin River Lake is one of the most westerly of Kentucky's tailwater trout fisheries; only the Rough River tailwater lies farther west. It is located in Edmonson County in the west-central portion of the commonwealth. There are 5975 acres of water in the impoundment behind Nolin River Dam. There is no power-generation facility at this Corps of Engineers flood-control project.

Flowing to the southwest, the Nolin skirts the western edge of Mammoth Cave National Park, then empties into the Green River directly north of the village of Brownsville.

The cool waters from the bottom of the fairly shallow reservoir have only a minimal effect on water conditions in the river downstream. As a result, the trout water extends for only about a mile below the lake. Along that distance, the Nolin River is only a medium-sized stream. Mature rainbow trout are stocked each month from April to November, with an annual total of 18,600 released here. Although most of the angling pressure on the Nolin appears to come from bank-fishing in the immediate area of the tailrace, there is a good boat ramp just below the dam to accommodate float-fishing.

The tailrace at the foot of Nolin River Dam is unique in that there are concrete fishing platforms along both shores for easy access. Then the shoreline changes to riprap that has been poured with concrete to form a solid surface along either bank. At the end of the tailrace the river widens to roughly 100 feet and flows through a shallow riffle area. A small creek feeds into the river at this point as well. Below the riffle, the boat ramp is on the western shore. The eastern bank is dominated by an impressive limestone head that juts a couple hundred feet above the water.

Access to the Nolin River tailwater is afforded by a Corps of Engineers recreation area on the western side of the stream at the foot of

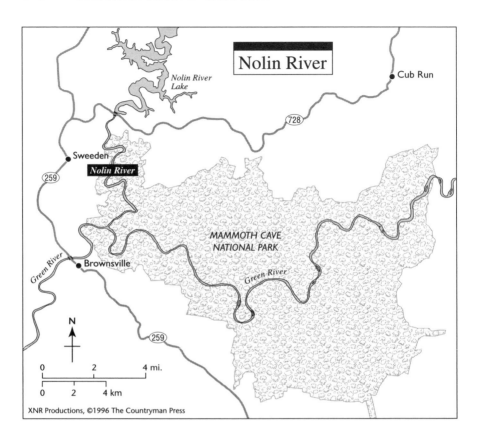

the dam. A road from the western end of the dam connects the park to KY 728, which runs across the dam. Parking and picnic areas, a boat ramp, and rest rooms are provided in the recreation area, but no camping is allowed.

Shore access is short on the eastern side of the river, extending only to the end of the tailrace, where the beginning of the stone cliff blocks further movement down this side of the stream. On the western shore, an anglers' footpath leads downstream from the boat ramp area for an additional ¼ mile to the point where a deep ditch and a bluff are located. In all, there is about ½ mile of access on this side of the Nolin River.

Float-fishing is possible on the Nolin farther downstream, for it deepens and slows below the boat ramp. Eventually the river becomes the western boundary of Mammoth Cave National Park. Nolin River Dam is located on KY 728, between the crossroads of Sweeden to the west and Cub Run to the east in north-central Edmonson County.

22
Paint Creek

USGS Paintsville

Paintsville Lake is a Corps of Engineers flood-control facility located in the east-central portion of the state, in Johnson County. Below the reservoir, Paint Creek is managed as a tailwater trout fishery, despite its small size. Created in 1983, it is one of the newest tailwaters in Kentucky. It is also one of the more interesting and prettiest such fishing sites in the commonwealth.

For the first few years after the dam was closed, around 14,000 rainbow trout were stocked in the creek from April to October. Presently the number of catchable-sized fish being released has swollen to 18,000 annually, and the plantings run from April to November. These fish are stocked via a 1-foot-diameter pipe that connects the parking

Riffles and pools have been hand-crafted in the park on the tailwater just below Paintsville Lake.

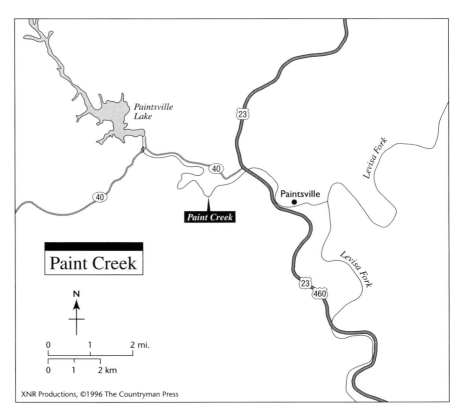

Paintsville
Lake

23

40

40

Paintsville

Paint Creek

Levisa Fork

Levisa Fork

23
460

Paint Creek

N

0   1   2 mi.

0   1   2 km

XNR Productions, ©1996 The Countryman Press

area at the foot of the dam to the creek, allowing easy access to the hatchery trucks. Thanks to the excellent facilities on this tailwater, fishing pressure is quite heavy immediately following stockings, especially from bank-fishers using bait.

Where the tailrace comes out of the dam, it is surrounded by a concrete walkway that leads into paved fishing platforms along either shore. Below these platforms, steeply inclined riprap lines both banks for several hundred yards down to the end of the Corps of Engineers land. This channel courses through a well-maintained park. Some riprap-sized rocks have also been placed in the water to break the flow into a half-dozen pools separated by these handcrafted shoals. A footbridge crosses here, making for easy access to the entire tailrace area from either bank.

At the downstream limit of the corps land, KY 40 crosses the river on a metal bridge. Just above the bridge, on the western shore, a feeder creek enters the flow. This tributary's flow has pushed a gravel bar out into Paint Creek, creating a natural shoal. Above the shoal a deep, slow pool extends back upstream to the end of the riprap. As in the riprap area, the bank is quite steep on this lower end of the public access.

Below the corps land, Paint Creek flows through private lands as it courses on down to its junction with the Levisa Fork at the town of Paintsville. Through here, however, it is possible to drift and wade using a float tube. There is much less fishing pressure downstream of the public land, and anglers casting small lures or spinners often tangle with smallmouth bass, as well as the stocked trout. Also, since Paintsville Lake and the creek have been stocked with river otters, anglers are sometimes entertained by encounters with the frisky critters.

Access to Paint Creek is provided by a Corps of Engineers recreation area at the foot of the dam. There are parking lots, playgrounds, and rest rooms.

To reach Paintsville Dam and Paint Creek, travel 4 miles west from the town of Paintsville via KY 40. The park is located on the north side of this road, 2¼ miles beyond the intersection of KY 40 and US 460.

23

Rough River

USGS Falls of Rough

The final trout water in the commonwealth of Kentucky to be covered is the Rough River, the most westerly of all of the state's tailwater trout streams. Rough River Lake is the 4830-acre Army Corps of Engineers flood-control reservoir from which the trout water flows. There is no hydroelectric generating facility at Rough River Dam. The impoundment and tailwater form the boundary between Breckenridge County to the north and Grayson County to the south. Lying in west-central Kentucky, the tailwater is roughly 70 miles southwest of Louisville.

The KDFWR stocks the Rough River with catchable-sized rainbow trout each month from April through September. Usually, the total number of trout planted is 11,600 per year; it is composed of 8- to 12-inch fish. The fishing is mainly bank-angling, done in the corps park at the foot of Rough River Dam. Fishing pressure is fairly heavy during periods of stocking, and even continues on the shoreline through the winter.

During periods of maximum water release, the flow in the tailwater is sluggish, and it turns rather murky. At ¼ mile downstream, at the end of the corps property, the river narrows abruptly from about 100 feet to roughly 50 or 60. This causes water to back up, giving this portion of the tailwater a lakelike appearance. Shoreline access is excellent down to the end of the public property on the southern side of the river. It is also possible to walk down the northern side from the dam. The river does offer the possibility of float-fishing from the park to the KY 110 bridge or even to the Green Mill Historic Site farther downstream. Since there are no boat ramps on the tailwater, a float tube would appear to be your best bet.

Access to the Rough River's trout-bearing water is available in the Tailwater Recreation Area at the foot of the dam. There is a parking area, plus a seasonal (closed in winter) RV and tent campground.

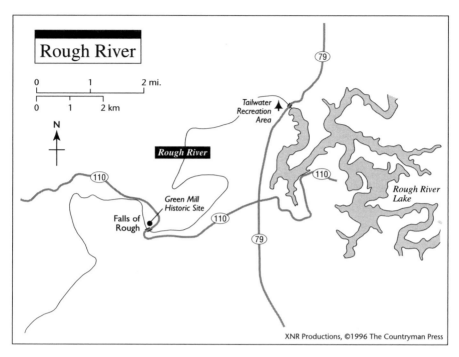

Rough River

0   1   2 mi.

0   1   2 km

N

79

Tailwater
Recreation
Area

Rough River

110

110

Green Mill
Historic Site

Falls of
Rough

110

79

Rough River
Lake

XNR Productions, ©1996 The Countryman Press

The park is reached via an approach drive off KY 54 at the southern end of Rough River Dam. Other access is found at the KY 110 crossing, and at the Green Mill Historic Site, ½ mile farther downstream at the Falls of Rough. This gristmill was operated by the Green family continuously from 1823 to 1963. An old metal bridge, no longer used, spans the river here, as well as a low-head dam that creates a small waterfall. Caution should be exercised in approaching the dam from upriver.

Missouri

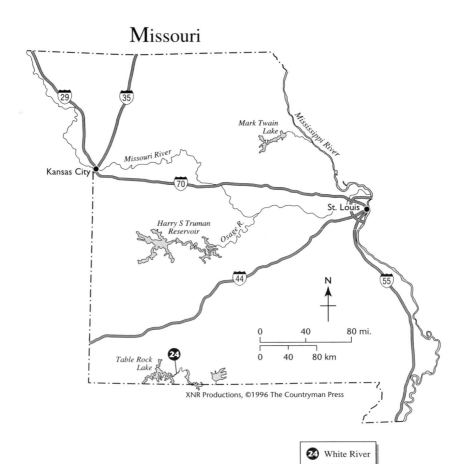

Kansas City

Missouri River

Mark Twain Lake

Mississippi River

29 35

70

St. Louis

Harry S Truman Reservoir

Osage R.

44

55

N

0   40   80 mi.

0   40   80 km

Table Rock Lake

24

XNR Productions, ©1996 The Countryman Press

24 White River

SECTION FIVE

MISSOURI

Although Missouri had no natural trout populations in historical times, the Show Me State nonetheless has a fairly long tradition of trout fishing. The first of these cold-water species introduced to Missouri waters were brook trout transplanted from Wisconsin in 1879. These fish were stocked into several Ozark Mountain streams in the southwestern portion of the state.

As soon as it was realized that the brookies were surviving, rainbow trout from California's McCloud River were planted in Missouri waters; this began in 1880. These West Coast–native fish quickly adapted to the heartland, and by the late 1880s there were reproducing populations in Crane Creek, the Spring River, and Maramec Spring. The stocking of trout, however, was only possible because these rivers are fed by a number of substantial springs that gush forth water at a constant 50 degrees year-round.

In the ensuing years, the Missouri Department of Conservation (MDC) experimented with a number of other exotic species. Eventually, brown trout, steelhead, Pacific salmon, Atlantic salmon, and grayling were introduced to the Show Me State. As it turned out, only the brown trout became established and joined the brookies and rainbows in furnishing today's fishery.

Probably the most familiar image of Show Me State trout fishing that anglers from other areas have is of opening day in Missouri's state parks. Four facilities—Bennett Springs, Montauk, Maramec Spring, and Roaring River—are designated as state trout parks. Here an estimated 400,000 fishing trips per year produce a million trout. The streams in these parks are stocked daily during the spring-through-fall season. Every year, just after Missouri's opening day on March 1, newspapers across America carry photos showing anglers forming large circles of humanity on the streams and fishing inside them. While such angling is productive, its aesthetics are not overly appealing to many trout fishers!

Although memorable, these scenes hardly typify the variety of trout fishing opportunities Missouri provides. During the winter months, the trout parks are open to catch-and-release fishing for a limited number of days each week, and offer more solitude. The MDC also provides eight trout management areas that are stocked periodically with 10-inch rainbows, and are open to year-round angling. Finally, there are three trophy trout fishing areas and one catch-and-release trout fishing area in Missouri. The fishing regulations booklet published yearly by the MDC and available at most sporting-goods outlets identifies these areas and provides complete regulations for each.

Among the MDC's trout management areas is Missouri's only tailwater trout fishery. Located below Table Rock Lake, the White River is the state's premier trout fishing destination. In all, Missouri contains 177 miles of river, creek, and tailwater trout habitat.

All anglers from 16 to 64 years of age are required to have a regular fishing permit, as well as a trout stamp, to catch trout in Missouri. A trout stamp is not required in the trout parks, however; instead, anglers must purchase daily trout tags. On the White River tailwater, neither a trout tag nor a trout stamp is needed. The regular state creel limit is 5 trout per day, regardless of species or size. On the tailwater below Table Rock Lake, only 1 of the 5 may be a brown trout, and it must be at least 20 inches long.

24
White River

As mentioned earlier, the White River below Table Rock Lake is the only tailwater trout fishery in Missouri. This is, in fact, the same river that provides tailwater fisheries in the Ozark region of Arkansas just to the south. After passing through Beaver Lake in northwestern Arkansas, the White River enters Missouri and 43,100-acre Table Rock Lake. Below Table Rock Dam, the river forms an arc that flows into Bull Shoals Lake and, thus, back across the state boundary into north-central Arkansas.

The White River's tailwater in Missouri is more commonly known as Lake Taneycomo due to its unusual makeup. Some 22 miles downstream of Table Rock Dam is Power Site Dam (also known as Ozark Beach Dam), which backs up 2080 acres of water in Lake Taneycomo. (Power Site Dam is the oldest hydroelectric facility on the White River—it was constructed back in 1913.) As a result of this configuration, the White's tailwater in Missouri is a hybrid between a lake and a river. Much of the lower end of the tailwater looks and acts like a reservoir, while the several miles just below Table Rock Dam fluctuate between being a river and being a lake. The variation, of course, depends on the discharges of water from Table Rock's four generators. From the practical standpoint of trout fishing, however, this discussion will cover only the 8 miles of river from Table Rock Dam down to the twin towns of Branson and Hollister. Below there, Taneycomo takes on, full-time, the characteristics of a lake.

Another fact unique to this portion of the White River is that it receives the heaviest stockings of trout per mile of any tailwater in the South. Plantings of rainbow trout began shortly after Table Rock Dam was completed in 1958 and turned Lake Taneycomo into a cold-water resource. The trout come from the Shepherd of the Hills Trout Hatchery. Located in Table Rock State Park at the foot of Table Rock

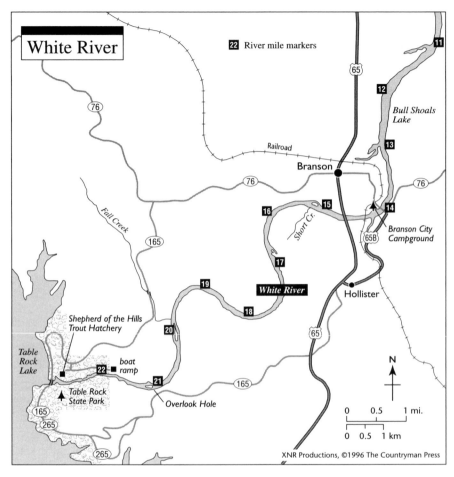

Dam, this is the largest state-owned facility east of the Rocky Mountains. From a high of 1.6 million trout stocked in 1984, the MDC now releases roughly 400,000 pounds of trout into the tailwater annually, or about 760,000 fish.

Additionally, beginning in 1980 up to 50,000 brown trout were added to the fishery annually, although that number has since settled to about 10,000 per year. Up until 1975, some steelhead trout were also planted in this tailwater.

With such heavy stocking, up to 90 percent of the trout taken from Taneycomo are rainbows of 8 to 10 inches in length. But that does not mean larger fish are not present. In fact, the last two Missouri state-record brown trout have come from this part of the White; it can also lay claim to three previous state records for rainbow trout.

On March 29, 1991, Marty Babusa of Hollister was fishing a Muddler Minnow when he landed a 23-pound, 4-ounce bruiser of a brown trout to claim the record for that species. Babusa's trout, however, was bested on June 27, 1994, by a 24-pound, 15-ounce brown hauled out of the White River by Kevin Elfrink of Jackson. He was fishing a Shad Assassin soft-plastic jerkbait at the time.

The first of the Taneycomo record rainbow trout was caught on January 26, 1970, by Charles Gott of Green Forest, Arkansas. He was fishing a Little Cleo spoon near the mouth of Fall Creek when the 13-pound, 14¾-ounce lunker took the lure. The next time the White River produced the Missouri record for rainbows came on July 14, 1976. That 14-pound, 7-ounce fish was hooked by Craig Wolf of Branson, who was fishing a Flatfish lure at the US 65 highway bridge. Finally, on December 23, 1984, while fishing the upper part of Lake Taneycomo with a salmon egg, Bill Hecker of Rogersville caught at 16-pound, 12-ounce rainbow. That fish held the record for just under 3 years before being bested by 1 ounce by a Roaring River State Park catch, which continues to set the standard for the species in Missouri.

Despite these impressive fish—all taken from the White River below Table Rock Dam—the rainbow trout fishery has declined noticeably over the years. Many local anglers and fisheries managers point to the 1960s and 1970s, when 5-fish limits of rainbow trout were regularly brought in that weighed a total of more than 35 pounds! Such a catch would raise eyebrows today on Taneycomo. Though occasional 6- to 7-pound rainbows are taken, they are not common.

Part of the decline can be traced to the collapse of the scud population that occurred on this part of the White River in the mid- to late 1980s. Biologists reported that by 1987 the numbers of these small freshwater crustaceans had fallen by 90 percent. Poor water quality resulting from development along the river, and a population increase of the white sucker—which competes with trout for this food staple—in the flow, are two possible causes for the scud decline. Another problem may have been that too many trout were being stocked into the river for its forage base. Though a definitive cause for the problem was never found, the number of trout being stocked has declined steadily from the highs of the mid-1980s to present levels. A 5-year study was begun in 1992 using tagged trout to learn more about the dynamics of the rainbow population in the Table Rock tailwaters.

At the same time that Taneycomo's rainbow fishery has exhibited signs of a decline, its brown trout fishery has been heading in the opposite direction. Besides the two state-record fish of the early 1990s, the same period saw biologists on an electrofishing expedition stun, revive, and release a 36-inch brown. Most anglers and state fisheries managers consider it only a matter of time before the next record-breaking brown trout is brought in from this stretch of the White River. In large part, the quality of the brown trout angling here is a result of the regulations covering the species. Since 1985 there has been a creel limit in effect permitting the daily harvest of only 1 brown trout, which must be at least 20 inches in length. This restriction has allowed many of the tailwater browns to grow large.

Most of the trout fishing pressure on Taneycomo occurs from dawn to roughly 11 AM, regardless of the time of year. Another, lesser, period of activity usually follows from 2 to 5 PM. Though the trout are caught at any water level here, local anglers do prefer a stable flow. If the river is rising or falling, the fish often seem to be thrown off their feeding routines.

Regarding time of year, trout in Taneycomo are not notoriously picky. They will take a bait during any month. Still, the period of December through early March is noted for producing the best fishing for trophy-sized brown trout. Another appeal of fishing at this time of year is the chance to avoid crowds on the tailwater. As far back as 1970, the MDC estimated the fishing pressure on Taneycomo to be 5 million angling hours per year. This figure jumped to 15 million by the early 1980s, and is undoubtedly much higher today.

By far the most often used angling technique on this water is bait-fishing with corn, cheese, marshmallows, or night crawlers. These are employed while drift-fishing on high water, or still-fishing from boats when the generators are silent. Most drift-fishers, however, change over to artificial lures when the turbines quit turning at Table Rock Dam. Little Cleo spoons, Blakemore Road Runners, Mepps spinners, and Rooster Tails are all popular (this latter lure in green is often mentioned as especially productive). Still, the most popular spinning lures for trout on this tailwater are tiny $\frac{1}{80}$-ounce micro jigs. These are often drifted below a strike indicator during low water. The most popular color tends to be brown, but black, olive, gray, pink, and white jigs also take fish. These jigs are also very effective when a shad die-off takes place in Table Rock Lake, loading the tailwater with dead and dying baitfish.

Public access to the shores of Taneycomo is limited. Table Rock

*The outflows from the Shepherd of the Hills Trout Hatchery
are hot spots for trout that make spawning runs to the area.*

State Park, which lies at the foot of the dam, provides the best access to the river. Besides containing the Shepherd of the Hills Hatchery, the park offers gravel and paved parking areas, trail access to the water, and a paved boat ramp. There are roughly 1¹⁄₁₀ miles of streamside access to the fishing on the northern shore of the river in the park.

A major attraction for anglers in Table Rock State Park are the three water outlets that empty into the river from the hatchery. These highly oxygenated and nutrient-loaded flows attract and hold trout in their vicinity. Marty Babusa's 1991 record brown was taken at the mouth of one of these outlets. In fact, many local anglers know this area around the outfalls of the hatchery as the Lunker Hole. Big brown trout are often seen here in the fall and winter, but it is not clear if they are making spawning runs to the outfalls or simply moving to the places where food and oxygen are most abundant. At any rate, these outlets are primary target areas for angling. Be aware, however, that fishing above the high-water mark in these outlets is prohibited.

This is the only area of Taneycomo where fly-casters can be called a common sight. During low water levels some wading is available, and intrepid anglers even wade around the hatchery outfalls during the highest water levels. Minnow-imitating streamer patterns are a good bet at most times, with black Woolly Buggers noted for being particularly good. Fishing scud imitations under a strike indicator should also prove effective. Fish these latter flies 3 to 4 feet below the surface to attract the most attention from the fish.

The next area of note among local anglers is called the Overlook Hole. It is found just below the major island in the river at Mile Marker 21. The markers were placed on Taneycomo by the Empire District Electric Company and are located at 1-mile intervals along the shore. They begin at Power Site Dam and mark the distance from that point upstream to the foot of Table Rock Dam.

The Overlook Hole gets its name from the scenic overlook on MO 165 highway, which is on the southwestern shore above this part of the river. The major fishing feature of the hole is the three large rocks on the southwestern side of the river. These are visible during low water, and are good holding places for trout when the water goes up.

The area with the reputation for the best fishing ends at the mouth of Fall Creek, some 3¼ miles below Table Rock Dam. Downstream of this point the river takes on many more of the characteristics of a lake. When using small jigs with spinning gear or scud imitations with a fly-rod through here, fish at depths of at least 7 to 8 feet for best results. There are, however, still some honey holes worth mentioning on this section of river.

Between Mile Markers 18 and 17 is a major submerged gravel bar referred to as Monkey Island. The disruption in the current here generally attracts large numbers of rainbows and is a good area to target year-round. Then, at Mile Marker 17, you will encounter the School of the Ozarks Hole. This spot is noted for having produced some lunker-sized rainbows over the years. It is a deep hole in the riverbed that contains a fair amount of structure and debris, making it best suited for fishing from a stationary boat during low water.

Between Mile Markers 17 and 16 there are no notable structures, nor other distinguished angling hot spots, but this *is* the area of the tailwater that produced Kevin Elfrink's state-record rainbow. Obviously, drift-fishing this section can be productive.

The final section upstream of Branson worth special attention is found along the northern shore from the mouth of Short Creek down to the village waterfront. Through here a lot of downed trees are in the water along the bank; either a crankbait or a big minnow-imitating streamer offers a good chance at a lunker brown trout.

Besides the park at Table Rock Dam, the only public shore access on the upper portion of Taneycomo is located in town at the Branson City Campground. In addition to RV and tent-camping areas, the campground offers fishing docks and two public boat ramps. Also, during low water levels, there is the possibility of doing some wading around the US 65 bridge in Branson.

Downstream of town, Taneycomo offers another 14 miles of trout habitat to Power Site Dam, but the water loses all resemblance to a river. This final stretch of tailwater is virtually a reservoir.

While Branson offers various accommodations for visiting anglers, it is far better known for its country music and other theaters. This is a tourist mecca, particularly from spring through fall. The influx of music fans can make for heavy traffic on the roads. Particularly in the summer, traveling through town can be a nightmare.

For information on water releases on the Taneycomo section of the White River, call the Army Corps of Engineers' automated telephone message at Table Rock Dam at 417-336-5083.

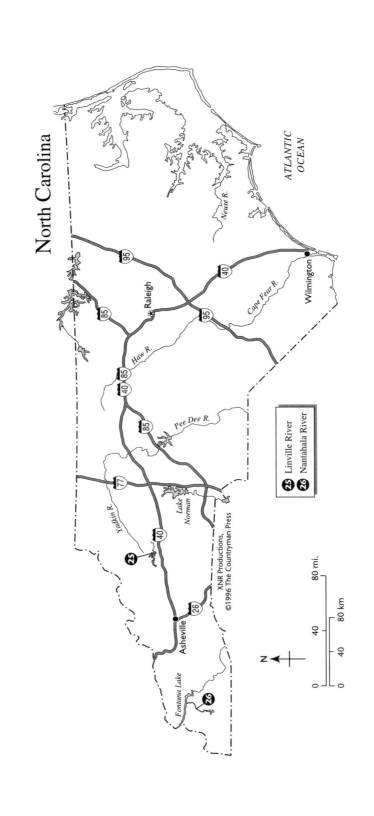

North Carolina

ATLANTIC OCEAN

Neuse R.

95

40

Raleigh

85

95

Cape Fear R.

Wilmington

Haw R.

40 85

85

Pee Dee R.

77

Yadkin R.

Lake Norman

40

25

26

Asheville

Fontana Lake

26

XNR Productions,
©1996 The Countryman Press

25 Linville River
26 Nantahala River

N

80 mi.

40

0

80 km

40

0

SECTION SIX

NORTH CAROLINA

Although the folks in Virginia might argue the point, the Tar Heel State of North Carolina is the epitome of southern trout fishing areas. It has more miles of trout water of every description than any other state in Dixie, ranging from tiny mountain brooklets to large mountain lakes and bold-flowing rivers. The state is probably home to more native brook trout than any other area in the South, as well as thriving populations of brown and rainbow trout.

All of the 4200 miles of Tar Heel trout streams are located in the 26 westernmost counties of the state. Rainbow trout first came to the Old North State in the 1880s, when the original populations of native brook trout were depleted in many streams. From these original stockings of the West Coast exotics, rainbows eventually became the predominant species in most of the state's trout water.

In 1905 the first recorded introductions of brown trout occurred in North Carolina. Like the rainbows, browns found the new territory to their liking and have expanded their range ever since. It is an expansion likely to continue for some time into the future.

With such an abundance of trout water, the North Carolina Wildlife Resources Commission (NCWRC) has been quite active in managing the streams, rivers, and lakes of the state. There are more regulations on waters here than there are in any other state of the Southeast. Regulations run the gamut from fly-fishing-only, catch-and-release waters through hatchery-supported, put-and-take streams. Between these extremes, a number of intermediate management philosophies are applied to some creeks and rivers.

Amid all this abundance, it may seem strange to discover that North Carolina has only two tailwater trout fisheries. The Linville River below Lake James in Burke County and the Nantahala River downstream of Nantahala Lake (sometimes identified as Lake Aquone) in

Macon and Swain Counties are true tailwater trout fisheries.

A couple of other rivers offer what appear at first glance to be tailwaters but, due to their unique circumstances, fail to qualify. Technically speaking, the waters downstream of Fontana Lake on the Little Tennessee River, which form the boundary of Graham and Swain Counties, fit the description of a tailwater trout fishery. On closer inspection, however, the Little Tennessee can't actually be called a river through here. Fontana empties its waters directly into Cheoah Reservoir, which in turn flows through its dam into Calderwood Reservoir. Additionally, water from Santeetlah Lake is piped to a powerhouse on Cheoah Reservoir, adding still more cold water to this system of lakes. This results in excellent trout habitat in both Cheoah and Calderwood, but in a totally lake environment.

Much the same situation can be found at the headwaters of the Tuckaseegee River. A couple of feeder streams and the main stem of the Tuckaseegee are dammed to form four small reservoirs in Jackson County. The waters of Wolf Creek and Tanasee Creek Reservoirs, however, run through a pipeline down to a power plant on the main river. When the water exits the power plant, it is released into Bear Creek Reservoir, which then empties directly into Cedar Hill Reservoir downstream.

On the West Fork of the Tuckaseegee, also in Jackson County, the same type of operation exits. Water is piped from Thorpe Reservoir down to a power plant at the head of Little Lake Glennville. From there the water is released into the lake. By the time the water comes out of Little Glennville, it quickly joins the flow of the Tuckaseegee, which has exited Cedar Hill Reservoir. While the Tuckaseegee River downstream of this point is trout water, it is a marginal, put-and-take fishery that is affected only slightly by the upstream dams.

Both the Linville and Nantahala tailwaters are managed as hatchery-supported trout waters by the NCWRC and adhere to the statewide regulations for waters carrying this designation. The creel limit is 7 trout per day in any combination of species. There are no bait or size restrictions. Both tailwaters are closed to fishing from March 1 each year until 6 AM on the first Saturday of April. All of North Carolina's trout streams except the Nantahala are also closed to night-fishing.

Stockings of trout in these waters are composed of the Old North State's standard mix of 40 percent rainbow, 40 percent brown, and 20 percent brook trout. These fish are basically 8 to 10 inches in length, but 3 percent of the released fish exceed 10 inches, and 1 percent exceed 12 inches.

To fish for these trout, all persons 16 years of age or older must have a valid comprehensive fishing license. There are some exceptions to this rule for resident anglers, so check the current "North Carolina Inland Fishing, Hunting & Trapping Regulations Digest" for more details. This brochure is available from most outlets that sell hunting and fishing licenses.

Since September 1993, it has been possible to order a North Carolina fishing license over the telephone at 919-715-4091. You can charge the cost of the license to a major credit card. Identification and license numbers will be issued to you over the phone. You can then begin fishing immediately. The actual license will arrive via mail later. To use this service, have a pen or pencil ready to write down the license and ID numbers; have your credit card number and driver's license or Social Security number at hand as well.

25

Linville River

USGS Glen Alpine • DeLorme 33

The Linville River tailwater fishery is pretty much overlooked in the Old North State. This situation is not hard to understand, since North Carolina is blessed with such a wide-ranging and diverse amount of trout water. The stretch of tailwater on the Linville is only about 1 mile long and has rather poor access, making it of only marginal interest to most anglers.

Located entirely in Burke County to the west of Morganton, the Linville tailwater originates at the foot of Linville Dam on 6500-acre Lake James. While many anglers may be familiar with the Linville's trout fishing, their knowledge is generally limited to the river's upstream portions. North of the Blue Ridge Parkway in southern Avery and northern Burke Counties, the Linville is one of the Tar Heel State's most fertile trout habitats, producing both chunky stockers and wild fish. Then the river plunges over Linville Falls and through the wilderness lands of the Linville Gorge for more than a dozen miles. In the gorge's seemingly enchanted landscape of stone chimneys and steep rock cliffs, the Linville is a big, brawling river that supports brutish brown trout. These browns are planted as fingerlings, produced in NCWRC hatcheries from half-wild brood stock. Once out of the gorge, the river empties into Lake James.

Lake James's configuration is a bit unusual in that there are dams on both the Linville (to the east) and Catawba (to the west) Rivers. As the waters of the lake rose, they spilled through a gap in the hills, dividing the two river valleys to form a single reservoir. The Linville Dam, however, is the only one with a powerhouse, so all of the water exiting Lake James goes down the Linville. The bed of the Catawba is dry from its dam down to where the Linville empties into it.

The trout water on the Linville tailwater is listed by the NCWRC as running from the Linville powerhouse down to the mouth of Muddy

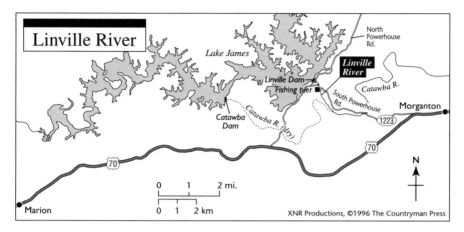

Creek. A look at a map, however, shows that Muddy Creek actually empties into the Catawba upstream of where the Catawba and Linville join. The confusing terminology probably results from the fact that all of the water in the Catawba at the junction came from Muddy Creek, even though it is flowing in the old bed of the Catawba. Anyway, whether you choose to call it Muddy Creek or the Catawba River, the point at which this stream joins the Linville is the downstream limit of trout habitat on the tailwater. Below the junction the stream is known as the Catawba River.

The trout fishery on the Linville below Lake James is a purely put-and-take resource. It is unlikely that any appreciable carryover of trout occurs, let alone any reproduction. This is marginal trout habitat. The NCWRC releases roughly 10,000 catchable-sized rainbow trout into the tailwater each year between March and August. These stockings take place at the State Route (SR) 1223 bridge near the foot of Linville Dam.

Just below this bridge is a large pool that features a public fishing pier. This is the only public access on the Linville tailwater and gets heavy usage at all water levels from bait-anglers. It is a placid pool when minimum flows are coming through the powerhouse, but turns rowdy when the water level goes up. There are some shoals just downstream of the pool where wading is practical, especially during low water.

It is also possible to float the tailwater in either a canoe or a float tube. The takeout point is a second SR 1223 bridge, about 2 miles downstream of the first. Unfortunately, the last mile of the float is through waters where trout are scarce.

There is a parking area on the western side of the Linville at the upper SR 1223 bridge. The public fishing pier is also located on that side of the river, beside the parking lot. The Linville tailwater is open to fishing under standard North Carolina regulations for hatchery-supported waters.

To reach the Linville River tailwater, travel east from the town of Marion via US 70. Turn north onto South Powerhouse Road (SR 1223) and stay on this paved road until it crosses the river for the second time, just downstream of Linville Dam.

26
Nantahala River

USGS Wesser • DeLorme 51

The Nantahala River is one of the more celebrated streams of western North Carolina. The renown that the river has achieved, unlike that of most tailwater streams, does not rest with the trout fishery created by humanity's tinkering with the environment. The headwaters of the river, far upstream of Nantahala Dam, have enjoyed the reputation of being a fine natural trout stream that supports even native brook trout in its more remote portions. Add to this a legacy of some of the best whitewater canoeing, kayaking, and rafting in the eastern United States and the package is so appealing that the tailwater fishery is actually often overlooked.

Another feature setting the Nantahala apart from most of the South's artificially created trout fisheries is that the tailwater does not start at the foot of the dam. Rather, almost all of the water exits Nantahala Lake via a pipeline that bypasses roughly 8 miles of the riverbed. Through this section the Nantahala is dependent upon its feeder streams for all of its water. The upper portion of this bypassed water is very marginal trout habitat, but it is stocked with several thousand trout each year. The lower 4 miles is open under special delayed-harvest fishing rules that have proven so popular since being instituted back in 1993 that this portion of the stream has also drawn attention away from the tailwater farther downriver.

When the pipeline ends at the Nantahala Powerhouse in Macon County, just south of the Swain County border, the water empties out of the turbines to refill the riverbed. For the next 8 miles the river flows through Swain County and the Nantahala Gorge. In the process it earns its name, which in the Cherokee language means "land of the midday sun." Steep mountainsides drop precipitously to both shores of the river valley, shutting out the sun except in the early afternoon.

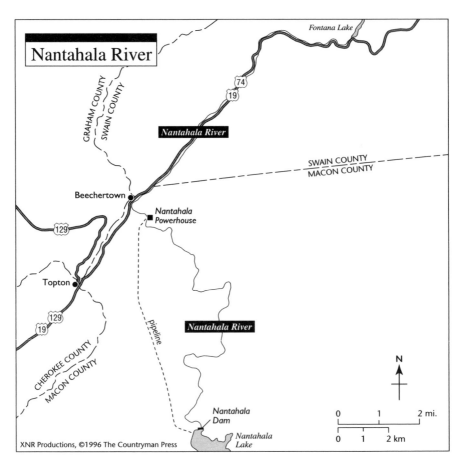

Unlike some other southern tailwaters, there are only two water levels on the Nantahala. When the water is "off," the flow is that of but a medium-volume creek, meandering along the bed of a full-sized river. Wading is possible on virtually the entire stream at this stage; its pools are fairly placid throughout. Such conditions are usually found during the night and early-morning hours, especially during the peak fishing months of spring through fall.

Periods of low water tend to be favored by fly-casters on this tailwater. In fact—and in another departure from other southeastern tailwaters—fly-fishers are usually more common on the Nantahala than are bait- or spin-fishers. This is, in part, due to some large hatches of aquatic insects on the river. Unfortunately, while they can be expansive in size, these hatches are no more predictable than those on other waters of the southern highlands.

The stretch of water running through Nantahala Gorge yields some hefty rainbows; they may be holdover or wild fish.

Fly-fishers usually employ one of two methods in their fishing. The first is to try to match the insect action taking place with dry flies of the appropriate color, in sizes from 16 to 18. This approach usually produces a lot of smaller fish. On the other hand, some local anglers cast large, bushy attractor patterns, like the Royal Wulff, in sizes up to 8. These folks get fewer strikes, but the fish they raise are often the larger rainbows and browns of 16 to 20 inches.

The bait- and spin-anglers who do appear on the Nantahala tailwater use all of the usual trout baits and lures. In the case of spin-fishing, in-line spinners or small Rapala minnow patterns are most common.

Another oddity about the Nantahala is its status as the only trout stream in North Carolina open to night-fishing. The use of large streamers or attractor dries after dark offers the fly-fisher the opportunity to tangle with one of the big nocturnal brown trout that inhabit the stream. It is wise, however, to be thoroughly familiar with the portion of river to be fished before attempting to tackle it in the dark.

When fishing the Nantahala, be aware that the water will rise without warning. Wading anglers should keep a close eye on the water for any hint that it is rising. Keep an ear alert as well. A noticeable rushing noise will become audible from upstream when the river begins to rise. When its volume begins to increase, it is wise to head for shore.

The other fishing condition encountered on the Nantahala occurs when the turbines at the powerhouse are on. During these periods, the river is a boisterous, rowdy, powerful flow that careens down the gorge. It is this water that attracts crowds of boaters to the river; hundreds of them descend the chutes and shoals in kayaks, rafts, and canoes. Such crowds discourage most anglers from approaching the water. Those who do, however, will find that the high water and numbers of watercraft do not seem to affect the fish. The trout have apparently become used to the mass of humanity floating over them and continue to feed just feet from passing rafts.

Additionally, the rafters and kayakers descending the river head for the rougher current, while the trout look for big eddies or ob-structions breaking the current. This puts the fish in a different part of the river from most of the raft traffic. During high water, other good places to look for the trout are in the side channels behind is-lands, or around logs and boulders in the river.

Regardless of the water level or the fishing method employed, the trout on the Nantahala can be impressive. Although both browns and rainbows reproduce naturally in the river, these populations are supplemented with about 6000 catchable-sized rainbows annually. The NCWRC plantings take place from March to August and, be-cause of them, the Nantahala is managed under regular North Caro-lina hatchery-supported regulations. The nutrient-rich waters released from Nantahala Lake support a forage base that turns both stocked and wild fish into plump, energetic battlers. Most of the fish will be under 12 inches, but trout of up to 20 inches are fairly common. Of course, as with any brown trout water, there is the chance of hanging a fish measured in pounds rather than inches, as well.

Access to the Nantahala tailwater is excellent through nearly the entire gorge. US 19 parallels the river from just below the power-house down to Nantahala Falls (previously known as Little Wesser Falls) at the foot of the gorge. At that point, the river leaves the high-way to plunge over Big Wesser Falls and empty into Fontana Lake. There are a number of parking areas along the highway in the gorge. During rafting season, the highway and parking areas can be very crowded around midday.

To reach the Nantahala tailwater, follow US 19/129 north from the town of Andrews. Stay on US 19 when the two routes separate at the crossroads of Topton (US 129 heads northwest). US 19 strikes the Nantahala near the village of Beechertown and just downstream of the powerhouse.

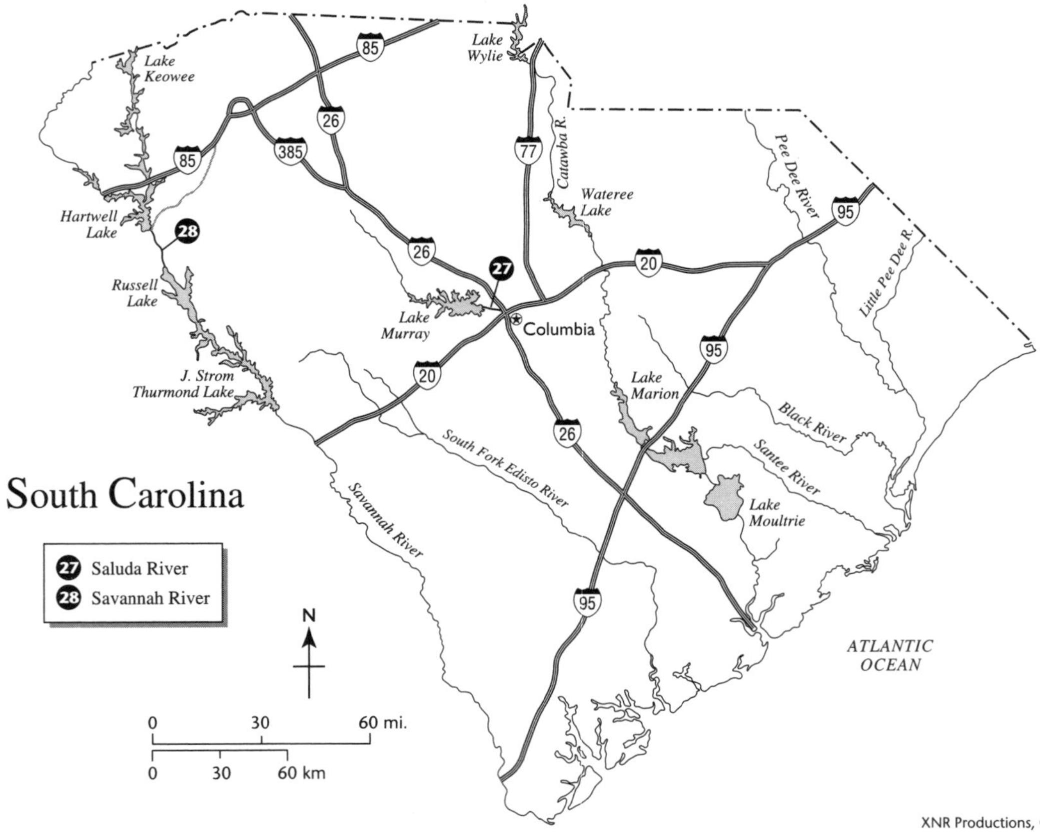

South Carolina

ATLANTIC OCEAN

Pee Dee River

Little Pee Dee R.

Black River

Santee River

Lake Moultrie

Lake Marion

South Fork Edisto River

Savannah River

Wateree Lake

Catawba R.

Columbia

Lake Murray

Lake Wylie

Lake Keowee

Hartwell Lake

Russell Lake

J. Strom Thurmond Lake

95

95

95

20

20

26

26

26

77

85

85

385

27 Saluda River
28 Savannah River

N

0   30   60 km
0   30   60 mi.

XNR Productions, ©1996 The Countryman Press

SECTION SEVEN

SOUTH CAROLINA

It comes as a surprise to many anglers to learn that South Carolina has always had a population of trout within its borders. Their range has traditionally been quite small, however. In fact, the natural trout waters of the Palmetto State are confined to the three counties comprising its westernmost corner. Oconee, Pickens, and Greenville Counties today contain about 200 miles of streams and rivers that support some type of trout fishing for at least part of the year.

As with the other natural trout waters of Dixie, South Carolina's native fish was the southern Appalachian strain of brook trout. Unfortunately, these holdovers from the last Ice Age were virtually eradicated from the state's waters during the last half of the 19th century by logging and farming in South Carolina's small portion of the southeastern highlands. Today, relics of the original brook trout population hang on tenuously in a few remote headwater creeks and brooks.

Introductions of rainbow and brown trout soon followed the decline in native brookie numbers and, as elsewhere, accelerated that downward trend. Since the early 1950s, the South Carolina Wildlife and Marine Resources Department (WMRD) has been actively managing and stocking most of the state's suitable trout waters. Presently, 250,000 catchable-sized trout are released into state waters annually, along with another 40,000 to 100,000 fingerlings. Almost all of these are rainbows and browns. These go into more than 30 creeks and rivers, as well as 7500-acre Lake Jocassee. This reservoir on the Greenville and Pickens county boundary is the Palmetto State's bona fide trophy trout fishery, regularly producing browns and rainbows in the 2- to 6-pound range. The impoundment is managed by the Duke Power Company.

When a pair of South Carolina tailwaters were stocked by the WMRD, the range of trout in the state was increased to include two more counties. The Saluda River below Lake Murray and the Savannah River below Hartwell Lake constitute the man-made trout resources of this state.

To fish for trout in South Carolina, anglers 16 to 64 must possess a valid state fishing license; nonresident anglers under 64 must also have a license. The creel limit on trout is 10 per day, regardless of species. There are exceptions to these rules on some state waters (especially the Savannah River; see chapter 28), so check the WMRD brochure, "Hunting and Fishing Rules and Regulations." This annual publication is available from many bait and tackle shops, or by mail from the WMRD offices. There is no closed trout season in South Carolina.

27
Saluda River

USGS Irmo, Columbia North, Southwest Columbia •
SCWFA 84, 85

The tailwater of the Saluda River is located deep in the Piedmont region of central South Carolina in Lexington County. This area, west of the state capital of Columbia, is far removed from the portion of the Palmetto State that is ordinarily thought of with regard to trout fishing.

The tailwater originates from the 90-foot depths of Lake Murray, an almost 50,000-acre reservoir built in 1930. The Saluda flows to the southeast from the dam, joining the Broad River to form the Congaree River at Columbia's western edge. Along the Saluda's roughly 10-mile course from Lake Murray to the river junction, the entire flow is capable of supporting trout. In fact, during cooler months it is not unusual for trout to turn up for a mile or more down the Congaree below the mouth of the Saluda.

In general, the Saluda tailwater is a large river with limited public access. Also, very little wadable water exists along the flow. Those few wading areas it has are most accessible when the five generators at the dam at Lake Murray are not in use.

The Saluda trout fishery has had a spotty history, with a number of peaks and valleys. Until recently, the South Carolina Electric and Gas Company managed the Saluda Hydroelectric Plant for the generation of electricity alone, with little regard for the fishery downstream. As a result, water containing almost no oxygen would be released into the river in the late summer and early fall, leading to fish kills. The local chapter of Trout Unlimited in Columbia has since brought pressure on the company to be more cognizant of how its management practices affect the fishery. In response, the energy company has now instituted a program of venting the turbines in the powerhouse at critical times to maintain the oxygen levels.

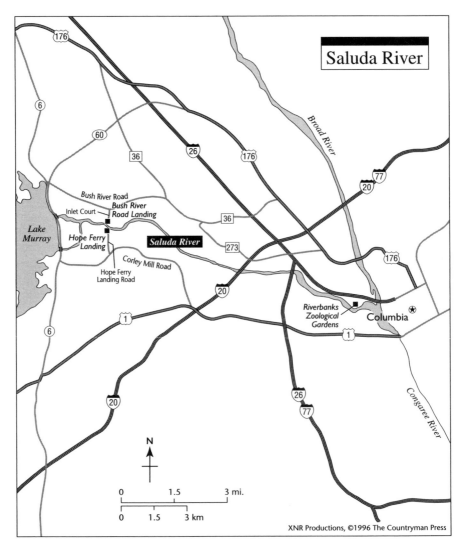

The WMRD stocks the Saluda with rainbow trout twice weekly in the months of January through May. Another stocking takes place in November or December. The stockings total 25,000 to 30,000 catchable-sized, 9- to 10-inch trout annually. Of that number, 4000 are planted in the fall. Additionally, the fall stocking includes about 40,000 brown trout fingerlings in the 6-inch range. Because of the lack of easy access points along the Saluda, some of the trout are stocked using helicopters in order to disperse them through the entire tailwater.

Although water temperatures are low enough to support trout even in the summer, no fish are released from mid-June through October. Striped bass from the Santee-Cooper Lakes downstream migrate into the Saluda tailwater in search of refuge from the warming lake waters. Trout stocked during the summer would be little more than forage for these stripers, but rainbows and browns released earlier are streamwise enough to avoid the large predators.

Though fishing pressure on the Saluda is ordinarily only moderate, the stockers are caught out rather quickly. Some fish will hold over, particularly those in areas several miles downstream of the dam, and trout of up to 20 inches are sometimes taken.

While most tailwater fishing tactics prove successful here, the bulk of the pressure comes from bank-anglers using natural baits. There are, however, some notable hatches of caddis flies on the river during spring and summer evenings. These tend to occur farther downstream, toward Columbia, attracting the local fly-casting enthusiasts.

The major drawback to fishing the Saluda is its lack of public access. There is an access road at the northern end of Lake Murray Dam, but it is only open at the discretion of the South Carolina Power and Gas Company, and is not a dependable route to the river.

On the southern shore of the stream, the only public access is found at Hope Ferry Landing. This park is open from sunrise to sunset daily, and provides a paved boat ramp and a limited amount of parking. The accessible portion of the river is minor here, since the park is surrounded by private farmland.

To reach Hope Ferry Landing, travel south on SC 6 from the point at which the highway crosses Lake Murray Dam. Turn east onto Corley Mill Road and drive 1¾ miles to its junction with Hope Ferry Road, which enters from the left. Follow this paved road until it changes to gravel and reaches the parking area and boat ramp at ½ mile.

The northern bank of the Saluda is a bit more accommodating to anglers. Directly across the river from Hope Ferry Landing is the Bush River Road Landing. Both of these access points are between 1 and 2 miles downstream of Lake Murray. This park is also open daily from sunrise to sunset, and offers a paved boat ramp and parking area. An appreciable amount of shore access is available by foot here.

To reach Bush River Road Landing, travel northward from the dam on SC 6 to the intersection with SC 60 and Bush River Road (SC 107). Turn southeast onto Bush River Road and drive 2¹⁄₁₀ miles to the intersection with Inlet Court. Follow Inlet Court to the west, where it ends at the parking area and boat ramp.

*Hope Ferry Landing is one of only a few points of
public access to the Saluda tailwater.*

A complex of Jeep and foot trails runs upstream from the parking area. At ¼ mile above the boat landing, the river makes a bend that contains a small island and a shoal area. This is ideal wading water at minimum flows, and even offers limited wading at higher water levels. It is also possible to run a small boat with an outboard upstream through this shoal during medium to high water.

The foot trail continues up this eastern shore for about another ¼ mile, where it ends on a 40- to 50-foot bluff overlooking the river. It is possible to climb down the dirt bluff to reach the water at this point. It makes a good spot to launch a float tube for drift-fishing back down to the landings.

There are additional trails running down the northern shore from Bush River Road Landing. These are not well marked, run for just ¼ mile, and provide only bank-fishing access.

One other point of public access exists on the eastern shore of the Saluda. The Riverbanks Zoological Gardens are located on the river just upstream of its junction with the Broad River in Columbia. The zoo lies along a rocky section of the flow that is shallow enough to wade during low water. The boulders in this part of the stream are used heavily by sunbathers from local colleges during warmer months, so parking can be at a premium. Access to this area is available off I-26 via the Greystone Boulevard exit in Columbia.

The South Carolina Electric and Gas Company maintains a toll-free number that provides information on water conditions on Lake Murray and release schedules for the Saluda tailwater. Call 1-800-830-5253.

28

Savannah River

USGS Hartwell Dam • SCWFA 12, 13

The final tailwater in South Carolina is located on the Savannah River, which forms the border between the Palmetto State and Georgia. Due to its location between Anderson County, South Carolina, and Hart County, Georgia, the Savannah River trout fishery is claimed and managed by both states. Unfortunately, the resource that they have to manage has been greatly reduced over the last decade and a half.

When trout were first introduced into the Savannah River tailwaters, their range stretched for 14 miles downstream of the dam and power plant at Hartwell Lake. Then in 1982 the gates were closed on Russell Lake just downstream, creating a new reservoir that backs up almost to the foot of Hartwell Dam. In the process, the demand for electric power destroyed nearly all of the trout fishing area. Today the Savannah River trout fishery is but a ghost of its original self. At virtually any level, the river more resembles a lake than flowing water.

Presently, South Carolina and Georgia each stock 12,000 catchable-sized rainbow trout in the Savannah River annually. The efforts of the two states are coordinated so that they do not release fish at the same time. Stocking is generally done twice a week from February through June. Additionally, Georgia has from time to time planted some brown trout in the Savannah.

Any trout that hold over in the tailwater below Hartwell Dam do have the potential to put on some size. A former South Carolina state-record rainbow of 5 pounds, 8 ounces was taken from the river in April 1971. More recently, in 1994, a 10-pound rainbow was caught by an angler fishing from the Georgia shore.

It appears that Hartwell Dam's tailwater trout fishery is in the process of suffering yet another blow. Georgia fisheries managers had for several years released up to 100,000 rainbows of over 10 inches into downstream Russell Lake. That reservoir had a 12-inch mini-

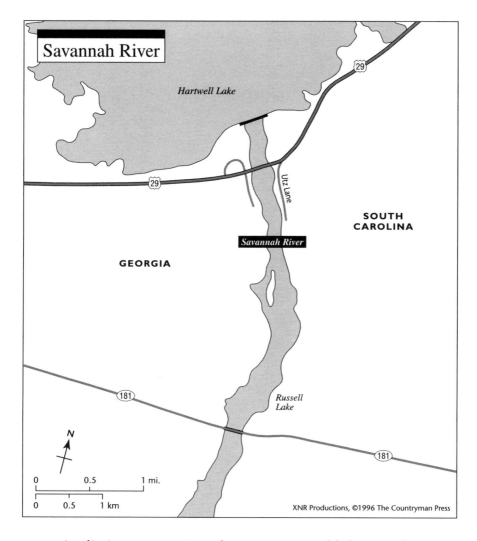

Savannah River

Hartwell Lake

Utz Lane

SOUTH CAROLINA

Savannah River

GEORGIA

Russell Lake

N

0   0.5   1 mi.
0   0.5   1 km

XNR Productions, ©1996 The Countryman Press

mum size limit on trout, in order to try to establish a trophy trout fishery. Undoubtedly, many of these fish moved into and out of the tailwater section of the river as well. In 1995, however, the stocking of Russell was discontinued, due in part to problems with oxygen levels in the water coming down from Hartwell, but mainly to a lack of interest among anglers in this lake fishery.

As a result of its position on the border of two states, the Savannah's fishing regulations represent a compromise between the South Carolina WMRD and the Georgia Wildlife Resource Division. Fishing is allowed with all types of flies, lures, and natural baits. The creel limit

*Below Hartwell Dam, the Savannah River tailwater
is more like a lake than a stream—at all water levels.*

adheres to Georgia's standard of 8 trout per day regardless of species. On the other hand, as with South Carolina's streams, there is no
season closed to fishing on this tailwater. Finally, anglers may fish the
main branch of the Savannah River from either bank as long as they
possess either a Georgia or a South Carolina fishing license.

Almost all of the fishing that takes place on the tailwater of the
Savannah is in the form of bait-fishing from shore. Although some
rocky portions of the river just below the dam are visible and shallow
enough for wading, signs are posted along this section warning that
no one is allowed on the rocks even during low water. Even boats
coming upstream from Russell Lake are denied access to several hundred yards of the tailwater by a cable and buoys strung across the
river below the dam. Anglers occasionally try casting in-line spinners
or crankbaits from the bank, but a fly-caster is a rare sight on the
Savannah.

The US Army Corps of Engineers maintains parks on both shores
of the Savannah River below Hartwell Dam. On the South Carolina
side, three concrete fishing piers are provided. The Georgia shore has
a walkway for fishing near the dam and one pier farther downstream.
Access to the Georgia park is via an approach drive off US 29 at the

western end of the highway bridge, immediately below Hartwell Dam. To reach the South Carolina bank access, go ½ mile east of the bridge on US 29, then turn south onto Utz Lane. This dirt road dead-ends in the river park at ¾ mile. Boats can be launched at ramps on the upstream end of Lake Russell near the SC 181 bridge.

To hear a recording of the water-release schedule at Hartwell Dam, call the Corps of Engineers at 706-376-3500.

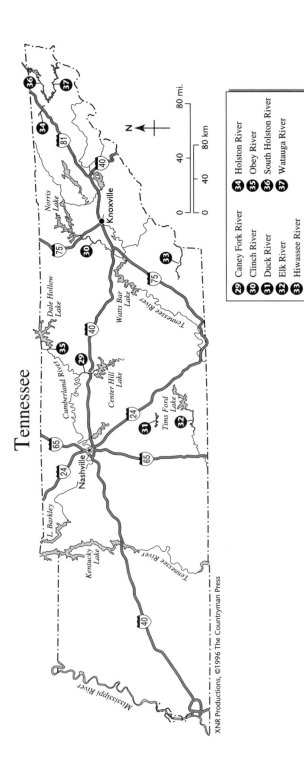

Tennessee

29 Caney Fork River		**34** Holston River	
30 Clinch River		**35** Obey River	
31 Duck River		**36** South Holston River	
32 Elk River		**37** Watauga River	
33 Hiwassee River			

XNR Productions, ©1996 The Countryman Press

SECTION EIGHT

TENNESSEE

When trout fishing in the Volunteer State is mentioned, the inclination is to think of the Great Smoky Mountains National Park or the Cherokee National Forest of extreme eastern Tennessee. The 10-county strip of mountainous land along the North Carolina border where the national park and forest are found does contain some of the wildest and most beautiful trout streams in eastern North America. The presence of these gems among Tennessee's 1900 miles of trout water, however, means that many of the state's other trout fishing resources are overlooked. This is especially true of the man-made resources.

Tennessee's "artificial" trout waters fall into two categories—stocked streams and tailwaters, both of which are managed by the Tennessee Wildlife Resources Agency (TWRA). In the case of stocked streams, the planting of fish has extended the range of trout in free-flowing water westward all the way to the lower Tennessee River valley, some 50 miles west of the state capital, Nashville. Here some spring-fed tributary streams in the ridge country along the Tennessee and Cumberland Rivers now provide habitat for hatchery-raised brown and rainbow trout.

In the instance of the other form of man-made trout habitat—tailwaters—the Volunteer State is blessed. Although its tailwaters are less numerous than Kentucky's and may not be quite as awesome as Arkansas's, Tennessee still lays claim to some of the top blue-ribbon fishing destinations in the eastern portion of the nation. In all there are nine tailwater trout fisheries, totaling 127 miles of rivers.

Three of the tailwaters—the Clinch, Hiwassee, and South Holston Rivers—deserve mention in any listing of the top trout rivers in America. The other six—the Caney Fork, Duck, Elk, Holston, Obey, and Watauga Rivers—run the gamut from very good to only marginal as fishing destinations.

To fish for trout in Tennessee, a resident angler over 13 years of age and born after March 1, 1926, must possess a regular fishing license and an annual trout permit. For all nonresidents over 13, an All Fish License is required. The statewide creel limit is 7 trout, regardless of species. There is no minimum size limit for brown or rainbow trout, but all brook trout must be at least 6 inches long. There are exceptions to these regulations that apply on the Hiwassee and Watauga tailwaters, but those are covered in the appropriate chapters. There is no closed season for trout on Tennessee's tailwater rivers.

29
Caney Fork River

USGS Center Hill Dam, Buffalo Valley, Gordonsville •
DeLorme 55

The Caney Fork River is noted as the best trout water in Middle Tennessee. Since this region did not originally support trout, one might assume that the competition for this title is not very tough. There are, however, 39 streams in this part of the Volunteer State that now hold rainbow and brown trout. Most of these are spring-fed tributaries of the Cumberland or Tennessee Rivers. These feeder streams drop down from the highlands of the Cumberland Plateau and flow into the rivers from the south or east. Although some are quite good trout fisheries, the Caney Fork tailwater stands head and shoulders above the rest.

From Center Hill Dam near the community of Laurel Hill, the Caney Fork flows for 28 miles to the northwest, eventually emptying into the Cumberland River at the town of Carthage. Located about an hour's drive due east from Nashville, the Caney Fork is also the midstate area's most popular trout fishing destination. Particularly in spring and summer, this tailwater attracts a lot of canoeists, bank-fishers, and wade-anglers. Due to its limited shoreline access, float-fishing in a canoe is the best option for covering the water during its low periods. There are so many shallow riffle areas that venturing out in a float ring requires plenty of downstream walking along the way.

It is, of course, the trout fishing that attracts most of the visitors to the Caney Fork below 18,220-acre Center Hill Lake. Each year the TWRA releases up to 125,000 brown and rainbow trout into the flow (usually 80 percent are rainbows). The fish range from 4-inch fingerlings to catchable-sized adults. The TWRA uses boats to stock the Caney Fork along its entire length, unlike the procedure on most tailwaters, in which fish are simply dumped from bridges or other access points. For this reason, the entire 28 miles of water provide fairly dependable fishing.

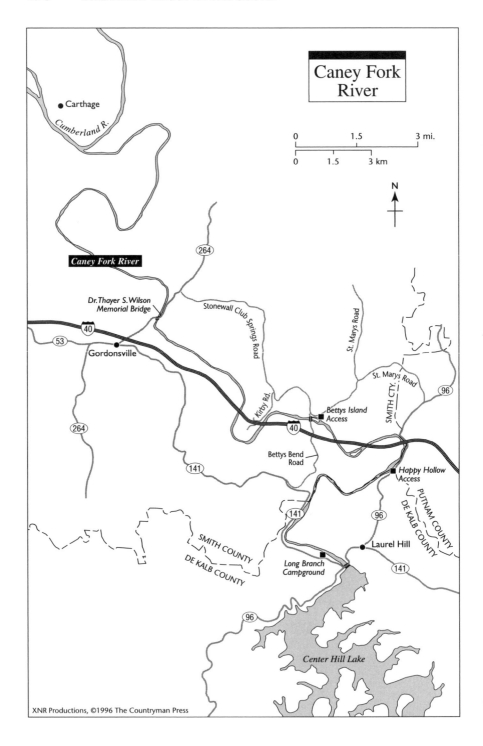

Carthage

Cumberland R.

Caney Fork River

Caney Fork River

264

Dr. Thayer S. Wilson
Memorial Bridge

Stonewall Club Springs Road

St. Marys Road

40

53

Gordonsville

St. Marys Road

SMITH CTY.

96

264

Kirby Rd.

Bettys Island
Access

40

Bettys Bend
Road

Happy Hollow
Access

141

PUTNAM COUNTY
DE KALB COUNTY

141

96

SMITH COUNTY

DE KALB COUNTY

Laurel Hill

Long Branch
Campground

141

96

Center Hill Lake

0   1.5   3 mi.

0   1.5   3 km

N

XNR Productions, ©1996 The Countryman Press

The Caney Fork is noted for producing quality trout as well as quantity. Rainbows of 2 to 3 pounds tend to be common, while fish of that species in the 6- to 10-pound range also occasionally turn up. As with any water in which brown trout are found, catching a large fish is a consistent possibility. These battlers turn up in the 5- to 10-pound range regularly, and 15-pound behemoths also have been reported.

Two distinct patterns are used by anglers on the Caney Fork, depending upon whether they are after a limit of fish or a lunker. To produce numbers of trout, corn, worms, or other natural baits are hard to beat. Tossing Rooster Tail, Panther Martin, or Beetle Spin spinners will take the stockers as well, along with Little Cleo spoons or small jigs. Fly-casters have particularly good results using Woolly Buggers in dark hues, or Tellico Nymphs. Despite the presence of rising trout in downstream areas, aquatic insects are rather scarce on the Caney Fork's rocky bottom.

For the larger trout, fish during low water and look for the deeper runs, rocky banks, and downed trees in the water. Especially where the trees and rocks are found together, expect to encounter some bigger brown trout. Most such areas are located 4 to 5 miles below Center Hill Dam. During hot summer months, the browns will be in this type of cover almost exclusively during the daylight hours.

Spin-casters often resort to crawfish-pattern crankbaits for the big browns and rainbows, and will even tie on large topwater jerkbaits like the Red Fin, Thunderstick, or Rapala. Fly patterns to use for the lunker trout are leech, crawfish, or minnow imitations.

Although the most oft cited problem with fishing the tailwaters of the Caney Fork is lack of shoreline access, there are several places open to the public. The most popular is at the foot of Center Hill Dam. This part of the river comprises the tailrace from the dam, plus a backwater eddy. An underground creek empties into the eddy via a waterfall after popping out of the rocky cliffs on the northeastern shore. In all there are several acres of water backed up here, before the flow exits to the northwest through a shallower riffle area.

When the flow from the dam is low, the best area to fish for browns is around the waterfall. For rainbows, the vicinity of the boat ramp on the eastern shore is good. The water between these two points is deep, but at the foot of the falls becomes quite shallow. It is not unusual to see anglers wading around the east-side boat launch during low water. However, when wading this pool, be aware that the water can rise up to 8 feet when power generation begins.

An underground stream bursts forth into a waterfall and drops into the pool at the foot of Center Hill Dam.

Also visible in low water are carp, gar, bass, bream, and other warm-water fish. Some of the anglers you encounter here will be using heavy gear to target the striped bass that inhabit the pool.

When the water begins to rise, angling interest is redirected to the western shore along the riprap below the tailrace. Through here, stunned minnows will surface after coming through the turbines. Fishing this area with minnow-imitating lures may yield some of the biggest trout in the river.

Below the pool, foot access is possible for roughly a mile down the eastern shore, along the part of the tailwater that is more riverine. Access to the western side is via the Long Branch Campground and the paved boat ramp beside it. The campground and parks on both shores are managed by the Corps of Engineers. There are drives off TN 141 (which crosses the dam) at either end of the dam that lead to both parks. The east-side access is through the Center Hill Lake Resource Manager's office parking lot.

On the western shore, some access is available off TN 141 along the first 2 miles of river below the dam. At 1½ miles downriver there are parking spaces for three to four cars, with trails leading down to an outside bend with deep water. Just ¼ mile farther down, at the point the road leaves the river at the Smith County border, a long gravel bar gives ½ mile of water access. Parking is in short supply at this point as well, consisting of a few roadside turnouts. Both of these areas appear to get heavy fishing pressure on weekends.

The first "official" downstream access to the river is found at the TWRA's Happy Hollow Access. A parking area is provided at the Putnam-DeKalb county line on the southeastern side of the river. Although there is no boat ramp, it is possible to get a canoe down to the water here. The river skirts a long gravel bar at this point, and the river bottom is made up of marble- to baseball-sized rocks. This provides excellent footing for wading. Walking the bar or wading provides about a mile of access along the river from this entry point. When water is released at the dam, it takes about an hour for the surge to reach Happy Hollow Access.

One unique aspect of the Caney Fork's gravel bars is that when the water falls rapidly in nongeneration periods, isolated pools of it are left on the bars. These often contain trout and provide beaver-pond-type fishing. The trout cruise these pools, continuing to feed as they await rising water and an opportunity to escape back to the main flow. Since the water in the pools is very clear, use extreme caution when stalking these fish.

Expect fishing pressure and competition for parking spaces to be heavy on weekends at all of the access points along the river, since this spot is a particular favorite of anglers. Also expect to see a lot of cars in the Happy Hollow parking area bearing license plates from Nashville's Davidson County.

To reach Happy Hollow Access, take TN 96 north for 2½ miles from its intersection with TN 141 just east of Center Hill Dam. The parking area is on the western side of the highway.

The next downstream access point is Bettys Island Access, which is managed by the TWRA. This spot is just upstream of Laycock's Bridge. Though the high iron-and-wood bridge is still in use on Bettys Bend Road, it can be unnerving to cross. Positioned on the northeastern shore, a gravel bar, from which small boats or canoes can be launched, runs for about ½ mile along the river. All of this area is wadable during low water.

Through here, there are more of the "beaver ponds" described at Happy Hollow. Be aware that you do not want to leave a vehicle on the gravel bar even though it is possible to drive onto it. When the river rises during power generation, the bar is inundated. It takes the rising water roughly 2½ hours to reach this point from the dam. The gravel bar also provides a takeout point for a good 6-mile day of float-fishing beginning at Happy Hollow.

To reach Bettys Island Access, take St. Marys Road west from TN 96. This intersection is 5½ miles north of the junction of TN 96 and TN 141 near the dam. Follow St. Marys Road until it changes to Stonewall Club Springs Road (the transition point is not clearly marked, but proceeding straight at each intersection will keep you on the proper road). At 4¹⁄₁₀ miles a gravel spur marked with the access sign is on the left. It runs down to the gravel bar on the river.

Another point of access is located just downstream of Bettys Bend, where Kirby Road skirts the shoreline of the Caney Fork. At the point where Kirby Road first strikes the river, there is a gravel bar and a mild shoal that is reached by wading. Then, for a little over ¼ mile, the river runs deep and slow along the roadside. Where the river and Kirby Road run under I-40, there is some more wadable water.

Kirby Road is a gravel track that runs south off Stonewall Club Springs Road. It is ⁸⁄₁₀ mile from that intersection to the river. Kirby Road then follows the river for ³⁄₁₀ mile, passes under the I-40 bridge, and comes to a dead end. The intersection where Kirby Road leaves the paved highway is not presently identified by a sign, but it is located 1⁸⁄₁₀ miles west of Bettys Island Access via Stonewall Club Springs Road.

The final point of public access on the Caney Fork before it empties into the Cumberland River is found on the outskirts of the town of Gordonsville. At the point where TN 264 crosses the river just northeast of the village, a canoe put-in is provided. It is found at the northeastern end of the Dr. Thayer S. Wilson Memorial Bridge at the Gordonsville city limits.

Though the access here is limited, there is a path running downstream to a gravel bar and shoal below the bridge. The rest of the water in this vicinity is too deep for easy wading. It takes rising water 3½ hours to reach this point from Center Hill Dam.

To obtain the Caney Fork water-release schedule, call the Corps of Engineers' recorded message at 1-800-261-5031. The Tennessee Valley Authority (TVA) also provides generation schedules for Center Hill Dam if you call 1-800-238-2264 or 615-632-2264. These numbers require a Touch-Tone phone. The code for the Cumberland River system is 9. The code for Center Hill Dam is 37.

30
Clinch River

USGS Norris, Lake City, Powell, Clinton • DeLorme 59

The Clinch River is located in northeastern Tennessee's Anderson County, just over 20 miles to the northwest of Knoxville. This tailwater has some distinctive history and geographic features that set it apart from similar waters in the Volunteer State. The Norris Dam, from which the tailwater originates, was the first building project begun by the Tennessee Valley Authority (TVA); it came on-line in 1933. The Clinch was also the first tailwater in the South to be stocked with trout, receiving its first fish in the early to mid-1940s. The success of those plantings provided the impetus to introduce trout below other TVA and Corps of Engineers projects where the habitat looked promising.

From the standpoint of geography, the Clinch is a big river. For the entire 14 miles of its trout-bearing tailwater, from 24,000-acre Norris Lake down to the town of Clinton, the river is up to 100 yards wide. It is pretty easy to find supporters for the position that it is also the best big-fish trout destination in Tennessee. Backing up this view is the feat accomplished by Greg Ensor on August 30, 1988. While fishing about 2 miles below Norris Dam, the angler from the nearby hamlet of Powell hooked and landed a 28-pound, 12-ounce brown trout, which remains the Tennessee record for the species. Many anglers believe that the river holds browns of over 30 pounds as well. In the spring of 1993, TWRA biologists performing an electroshock survey raised a brown that was longer than the record fish and pulled their 25-pound scale all the way to its limit! Browns of 8 to 15 pounds turn up in the Clinch every year, and rainbows in excess of 10 pounds have been caught as well.

Despite these glowing tales of big fish, however, up until the last decade or so the Clinch was not highly thought of as a trout destination. A quick look at its history reveals why, and also explains why the stream's reputation has improved markedly.

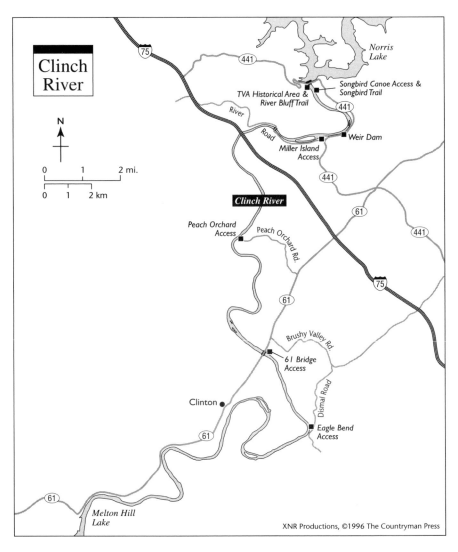

During the early years the brown and rainbow trout stocked by the TWRA and federal agencies did fairly well in the river, but a triumvirate of problems dogged the tailwater. Wildly fluctuating water levels scoured the river bottom at all times of the year, while in summer water coming through the powerhouse turbines contained low levels of dissolved oxygen. Finally, minimum releases in June and July raised water temperatures in the tailwater to marginal or lethal levels for trout. Until the Little Tennessee River tailwater was inundated by Tellico Lake in the late 1970s, the Clinch languished in the shadow of that famed fishery as well.

The Clinch's turnaround began in 1984, when a weir dam was built some 2 miles downstream of the reservoir to even out the flow of water during power-generation releases. Another benefit of the weir is the waterfall effect created when water plunges over it during low levels. This helps add oxygen to the tailwater downstream.

More recently, hub baffles have been added to the turbines in the dam's powerhouse. These are designed to suck air into the flow when electricity is being generated. Along with this innovation, release schedules have been altered to ensure that a minimum flow is maintained downstream.

While these physical and management changes were taking place, some biological tinkering was also being effected on the Clinch. The flow's sand-and-gravel bottom is among the richest in nutrients of any trout water in Tennessee, but was made barren by scouring. To address the absence of insect life in the river, some insects common to the highland streams of southern Appalachia were transplanted to the tailwater. As conditions improved in the Clinch, the TWRA and the US Fish and Wildlife Service increased the stocking of rainbow and brown trout by 40 percent in the mid-1980s.

It would appear that all of these efforts have borne fruit. Recent tagging studies revealed that the Clinch's rainbows grow at a rate of 1 inch per month. Additionally, there are indications that some brown trout may be spawning in the river. All in all, it would be hard to imagine a trout fishery in America that has improved any more in the last decade than has this river below Norris Dam.

Another effort to improve the fishing on the Clinch did not fare quite as well. Back in 1993, a Quality Trout Fishing Area was established for the 4¹/₁₀ miles from the mouth of Cane Creek to the downstream end of Llewellyn Island. On this portion of the flow, the original regulations called for artificial lures only and a daily creel limit of 2 trout over 14 inches long. In 1994 the rules were changed to allow any type of bait and liberalize the creel limit to 3 fish per day, only 1 of which could be 14 inches or longer. Finally, on July 1, 1995, the Quality Trout Fishing Area rules were rescinded. The entire tailwater below Norris Dam now is open under general Tennessee trout regulations and creel limits.

Despite all of this activity to improve the fishing, most of the trout taken from the Clinch tailwater are still stocked rainbows of 10 to 12 inches. These stockers are vulnerable to anglers at all water levels and during all seasons. The same, however, cannot be said of the larger trout.

During periods of low water the lunker-sized browns and rainbows will hug the bottom in deeper water, usually around any structure available. Much of the Clinch runs shallow and calm on minimum flows, and all of the trout become quite spooky. This is particularly true of the bigger fish.

It is during medium to maximum water releases that the angling for large trout picks up. Although virtually the whole river becomes unwadable at these times, it is possible to float the stream in a float ring, canoe, or johnboat. This allows anglers to get to the big trout that feed more recklessly in the stronger currents. High water levels are most prevalent on the Clinch from July through September when energy demands are at their peak.

For bait- and spin-fishers, the lures and the natural baits that work on other tailwaters will score here as well. For fly-casters who challenge the heavy currents, weighted streamers and sinking lines are needed. Black Woolly Buggers are a favorite with local anglers.

When the river is running at minimum water levels it becomes a fly-fisher's dream. Although both caddis and mayfly hatches occur on the Clinch, one bug of particular interest is the light Hendrickson. Due to the constant temperature in the tailwater, these mayflies, in sizes 14 to 16, are likely to appear at any time of the year. Midge hatches are fairly common during the summer months as well. A Griffith's Gnat in sizes 20 to 22, fished on a 7X tippet, is often needed to fool the fish during this action.

If no surface feeding is evident, attractor flies such as the Royal Wulff and the Adams are good options. Elk-Hair Caddis will also work, along with Tellico, Hare's Ear, and George's Nymphs. By far the most popular fly for fishing wet, however, is a scud imitation suspended beneath a strike indicator. This should be in the size 18 to 20 range; black, brown, gold, and green are dependable colors.

Although access points are not abundant on the Clinch tailwater, the TWRA has improved the situation in recent years by adding several public areas. The first access points below Norris Dam, however, are provided by the TVA. On the western side of the river the TVA Historical Area provides a paved drive down to a picnic area at the foot of the dam. This shore is fairly steep, but the River Bluff Trail runs down the river and is a better way to approach to the water at about a mile from the trailhead. The drive to the picnic area and trailhead is off the Norris Freeway (US 441, which crosses the dam) at the western end of Norris Dam.

During low water, much of the Miller Island Access is wadable. It is also a good spot from which to begin a float trip.

On the eastern side of the river, the Songbird Canoe Access and Songbird Trail provide almost a mile of shoreline access. Through here the river is like a very shallow lake when no turbines are in operation at the powerhouse. Although there is no boat ramp here, it is possible to launch canoes and johnboats. This access point along with the next two—one downstream at the weir dam, the other at Miller Island—are all reached by following the Norris Freeway south along the Clinch.

At the weir dam, which is roughly 2 miles downstream from Norris Dam, the river is split by an island. There are weir dams on both channels of the river, along with a canoe portage to make it easy for floaters to get around these drops. On low water, the area just below the dams breaks into multiple small channels coursing through the rocky riverbed. Just below the island are State Record Shoals, where Greg Ensor took his mammoth brown trout.

One mile below the weir dam is the Miller Island Access, also on the river's eastern shore. Access here is excellent and includes a paved boat ramp. During low water, a long stretch of the river in front of the ramp and down both sides of Miller Island downstream is easily waded. In fact, around the island the river is almost too shallow for fishing in many spots.

200 TAILWATER TROUT IN THE SOUTH

From this point down to Massengill Bridge, the eastern shore is paralleled by River Road. There are several spots with turnouts and trails to the water along the 1¼-mile stretch, but there is also much private land. A lot of bait-anglers fish from Massengill Bridge during higher water levels.

The next access point encountered heading downriver is the newest one established by the TWRA. The Peach Orchard Access provides only limited shore or wading access. When you are traveling north from Knoxville, you can reach it by turning southwest off I-75 onto TN 61. Go to the intersection of TN 61 and Peach Orchard Road, then turn northwest to drive 3 miles to the access point.

Access to the section of the river around Llewellyn Island is possible just upstream of the town of Clinton. Park at the new county jail on the southwestern side of the river at the TN 61 bridge. There is a park with soccer fields adjacent to the jail at this point as well. A streamside anglers' trail leads from the jail parking lot up to the island. This area of the river is noted as a good place for fly-fishers to try scud imitations.

On the northeastern side of the river and at the other end of the TN 61 bridge is the 61 Bridge Access point. This TWRA access provides a boat ramp, but the river is too deep to wade here. The same conditions exist about a mile downstream at the last public access point at Eagle Bend Access, off Dismal Road.

To obtain information on water releases at Norris Dam, call the TVA's recorded message at 1-800-238-2264 or 615-632-2264. A Touch-Tone phone is required for this service. The code for the Clinch River system is 1. The code for Norris Dam is 17.

31
Duck River

USGS Normandy Lake, Normandy • DeLorme 22

The Duck River tailwater is located in south-central Tennessee, almost directly north of Tims Ford Lake and the Elk River tailwater (see chapter 32). The river emerges from the foot of Normandy Dam at the Bedford-Coffee county line, then flows westward through Bedford County. This close proximity to the Elk, along with some problems with water quality, have combined to make the Duck an often overlooked trout fishing destination. Still, the river does have some following as a trout fishery, because it and the Elk are the most westerly tailwaters in the Volunteer State. Virtually all of the anglers encountered on the Duck River will be local residents.

At only 3230 acres, Normandy Lake is a small reservoir, and it has had recurrent problems with releases of poorly oxygenated water over the years. Even at its best, this river offers only a 10-mile stretch of marginal trout habitat. To combat this, a multilayered piping system draws water from varying levels of the lake, and the TVA, which manages the dam and lake, has installed ½ mile of "soaker hoses" on the lake floor to release air bubbles into the water. This oxygenates the water before it is released into the river.

As late as 1994 the Duck's flow failed state criteria for water contact. In other words, swimming and wading wet are not advised in this river. The major problems noted by the TVA are excess nutrients, resulting from the high phosphorus content of surrounding soils, plus run-off silt and bacteria from dairy farming and other agricultural activity in the region. Anglers have complained in recent years that the Duck sometimes looks cloudy, and even gives off a faint sulfurous odor.

Despite these dreary water conditions, the TWRA has continued to stock rainbow trout in the river. In the spring of 1993, the Dale Hollow National Fish Hatchery provided 7000 catchable-sized rain-

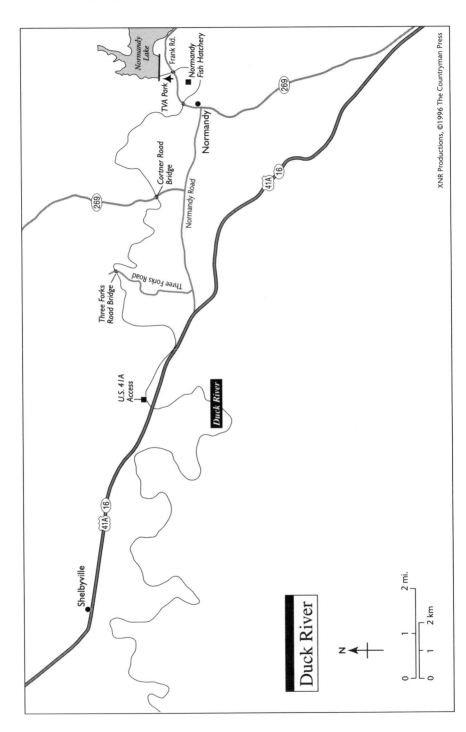

Duck River

bow trout for the tailwater beginning in February. The next year, 5000 were stocked beginning in March. On the brighter side, TVA sampling has shown a slight improvement in the condition of the tailwater's fish community in recent years. Still, the likelihood of any carryover fish in the Duck is small. Although at a few access points the tailwater does have wadable stretches, the best way to fish the Duck is floating in a canoe or a johnboat.

Access is provided to the Duck River tailwater between the foot of Normandy Dam and the upper bridge on Frank Road by a TVA park on the western side of the stream. Below the park, the Normandy Fish Hatchery property borders this shore between the two bridges on Frank Road, all the way downstream to the town of Normandy.

Much of the water in the park is wadable during low water, and the eastern shore just below the dam is lined by a steep wall of layered sedimentary rock. The park provides a boat ramp and a stairway to the canoe access, but no camping facilities. The park is 1 mile northeast of the village of Normandy via Frank Road.

Downstream of the town, the TWRA has constructed three other public access points along the river. At the Cortner Road Bridge (TN 269) there is a parking area and a stairway down to the water. There is also an old, abandoned highway bridge standing to the west of the one now in use. Just downstream of the two bridges is a short stretch of shallow water that is wadable at low levels.

The next access point is located where Three Forks Road Bridge crosses the stream, about 6 miles below Normandy Dam. A stairway to the canoe launch and a parking area are provided. There is a gravel bar and wadable riffle downstream of the access point.

The final point of access is upstream of the US 41A/TN 16 bridge just east of Shelbyville. A gravel drive intersects the highway from the west on the northern side of the river, then loops back under the bridge and follows the flow upstream for ¼ mile to the parking area. A gravel bar along the northern shore provides wading and boat-launch possibilities. This site is the end of practical trout water. It also receives obviously heavy use and is rather trashy.

To hear a message detailing the current water-release schedule for Normandy Dam, call the TVA automated phone line at 1-800-238-2264 or 615-632-2264. A Touch-Tone phone is needed. The code for the Duck and Elk River system is 8. The individual code for the Duck River is 56.

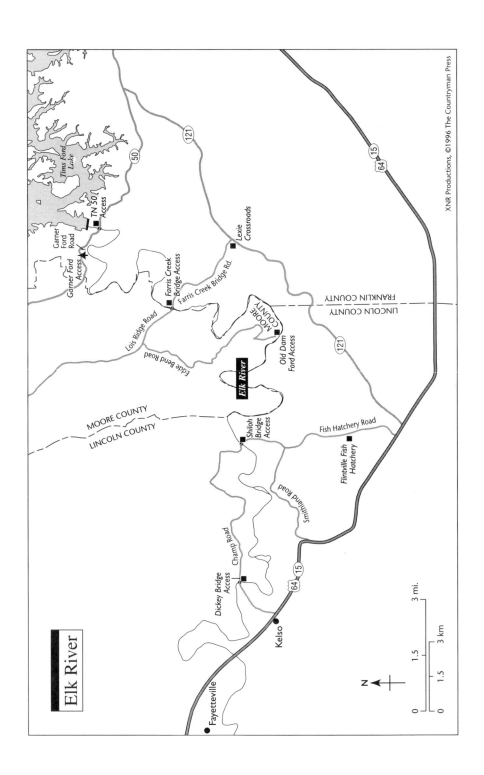

Elk River

Tims Ford Lake

Garner Ford Road

TN 50
Access

Garner Ford
Access

Farris Creek
Bridge Access

Farris Creek Bridge Rd.

Lois Ridge Road

Eddie Bend Road

MOORE
COUNTY

Old Dam
Ford Access

Lexie
Crossroads

LINCOLN COUNTY
FRANKLIN COUNTY

MOORE COUNTY
LINCOLN COUNTY

Elk River

Shiloh
Bridge Access

Fish Hatchery Road

Flintville Fish
Hatchery

Smithland Road

Dickey Bridge
Access

Champ Road

Kelso

Fayetteville

50

121

121

64 15

64 15

15

64

N

3 mi.

3 km

0   1.5   3

0   1.5   3

XNR Productions, ©1996 The Countryman Press

32

Elk River

USGS Lois, Mulberry • *DeLorme 22*

As noted in the previous chapter, the Elk River is located south of the Duck River tailwater. The reservoir spawning the Elk's tailwater is 10,700-acre Tims Ford Lake. Tims Ford Dam is located in western Franklin County, but the river soon becomes the north–south-running dividing line between Franklin and Moore Counties. It then turns west to form the border between Moore and Lincoln Counties. Eventually, the Elk River flows into Lincoln County, with its trout-holding water ending near the town of Fayetteville, roughly 28 miles below Tims Ford.

This river, which was known to the Native Americans of the area as the Chuwalee, is for the most part a small flow, alternating between shallow riffles running over a gravel bottom and pools that drop to depths of 10 feet. In most places the stream is no more than 50 to 80 feet wide.

The Elk is stocked with catchable-sized rainbow trout each spring by the TWRA, and some brown trout are also present in the river, though not regularly stocked. Some of these fish obviously carry over from year to year, since trout of both species show up in the 4- to 7-pound range. The gravel bottom and clear waters of this river are ideal for trout. Surveys done by the TVA, however, have shown that the stream has only a fair population of aquatic insects and crustaceans. Probably the most important of these organisms to the trout is the sow bug.

The lack of insect life is probably tied to the same type of problems mentioned earlier for the Duck River. Nutrient loading is a concern on the Elk due to the phosphorus-based soil it flows through, as well as agricultural runoff. Low oxygen levels in the water released from Tims Ford also plagued the Elk in the past. Fortunately, a pilot program to increase oxygen levels was begun by the TVA at Tims Ford

*Beneath the TN 50 bridge, just downstream of Tims Ford Dam,
is a good spot for fly-casting.*

Dam back in 1981, and ran through the summer of 1991. This involved putting a small, constantly running turbine in the powerhouse; later, an aeration and an oxygen-injection system were added. Oxygen levels in the Elk are no longer a problem, due to the equipment installed during the pilot program.

On the other hand, the lack of aquatic life has not been adequately addressed. TVA surveys in recent years have shown a decline in variety and mass of insect and fish life in the river. Additionally, at five of the six TWRA access points on the trout-bearing part of the tailwater, the TVA monitoring has shown the river's water quality to be too low to allow swimming.

Having noted all this bad news, the Elk River remains a popular fishing and canoeing destination in Middle Tennessee. Angling pressure just below the dam is usually fairly heavy on weekends, and all of the canoe access points get at least medium usage.

The bulk of the fishing pressure on the Elk is from bait-casters using corn, worms, and the other usual trout offerings. Casting small in-line spinners or floater-diver minnows such as the Rapala is also popular. Growing numbers of fly-fishers are showing up on this river as well. The area just downstream of the dam and the gravel bars found at several of the access points are popular with these long-rod enthusiasts. Some sporadic hatches of caddis flies or, in the summer, midges do take place on the Elk.

Access to the Elk River tailwater is possible off TN 50, only a couple hundred yards below Tims Ford Dam. A large pool forms just below the tailrace, then the river narrows as it flows under the highway bridge. A long gravel bar composed of fossil-bearing sandstone and limestone runs several hundred yards down the southeastern side of the river. This part of the stream is composed of slick pools and mild riffles, almost all of which are wadable during low water. The parking area is located on the southeastern side of the river just above the highway bridge. There is no boat ramp, but canoes and johnboats can be launched here.

The next point of entry to the Elk is at Garner Ford Access. This site is managed jointly by the TWRA and the Tennessee Elk River Development Agency, as are the rest of the downstream access points. It consists of a parking area at the end of Garner Ford Road. Again, a gravel bar on the northern side of the river provides a place to launch small boats. There is also room at the end of the road for some primitive camping.

For a couple hundred yards upstream of the access it is possible to wade the river along the gravel bar. This is an area where late-evening hatches of caddis and midges often occur. This part of the river also demonstrates why a float tube would be a poor choice for the Elk. The water is so shallow that for long stretches, more walking than floating would be required. A canoe is a much more practical choice.

To reach this access point, take TN 50 northwest from Tims Ford Dam to the intersection with Garner Ford Road. Turn south and travel ½ mile to the river.

The next downstream public access point is at the Farris Creek Bridge Access. There is a parking area at the end of a dirt spur running off the road at the bridge on the eastern side of the river. Downstream of the bridge there are a couple hundred yards of water that are shallow enough to wade.

Take Farris Creek Bridge Road northwest from the community of Lexie Crossroads on TN 121 to reach the access point.

The Old Dam Ford Access is the next public site encountered. At this location the river widens to a couple hundred feet, and most of the water is quite shallow. Needless to say, this makes for excellent wading. Several small islands and exposed gravel bars also break the river up into small channels.

Old Dam Ford is located at the end of a ½-mile gravel road running off Edde Bend Road. There is a sign for the access at the intersection of the approach track and the paved road. To reach this intersection, take Lois Ridge Road (the same road as Farris Creek Bridge Road—the name changes once it crosses to the northwest of the Elk) 1³⁄₁₀ miles northwest of Farris Creek Bridge Access. Turn left onto Edde Bend Road. There are no names on the roads at this intersection, but there is a sign for Liberty Hill Church of Christ. It is 4 miles along Edde Bend Road to the intersection with the gravel spur that leads to the access.

The next public access is the Shiloh Bridge Access. This part of the river offers no practical wading water, but has parking and a launch site for canoes. To reach Shiloh Bridge, take Fish Hatchery Road north from US 64 in Lincoln County. After passing the Flintville Fish Hatchery, you will encounter a three-way junction. Smithland Road (gravel) forks to your left. Take the right fork, Champ Road, and follow it to the bridge. It is 4⁶⁄₁₀ miles from US 64 to the bridge.

The final access point on the Elk before its waters become too warm to support trout is the Dickey Bridge Access. Through here the river runs deep and slow, offering no wading, though there is a canoe landing. The portion of the Elk from Shiloh Bridge to Dickey Bridge is very marginal trout water. To reach Dickey Bridge, take Champ Road to the northeast from the village of Kelso on US 64.

To obtain up-to-date water-release information on the Elk River tailwater, call the TVA automated message line. The numbers are 1-800-238-2264 and 615-632-2264. A Touch-Tone phone is needed. The code for the Elk and Duck River system is 8. The individual code for the Elk River is 50.

33
Hiwassee River

USGS Farner, McFarland, Oswald Dome • DeLorme 26

Located in southeastern Tennessee, approximately 50 miles to the northeast of Chattanooga, the Hiwassee River below Apalachia Lake rates as one of the premier trout fisheries in the Southeast. It also has the distinction of being one of the few tailwaters to run through a good deal of public land. In fact, most of the tailwater is located in the Cherokee National Forest. For its first 10 miles below the dam, however, it is not much of a stream. The water is diverted through a pipeline along this part of its course, reappearing at the Apalachia Powerhouse. It is at this point that the Hiwassee tailwater begins.

As with all tailwaters, the Hiwassee's flow fluctuates according to the need for electricity. Fortunately, the Hiwassee is a broad, shallow river for several miles below the powerhouse, so wading is possible in some areas even on high water. Of course, caution is necessary at those times, since the current can be quite strong.

During low water most of the riverbed is exposed, appearing as small channels running through a rocky maze. Although this low water offers the best fishing conditions, many anglers continue to take fish even at the highest water levels, especially when fishing from rafts, canoes, or float tubes.

The fish in the Hiwassee tailwater consist of stocked rainbow and brown trout, but holdover fish are common. More than 100,000 rainbows of 9 inches in length are released into the flow annually. As a result, the average rainbow caught is 10 to 14 inches long and shaped somewhat like a football. This is a fertile river, providing plenty of insect life for the fish, which explains their oval shape. In past years, brook trout were also routinely stocked in the tailwater, accounting for the Hiwassee yielding the Tennessee record for that species. Back in 1973, Jerry Wills hauled a 3-pound, 14-ounce brookie from the river to establish the mark.

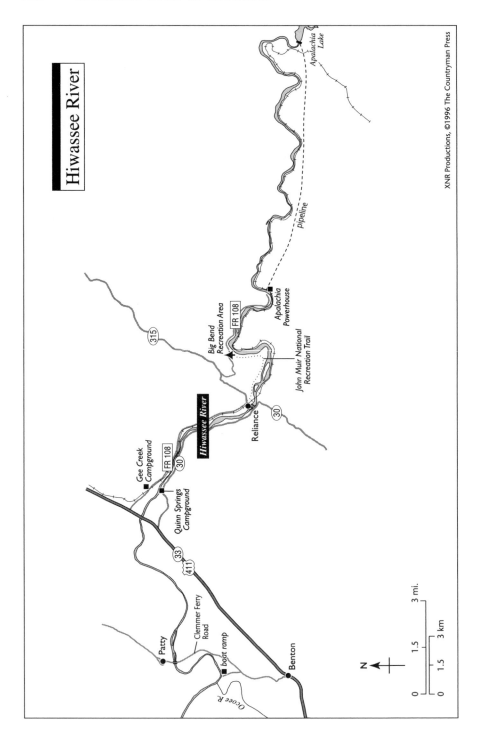

Hiwassee River

XNR Productions, ©1996 The Countryman Press

From the powerhouse to the US Forest Service's Big Bend Recreation Area, the river is open to fishing under Tennessee's general trout regulations and creel limits. The next 3 miles, however—down to the Louisville & Nashville railroad bridge just above the town of Reliance—are managed under trophy trout regulations. Artificial lures are mandated along this stretch, with a creel limit of 2 trout per day, each of which must be at least 14 inches long. These waters have been managed for trophy fishing since 1986 and the plan has worked admirably. Trout of 16 to 20 inches are regularly hooked on this part of the Hiwassee. Browns of 15 pounds and 9-pound rainbows have also been reported.

These larger trout, whether in the trophy or open sections of the river, fall victim to anglers more often during periods of high water. This is pretty typical of southern tailwaters, where larger fish do most of their feeding when they feel safe in the stronger currents.

From Reliance to the end of trout water on the Hiwassee, the river is again open under general regulations. On the portion of the flow down to the US 411 crossing, the angling is similar to that found above the trophy section, with plenty of 10- to 12-inch stockers present. There are some privately held lands along the river in the vicinity of Reliance, and just above US 411 the river flows out of the Cherokee National Forest.

Below US 411 the Hiwassee continues to be stocked and is cold enough to support trout, but access becomes a problem. Almost all of the land is private, on both shores, and has little road access. The tailwater here is more suited for float-fishing. One unimproved boat ramp is located near the junction of the Hiwassee and Ocoee Rivers to the north of the town of Benton and downstream of the village of Patty. This portion of the river is not very accommodating to fly-casters and gets little attention from them.

Needless to say, the upper reaches of the tailwater get plenty of attention from bait-fishers and anglers using in-line spinners or small minnow lures. This part of the river, however, is noted as a fly-fishing destination. It is one of the rare streams of the southern highlands on which insects hatch with some measure of predictability. Beginning in April, Blue-Winged Olives and Caddis are the mainstay of the daily activity, followed in May by Sulfurs and Light Cahills. When no surface action is visible, many anglers turn to floating Royal Wulffs in sizes 12 to 14 through the riffles.

Despite all of this glowing information on the Hiwassee's trout

*The Hiwassee tailwater just above the Big Bend Recreation Area
is a wide river with many shoal areas.*

fishing, there is a downside. The portion of the tailwater immediately
below the powerhouse has for some reason never supported the numbers of trout it seems capable of sustaining. Recently the TVA and
local Trout Unlimited chapters have been looking into possibilities
for improving this situation.

Also, the TVA has begun "pulsing" the generators at the powerhouse to maintain a minimum flow in the Hiwassee. Instead of running the generators for 8 hours, then shutting them off for 8 hours,
for instance, this method runs the generators for 2 hours, turns them
off for 2 hours, and so on. Thus, just as much electricity is produced,
but the river level is not allowed to bottom out. Without pulsing, the

extremely low water levels experienced when no water was being released were particularly detrimental to the insect life in the river. Aquatic insects unfortunate enough to be in shallow water when the river began to fall found themselves high and dry, thus wiping out much potential trout food. Keeping a minimum level of water in the river should largely alleviate this problem.

From the powerhouse down to US 411, access to the Hiwassee is excellent. Forest Service Road FR 108 runs along the northern side of the river from the powerhouse to Reliance. The only point at which it leaves the flow is the Big Bend section. There is, however, a foot trail along the 3 miles of water that are not at roadside. The John Muir National Recreation Trail follows the northern side of the river here and takes in most of the trophy trout water. Parking areas are provided at Big Bend, Towee, and the Hiwassee River Recreation Areas. This is by far the most popular portion of the tailwater and anglers flock to it on weekends.

Below the bridge at Reliance, TN 30 parallels the southern side of the Hiwassee tailwater. Due to the presence of some private land, not all of the water along this stretch is readily accessible. The water can be reached with ease in Reliance, or at Cherokee, Taylor Island, and Quinns Springs Recreation Sites, by driving west along TN 30 from the town. All of the recreation areas on the Hiwassee are managed by the US Forest Service as part of the Cherokee National Forest. A state-run campground is located on FR 108 at Gee Creek on the northern side of the river, while the forest service maintains one at Quinn Springs.

The lower portion of the river below US 411 can only be fished by floating, since there is practically no shore access. A boat ramp at Boyd Bottoms can be reached by taking Clemmer Ferry Road west from the Benton town square. The road makes several sharp turns along the route. At $1\frac{7}{10}$ miles, turn left onto the road (it presently has no sign) marked ROAD CLOSED. At ¾ mile, the boat ramp is down the steep gravel spur on the right.

Water-release updates for the Hiwassee tailwater can be obtained by calling the TVA at 1-800-238-2264 or 615-632-2264. Use a Touch-Tone phone to punch 4 for the Hiwassee River system and 22 for the Apalachia Powerhouse.

34

Holston River

USGS Kingsport • DeLorme 63, 71

The tailwater of the Holston River below Fort Patrick Henry Lake is located in extreme northeastern Tennessee's Sullivan County, very close to the Virginia border. The lake is a relatively small one, with a dam that is not particularly high. The result is a tailwater that supports trout for only about 2½ miles—from the dam down to the city of Kingsport.

The fishery consists almost entirely of stocked adult rainbows of 10 to 12 inches. There are, however, reports of trout of 2 to 3 pounds being caught occasionally. The trout habitat on the Holston is at best marginal. Recent TVA research has focused on studying how this fishery can be improved.

The Holston River below Fort Patrick Henry Lake
is definitely not in a wilderness setting.

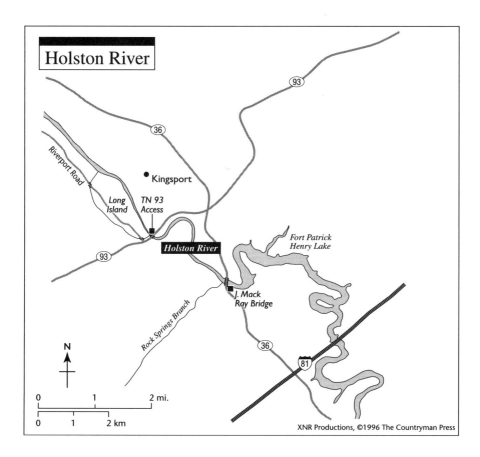

For all practical purposes, there are only two access points to the Holston's trout water. The upper of these is at the tailrace pool at the foot of Fort Patrick Henry Dam. There is a 100-yard trail from a parking area at the southeastern end of the J. Mack Ray Bridge on TN 36 (Fort Henry Road). The bridge is to the southeast of Kingsport and within sight of the dam. Rock Springs Branch empties into the tailrace pool beside the trail. This location offers only bank-fishing access. In fact, there is no really good wading available on the Holston's trout water.

The other access point is at the TN 93 bridge at the edge of Kingsport. There is a parking area at the northeastern end of the bridge and an unimproved boat-launch site under it. This is the area where the bulk of the angling pressure on the tailwater occurs. Most of it appears to come from bait-fishers. Although this is near the end of practical trout water, it is possible to boat downstream for several hundred yards. The downstream area is not very pleasing aesthetically, however, since both shores are lined by the Eastman Chemical Company complex. Shoreline access below TN 93 is not practical due to the presence of Eastman, the Holston Army Ammunition Plant, and other industries. Unfortunately, all of this industrial activity sometimes leaves a chemical odor hanging over the Holston as well.

The river splits around Long Island just below the TN 93 bridge. Some trout may venture down the narrow western channel during cooler months. Several stretches of this channel are shallow enough for wading, and are accessible from Riverport Road in Kingsport. All in all, though, the Holston is still of little interest to serious trout anglers.

To obtain the most recent water-release information for the Holston River, call the TVA automated line using a Touch-Tone phone. The numbers are 1-800-238-2264 and 615-632-2264. The code for the Holston River system is 3, while the number for Fort Patrick Henry Dam is 04.

35
Obey River

USGS Winfield, Oneida North • *DeLorme 66*

The Obey River tailwater lies below Dale Hollow Lake in north-central Tennessee, tight against the Kentucky border. In all, the trout habitat stretches downstream for about 8 miles, to the town of Celina at the junction of the Obey and Cumberland Rivers. Prior to the completion of the Cordell Hull Dam on the Cumberland, trout showed up for more than a half-dozen miles down that flow as well. The new lake, however, now backs up into the mouth of the Obey at higher water levels.

Despite the loss of the free-flowing portion of the lower Obey, the river still offers some quality trout fishing. From its emergence from the Corps of Engineers' 27,700-acre Dale Hollow Lake (4300 of those acres lie across the state line in Kentucky), the river travels a contorted course to the west, through Clay County to Celina. Along that route it is only a medium-width stream, but much of it is deep and carries a large volume of water. As a result, it is capable of floating even bass boats during periods of water release. On low water, a canoe or a johnboat is a better choice for float-fishing.

There is little in the way of good wading areas on the Obey even during low water. Those that do exist are more like flats off the main river channel than shoals or riffles. For the most part, the Obey is a float- or bank-fishing stream. Bank-fishers are much more prevalent during low water.

Another problem with fishing the Obey is the relative scarcity of shoreline access for the public. Basically, there are three parks along the river from the dam to Celina, with the rest of the Obey flowing through private property.

The Obey is a fertile river that supports a healthy insect population. In fact, back in its glory days—before the construction of the Cordell Hull complex—this tailwater at one time or another laid claim

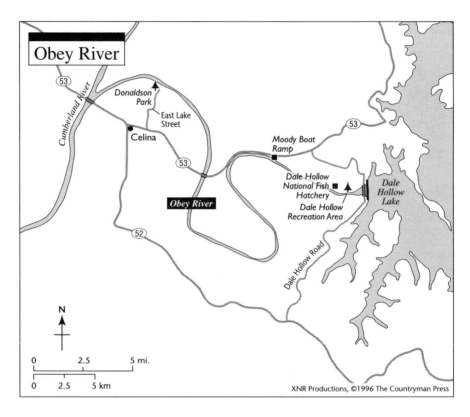

to the Tennessee records for both brown and rainbow trout. In 1955, a 26-pound, 12-ounce brown was wrestled from the Obey's water. That fish stood for a number of years not only as the Volunteer State standard, but also as the largest brown trout taken in North America. In 1971 the Obey yielded a rainbow that tipped the scales at 14 pounds, 5 ounces. That trout held the top spot in the state record book for more than a decade.

During those early years, cutthroat trout were also stocked in the Obey on an experimental basis. Today, however, the fishery is composed of freshly stocked rainbow and brown trout. A fair amount of carryover must take place in the river, since trout of both species in the 12- to 15-inch range are not uncommon. And of course, that rare fish measured in pounds rather than inches does still show up on the Obey. The dominance of stockers, however, is ensured by the presence of the Dale Hollow National Fish Hatchery on the banks of the river. Needless to say, a large number of the trout reared there find their way into the tailwater.

Fishing tactics on the Obey are similar to those on other southern tailwater rivers. Bait-anglers lean toward corn, salmon eggs, and worms. These anglers tend to dunk their baits in the deeper pools, especially during low water. In the case of spin-anglers, spoons and small minnow-type lures are popular. Nymphs and streamers tend to be the favored offerings of the rare fly-casters who tackle the Obey.

The Dale Hollow Recreation Area is a Corps of Engineers park located at the foot of the dam and stretching downstream for ½ mile. The entrance to the recreation site is on the western side of Dale Hollow Road, ½ mile north of the dam (Dale Hollow Road crosses the dam). Picnic and camping areas are in the recreation area, along with a paved boat ramp.

The campground stretches downriver from the boat ramp and separates the stream from the hatchery grounds. There are a couple of wooden fishing piers at the boat ramp, along with a sign warning of rising water. Believe the sign. At full generation the piers will be underwater. The pier just above the boat ramp will be completely submerged when the river is at high levels, with only a small ripple in the stream to mark it!

Downstream of the boat ramp, a trail runs along the river above the high-water mark. This path leads past the camping area, ending at the creek carrying the hatchery's outflow into the river. This creek is a good place to fish when the river is running at full bore. Trout will be backed into it all the way up to the miniwaterfall at the outflow pipe. Unfortunately, most of the really big fish spotted in the creek at these times turn out to be carp. There is a paved walking trail that follows most of the creek bank.

Another tip for high-water angling is to walk the path along the river watching the area around the bases of the trees standing in the edge of the flow. Trout usually are visible holding on the upstream side of some of the tree trunks. A fly or bait dropped in front of these fish will often tempt them.

The next downstream public access on the Obey is at the Corps of Engineers' Moody Boat Ramp. This site is located on TN 53, 2½ miles east of this road's junction with TN 52 in Celina. There is an improved boat ramp and several wooden fishing piers along the river, as well as a paved parking lot and rest rooms. In all, about ¼ mile of shoreline is available to the angling public here. When the river is high, up to a foot of water will be running over the fishing piers.

The final point of access to the Obey tailwater is in the town of

On high water levels, the fishing pier near the foot of Dale Hollow Dam is nothing but a ripple!

Celina. Donaldson Park is a Corps of Engineers day-use facility containing about a mile of shoreline and a boat ramp. There are also playgrounds, rest rooms, and parking and picnic sites in the park.

Through the park, which is on the southern side of the river, the water is too deep to wade, but does offer some bank-fishing possibilities. To reach Donaldson Park, turn north off TN 53 onto East Lake Street, just ¼ mile east of the courthouse square in Celina. The park is at the end of the street.

To obtain information on water releases for the Obey tailwater, use a Touch-Tone phone to call the TVA recorded message center at 1-800-238-2264 or 615-632-2264. The code for the Cumberland River system is 9, while the number for Dale Hollow Dam is 35.

36
South Holston River

USGS Holston Valley, Bristol, Keenburg, Bluff City •
DeLorme 63, 70, 71

A good way to start a debate in East Tennessee is to begin comparing
the trout fishing in the Clinch, Hiwassee, and South Holston tailwaters.
The argument can swirl on endlessly, with proponents of all three
rivers claiming that their choice represents the blue-ribbon trout destination in the eastern United States. And none of them will be far
from wrong.

In truth, all three tailwaters offer excellent fishing, but the natural
ebbs and flows of nature will make one a little "hotter" for a season
or two, only to be overtaken by one of the others later on. Over the
last couple of years, a very good case could be made for the South
Holston being the best of the best in southern trout fishing. In this
period the Clinch has suffered through some summers when the fish
have been hard to catch, and on the Hiwassee the larger fish have
played hide-and-seek as well. But on the South Holston the rainbows
have been plentiful, with their average size pushing 12 to 13 inches
and lunker rainbows and browns of over 20 inches turning up
regularly.

Much of the credit for the South Holston's outstanding fishing can
be laid at the door of the TVA for the recent improvements they have
undertaken on the tailwater. Chiefly, they installed a labyrinthine
aeration weir about a mile below South Holston Dam. By creating a
long, crested waterfall across the river, the dam adds a great deal of
oxygen to the downstream water. The weir, which was the first of its
kind anywhere in the world, also aids the fish population by evening
out water surges. This lessens the scouring effect on the bottom, allowing for more in-stream insects and plants. The lessening of the
surge also makes the South Holston a bit safer for anglers when the
turbines start to turn. The moderating effect of the weir allows them
more time to react when the water begins to rise.

*The weir dam on the South Holston evens out the flow
and adds oxygen to the tailwater.*

Of course, the downside of such a positive report on the South Holston's fishery is that more anglers flock to it, which thins out the trout population as creels are filled. The remaining fish, too, are more skittish from having seen so many lures, baits, and flies. Thus the stage is set for the Clinch or Hiwassee to overtake the South Holston in the coming years.

The South Holston tailwater originates at the foot of the 285-foot-high, earthen South Holston Dam, which was constructed by the TVA in 1947. Above the dam South Holston Lake backs across the state boundary into Virginia. Below the dam the river's trout-bearing water stretches for 14 miles through Sullivan County to the south of Bristol in extreme northeastern Tennessee. Eventually, the tailwater dumps into Boone Lake just north of Johnson City.

Along its course the South Holston is one of the more conveniently located tailwaters in Tennessee. It is almost constantly in sight of paved roads as it flows through a semiurban area mixed with some farmland. This ease of approach, coupled with the river's position among the Tri-Cities of Bristol, Johnson City, and Kingsport, makes it a popular destination. Adding to the number of anglers as well is its proximity to both Virginia and North Carolina. Many fishers in search of big

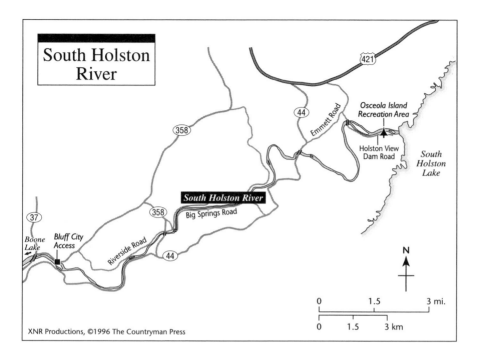

trout find their way across those borders to sample the South Holston fishery.

Regardless of where they come from, the visiting anglers find a medium-width stream composed of slick, glassy pools broken by gentle shoals. These pools and shoals are home to hordes of stocked rainbow and brown trout. Stories of 50- and even 75-fish days abound on the South Holston. Added to this mix is a healthy sprinkling of trophy-sized rainbows and browns in the 7- to 10-pound range.

Virtually all of the South Holston is wadable when the water is running low, while high water levels make the stream ideal for float-ing in a johnboat, in a canoe, or with a float ring. Some anglers float even on low water, mainly because of the scarcity of public land along the banks. There are only a very limited number of points where anglers can get to the river. Besides the public land sites, there are usually a number of enterprising land owners along the South Holston who rent parking spaces and access across their property to anglers. This is a constantly changing circumstance, but worth investigating while driving along the flow.

Due to its shallow and clear waters, the South Holston is one river where even many bait-anglers forsake the shore to wade the stream.

This allows them to get into position to float their baits under and around logs, rocks, undercut banks, and other structure. Wading is easy on the South Holston, since it flows at a much slower rate during low water than do many other tailwaters. Whether the bait-anglers take to the water or stick to the shore, they are armed with all the usual tried-and-true trout baits. Night crawlers, corn, and crickets predominate.

The easily waded and gentle flow of the South Holston make it perfect for fly-casting. Indeed, a large percentage of the anglers here carry a long rod. The insect populations in the tailwater are strong and active. Spring and summer see good hatches of caddis flies coming off. The Elk-Hair Caddis pattern in sizes 12 to 16 is a local favorite for this fishing. Hatches of Sulfurs, which are noted for taking place in late afternoon on most southern streams, are likely to take place anytime during the day on the South Holston. This is particularly true when the day is overcast. Another insect hatch important on this flow is the blue-winged olive. These bugs appear almost year-round on this Volunteer State river and call for imitations on hook sizes 12 to 18.

Most of the fly-fishing here involves casting to rising fish. When no such action is visible, using any of a number of regionally popular nymph patterns should turn up some fish. Tying a Tellico Nymph or Gold-Ribbed Hare's Ear is a good option.

Finally, if the fish you are targeting are the big rainbows and browns, your best bet is to float the stream during high water. Casting minnow or crawfish imitations on spinning gear will bring the best results. The fly-fisher should try a big, weighted streamer. These are often dressed with a gold spinner blade.

The best public access to the South Holston River is located at the Osceola Island Recreation Area at the weir dam. This TVA park is 1 mile below South Holston Dam. Above the weir the river is almost like a lake as it flows sluggishly along. Below the weir it offers plenty of wadable water. The weir dam is located on both channels of the river on either side of the island.

The parking area for Osceola Island is on the southern shore of the river off Holston View Dam Road. There are walking trails on the island that are accessible via a footbridge below the weir dam.

A hiking trail runs ½ mile down the southern shore from the Osceola Island parking lot to Holston View Dam Road bridge over the river. All of this stretch is open to public fishing.

Below the bridge there are several turnout parking spots offering access to the flow both along TN 44 (Rockhold Road) and off Big Springs Road. Both of these roads border the river at several points on its southern side. Riverside Road also offers some access to the river's northern shore, upstream of the Weavers Pike Bridge. The final access consists of boat landings at the head of Boone Lake in the town of Bluff City.

For information on water releases on the South Holston River, call the TVA automated phone system at 1-800-238-2264 or 615-632-2264. The code for the Holston River system is 3. The number for South Holston Dam is 01. The call requires a Touch-Tone phone.

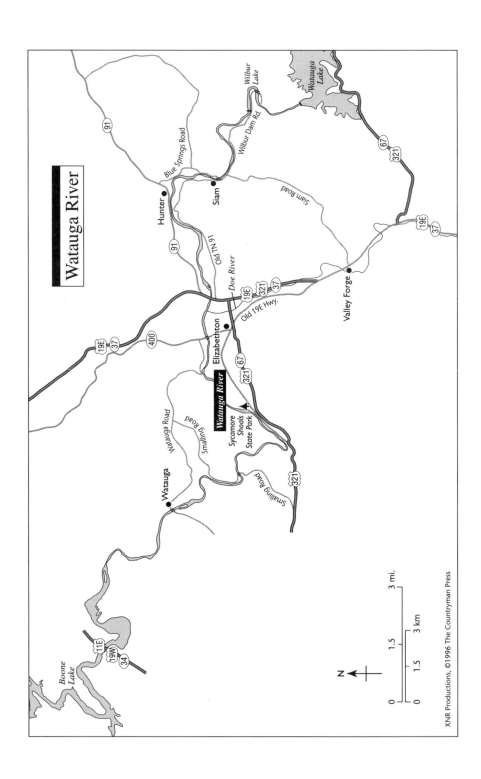

Watauga River

Wilbur Lake

Wilbur Dam Rd.

Watauga Lake

91

321

67

Blue Springs Road

Hunter

Siam

Siam Road

19E

37

91

Old TN 91

Doe River

19E

321

37

Valley Forge

19E

37

400

Old 19E Hwy.

Elizabethton

321

67

Watauga Road

Smalling Road

Watauga River

Sycamore Shoals State Park

Watauga

321

Smalling Road

Boone Lake

11E

19W

34

N

0   1.5   3 mi.

0   1.5   3 km

XNR Productions, ©1996 The Countryman Press

37
Watauga River

USGS Elizabethton, Johnson City • DeLorme 63

The Watauga River below Wilbur Dam is a large stream character-ized by long, deep pools. In all there are just over 19 miles of trout water down to the point at which the tailwater empties into Boone Lake. The Watauga traverses Carter County in northeastern Tennes-see, finally reaching the lake in Washington County.

The Watauga's tailwater gets a rather unusual start on its course. It flows out of Watauga Lake through a rock tunnel under the Iron Mountains and into Wilbur Lake. The water is then released from this small impoundment into the Watauga tailwater. Pulsing genera-tors have been installed in the powerhouse to help maintain water and oxygen levels downstream, but due to the influx of water from the Doe River several miles downstream, neither of these has been a problem on the Watauga.

The Doe River, however, creates a problem of its own. Especially during rainy weather it muddies up quickly, and will stain the Watauga as well. While bad for the fishing, this is also harmful to the habitat due to the amount of silt it brings into the tailwater.

Along its course, the Watauga passes through an area known as Siam, then runs through the towns of Hunter and Elizabethton. Just downstream of Elizabethton the river passes the historic site at Sy-camore Shoals where frontier settlers gathered before crossing the Appalachian Mountains to defeat the British at the Battle of Kings Mountain during the Revolutionary War.

Much of the country traversed by the Watauga is flat, providing gentle shoals that are easily wadable during low water. Like the South Holston, the Watauga is basically a float-fishing river at high levels, but a wader's paradise when the turbines are silent.

Bait-anglers are prevalent on the Watauga tailwaters, but they are mostly found near the river's heaviest stocking locations. Expect crowds near the foot of the dam, at the mouth of the Doe River, and at the water-gauging station in downtown Elizabethton.

Fly-fishers will find the same insect hatches on the Watauga as are found on the nearby South Holston tailwater. The Elk Hair Caddis is popular for imitating the abundant caddis hatching during falling water levels. Sulphurs in size 16 are also present, as are midges in the summer months. When the fish start attacking the midges, flies in sizes 20 to 22 are needed.

The Watauga tailwater is stocked with brown and rainbow trout. These are released as adults for put-and-take fishing, but fingerlings are also planted in the river for put-grow-and-take fishing. The TWRA, which stocks the Watauga, has noted that there is some natural re-production of brown trout in the tailwater. Some of these browns end up being taken when they have reached weights of 3 to 9 pounds.

The most popular areas for fishing on the Watauga are along the first 6 or 7 miles below Wilbur Dam down to Elizabethton. Through here Tennessee's general trout regulations apply, but there is a Quality Trout Fishing Area located farther downstream. From the Smalling Bridge down to the bridge in the village of Watauga, only artificial lures are legal, and the creel limit is 2 trout per day, which must be at least 14 inches long. From Watauga down to Boone Lake, the river continues to support trout and is again open to fishing under general regulations, but access is extremely limited and the river is not heavily fished. It is possible to float-fish through this stretch.

Access to the river at Wilbur Dam is available via Wilbur Dam Road to the southeast of the town of Hunter. From the point where the road crosses the river on the old metal bridge at Siam, it follows the river upstream to the dam. There is good access to the river at the Siam Bridge. To reach Wilbur Dam Road, travel north from the town of Hampton on US 321 to Siam Road at the village of Valley Forge. Turn northeast on Siam Road and drive to the bridge over the river.

From Siam northward to Hunter, Blue Springs Road offers some limited access and parking along the northern side of the river. The situation is similar along Old TN 91 (Broad Street) on the southern shore from Hunter to Elizabethton. In Elizabethton there are several bridge crossings, as well as the water-gauging site near the TN 400 bridge, all of which provide access to the river.

Downstream of Elizabethton, Sycamore Shoals State Park on US 321 is on the river's southern shore. Farther downriver, the Smalling Road and Watauga Road Bridges are the other two access points.

*The Revolutionary War mustering ground at Sycamore Shoals
lies right on the bank of the Watauga tailwater.*

For details on water releases from Watauga and Wilbur Lakes, call the TVA message center at 1-800-238-2264 or 615-632-2264. A Touch-Tone phone is required. The code for the Watauga River system is 3. The number for Watauga Dam is 02, while the Wilbur Dam is 42.

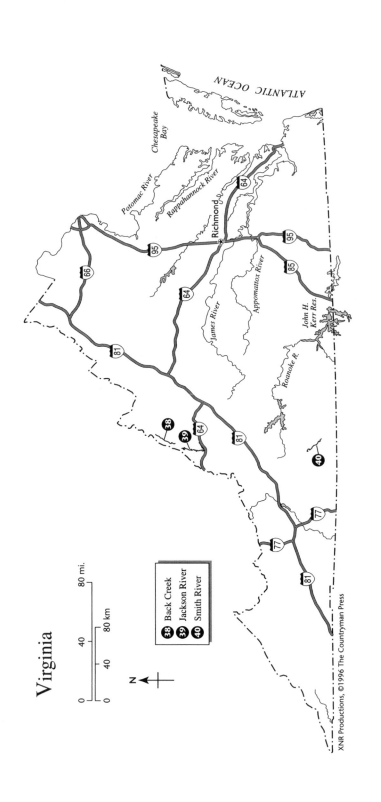

Virginia

N

80 mi.

40

80 km

40

80 km

40

0

0

0

38 Back Creek
39 Jackson River
40 Smith River

ATLANTIC OCEAN

Chesapeake Bay

Potomac River

Rappahannock River

Richmond

James River

Appomattox River

Roanoke R.

John H.
Kerr Res.

95

64

95

85

66

64

81

38

39

64

81

40

77

77

81

XNR Productions, ©1996 The Countryman Press

SECTION NINE

VIRGINIA

Virginia is the most northerly of the states covered in this book and, due to the position of the Allegheny and Blue Ridge Mountains within its boundaries, has some of the most beautiful natural trout waters of the region. In all, the Old Dominion contains 2800 miles of trout streams, of which only 600 miles require stocking to supplement natural reproduction. These include both high-elevation freestone streams and spring creeks flowing through lower valleys. The higher-elevation streams are noted for having the best native brook trout fishing south of New England.

With such outstanding natural trout water, it is hardly surprising that Virginia's tailwater fisheries have not received as much publicity or cornered as large a share of fishing interest as have the man-made trout streams of other southern states. Contributing to this situation as well is the relative scarcity of tailwater fisheries in Virginia. The state contains only three such flows: Back Creek, the Jackson River, and the Smith River.

Another stream that is sometimes lumped with the tailwaters is the North River below Elkhorn Lake in Augusta County. Although it bears some similarity to a true tailwater, it is not generally considered one by state fisheries managers. A 1½-mile stretch of this river in the George Washington National Forest between Elkhorn Lake and the Staunton City Reservoir is managed as a delayed-harvest stream. However, the North River is a trout stream upriver of Elkhorn Lake as well as below the dam. The 54-acre lake is not particularly deep, and it exerts very little influence on the river downstream of the dam. For these reasons, the North does not actually qualify as a true tailwater fishery.

Until recently Virginia trout waters were governed by a season running from the third Saturday in March through the following February 1. Beginning in July 1995, however, those regulations were changed. Year-round trout fishing is now legal in all of the state's waters, including the tailwater flows. The standard Virginia creel limit for trout is 6 fish per day with a minimum size limit of 7 inches. All three of the state's tailwaters, however, are managed under special regulations, which are covered in the appropriate chapters.

To fish for trout in Virginia, a regular fishing license is required. If you are fishing in any of the state's designated stocked trout waters, an additional permit is needed. However, fishing is allowed in these waters from June 15 each year to September 30 without the special trout license. Finally, when fishing on national forest lands, a special national forest fishing permit is necessary. An exception is the Jackson River. Although a portion of it crosses the George Washington National Forest, no permit is required.

With such a maze of permits and the possibility of changes in the regulations, it is wise to check the latest edition of "Virginia Freshwater & Saltwater Fishing Regulations" before venturing onto the tailwaters of the Old Dominion. The booklet is available at many retail sporting-goods outlets or by contacting the Virginia Department of Game and Inland Fisheries (VDGIF). Their phone number in Richmond is 804-367-1000.

38
Back Creek

USGS Sunrise, Mountain Grove • DeLorme 65

Undoubtedly the least known of the tailwater trout fisheries in Virginia is Back Creek in Bath County. Located in the Allegheny highlands of the Old Dominion's west-central portion, Back Creek flows from north to south through a scenic valley less than 10 miles east of the West Virginia border.

The history of the Back Creek tailwater is a short one. The headwaters have always been good trout water, but the lower section did not come into its own until the Virginia Power Company created the Bath County Pump Storage Station reservoir and power station on the creek in the mid-1980s. At that time the company also created a recreation area below the dam, as well as making extensive modifications to the stream itself. As a result, the creek has more holding water for trout in its tailwater portion than existed before the work began.

For several years after the creek below the reservoir dam was opened to fishing, it was stocked only with fingerling trout. The idea was to create a trophy brown trout fishery, so the regulations mandated single-hooked artificial lures only and a daily creel limit of 2 trout, which had to be at least 16 inches long. Fishing was permitted on the creek year-round. These rules were in effect from the Beaver Run Bridge on County Road (CR) 600 (Big Back Creek Road) just below the dam, downstream for 1½ miles to the Haul Road Bridge (the next bridge downstream, also on CR 600).

Unfortunately, the water coming through the 60-foot-high dam was too warm in the summer for the trout to carry over in large numbers. As a result, in the fall of 1992 Back Creek was changed to a delayed-harvest stream. Under this management scheme the portion of the tailwater below the dam is heavily stocked with catchable-sized trout in the fall, winter, and spring. From October 1 until May

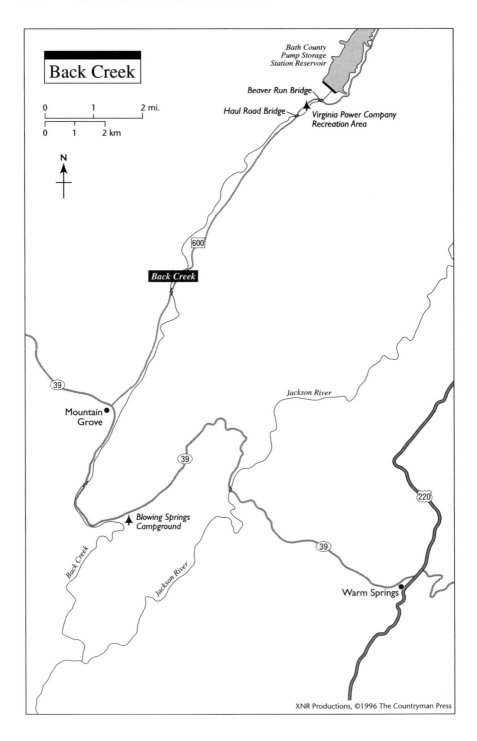

15 each year, fishing is permitted under catch-and-release regulations, with only single-hooked artificial lures allowed. From May 16 to September 30 the stream reverts to general trout regulations, using the state creel limit and allowing any type of bait or lures. The resulting fishery has proved to be a popular one that provides quality angling experiences to a large number of fishers each year.

From its beginning at the foot of the dam, Back Creek's tailwater is never more than a medium- to large-sized mountain stream. It averages no more than 25 feet wide along all of its trout water. Even during releases from the powerhouse, it is still possible to wade portions of Back Creek. When the water is low, virtually the entire run provides good wade- and fly-fishing. Most of the trout encountered are freshly stocked rainbows, but some fish do carry over, so it is possible to take a larger brown or rainbow.

Once below the lower CR 600 bridge at the end of the Virginia Power Company's property, Back Creek is open to fishing as "designated trout water." This is the Old Dominion fisheries managers' way of identifying stocked trout water. Back Creek receives plantings of mature rainbow trout through here in the spring and again during the fall. No trout are stocked during the summer, when water temperatures sometimes soar above the tolerance level of the fish. There are some holdover browns that attain respectable size through here, however.

In the spring, Back Creek is noted for the mayfly hatches to which it plays host. Quill Gordons and March browns are reported to be important. More often, fly-casters use attractor patterns in sizes 14 to 16. Royal Wulffs and Adams patterns are good for this fishing. Through the open, meadowlike areas of the Virginia Power Company's land, grasshopper imitations work well in the late spring. For fishers wanting to challenge the brown trout in Back Creek, in-line spinners, spinner-fly combinations, or—for the fly-caster—minnow-mimicking streamers are appropriate.

Access to the Back Creek tailwater begins at the Beaver Run Bridge below the dam. No angling is allowed upstream of this bridge to the tailrace. There is no parking allowed at this point either, but just downstream is the entrance to the Virginia Power Company Recreation Area. Besides offering parking (for a small fee), the recreation area has a campground, playgrounds, picnic pavilions, and two warmwater lakes (the smaller of which has a swimming area).

At the second bridge on CR 600, at the lower end of the Virginia

At any water level, Back Creek is only a medium- to large-sized mountain stream in its tailwater section.

Power Company land, there is a parking area beside the old bridge (which is no longer in use). This is an ideal spot to begin a day of wading upstream.

The next 8 miles down Back Creek along CR 600 and VA 39 are on private property and are not open to public fishing. The creek here is not large enough for float-fishing, so this portion is off-limits. From the VA 39 bridge, located to the southwest of the crossroads of Mountain Grove, the creek flows for 1¼ miles along VA 39 through US Forest Service land. Through here there are a number of roadside turnouts, a water-gauging station, and the forest service's Blowing Springs Campground. Below the campground, a foot trail along the shore leads down into the Back Creek Gorge portion of the tailwater. By this point, Back Creek is becoming marginal trout water.

To find Back Creek, take VA 39 west from its junction with US 220 near the village of Warm Springs. Continue past the Blowing Springs Campground to the intersection with CR 600, then turn right (north) to reach the delayed-harvest portion of the stream and the Virginia Power Company Recreation Area.

39

Jackson River

USGS Redwood • DeLorme 52

The Jackson River below Lake Moomaw in Allegheny County is Virginia's newest tailwater trout fishery. It was created when the river was first stocked in 1989. On the other hand, it is also the site of the Old Dominion's oldest ongoing controversy over trout fishing.

The Army Corps of Engineers first received congressional authorization for a dam on the Jackson in 1946. No work was begun, however, and in the 1950s the VDGIF purchased 18,000 acres of land, which included 12 miles of the river, to create the Gathright Wildlife Management Area. When the corps actually received funds for the lake project in the mid-1960s, Virginia's fisheries managers and many sportsmen opposed the construction of the dam. Basically, they did not want to lose the Gathright Wildlife Management Area or the free-flowing river.

In the end, the Gathright Dam was built, impounding 2530 acres of water in Lake Moomaw. As part of a mitigation agreement, however, the corps invested $10 million in a 260-foot mixing tower that takes water from nine different depths in the reservoir, then releases it into the tailwater. This creates ideal temperature and oxygen levels for trout in the Jackson. Oddly enough, Gathright Dam does not have electric-generation capacity, thus no powerhouse or turbines.

Even before the dam was closed, however, landowners along the river downstream began efforts to block the stocking of trout and the use of the river by the public. In October 1978, the river was declared navigable by the Corps of Engineers since the stream had been used for commercial hauling in historical times. This opened the way for the public to float the Jackson. The landowners appealed the decision and the battle dragged on in court until 1984, when the corps' decision was upheld. Meanwhile, in 1981, work on Gathright Dam was completed and the lake filled.

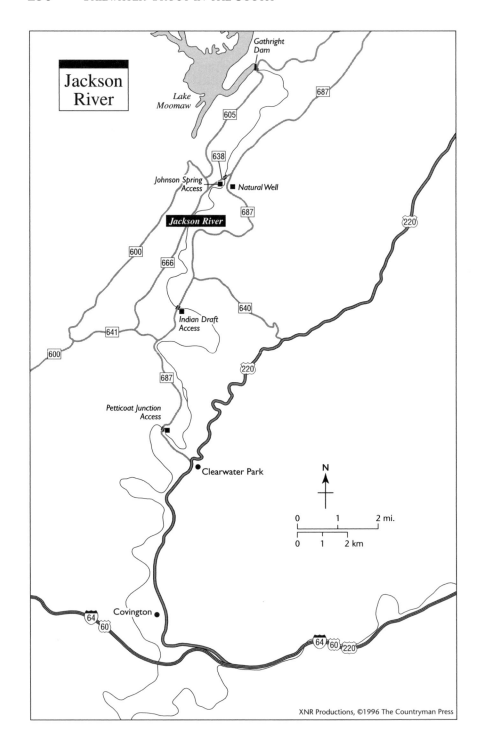

Jackson
River

Gathright
Dam

Lake
Moomaw

687

605

638

Johnson Spring
Access

■ Natural Well

687

Jackson River

220

600

666

640

Indian Draft
Access

641

600

220

687

Petticoat Junction
Access

● Clearwater Park

N

0   1   2 mi.

0   1   2 km

64
60

Covington ●

64 60 220

XNR Productions, ©1996 The Countryman Press

*Much of the Jackson River tailwater is easily waded
during minimum flows.*

At this point the landowners changed direction and challenged public use of the river based on crown grants made by George III before the American Revolution. These had given grantees the title to the river banks, the bottoms, and the fish in the stream. The present landowners contended that they still held that right. Under their interpretation, only the water in the river could be claimed by the state of Virginia.

Finally in 1989, the VDGIF stocked the first trout in the Jackson River. The controversy, however, did not end. In 1991 a landowner sued a guide and his clients for floating and fishing through his property. In the end, the landowner lost the case, but the ruling only established that the public could float down the Jackson. Unless you really enjoy court proceedings, you'd still be wise to skip fishing when floating across posted areas of the river (particularly the posted lands just above the public access point at Johnson Spring) until the courts decide the issue once and for all. And, of course, it is certainly illegal to go ashore on any of the posted lands.

With all the controversy and haggling over the Jackson tailwaters, you might be inclined to simply forget this stream and go fishing elsewhere. On the other hand, many anglers in the Old Dominion now consider the Jackson the state's premier trout fishery. In the first 2 years of stocking, 57,000 browns and 30,000 rainbow trout were released into the river. Another 53,000 trout of both species, including 5000 Kamloops-strain rainbows, were planted in 1993. The Kamloops rainbows originated in southern British Columbia and are noted for attaining large size. Presently, brown trout in the 14- to 20-inch range are showing up regularly on the Jackson tailwater, as are 10- to 17-inch rainbows.

The VDGIF originally envisioned a trophy brown trout fishery developing in this tailwater, but that idea is being rethought. In fact, the rainbows are showing much better growth in the river than are their European cousins. This is attributed to the scarcity of forage fish in the river. The carnivorous browns are having difficulty finding much to eat, while the very fertile aquatic insect habitat is providing plenty of food for the rainbows. Additionally, fisheries managers expect that trout will soon be reproducing naturally in the Jackson.

The entire 19-mile length of the Jackson tailwater from Moomaw Lake down to the town of Covington is open to fishing under strict catch-and-release regulations. Any type of bait, lure, or fly is allowed, but all fish must be immediately released back into the river. As a result, this is a very popular fishery with Old Dominion fly-casters. As mentioned earlier, the insect population is excellent in the stream, which adds to its appeal with the long-rod anglers.

The portion of the river just below the dam at Moomaw is noted for producing large hatches of black flies, especially early in the year. These are very small bugs, requiring midge imitations in the size 22 range. Farther downstream blue-winged olives, caddis flies, and true midges all appear on the water. In the fall, terrestrial patterns will attract some trout as well.

Although much of the Jackson is wadable during low water, float-fishing is the most popular method of tackling the stream. Public access points are set up to accommodate that activity.

To reach Gathright Dam take US 220 north from the town of Covington. At the village of Clearwater Park, turn northwest onto County Road (CR) 687 (Jackson River Road). Next, turn west onto CR 638 (Natural Well Road) near the crossroads of Natural Well. A turn north onto CR 666 (East Morris Hill Road) is next; then, at ½ mile, head northeast on CR 605 (Cole Mountain Road). A ¾-mile paved spur road runs down to the foot of the dam at an intersection marked with a MAINTENANCE AREA & DOWNSTREAM FISHING sign.

This first access point is a Corps of Engineers area with a parking lot and rest rooms. There is roughly ¼ mile of access. The site is very popular with wading fly-casters.

Although there will eventually be five other access points on the downstream portion of the tailwater, only three are presently completed and open. These are all in the George Washington National Forest but, as mentioned in the summary of Virginia angling regulations, a national forest fishing permit is not required for fishing on the Jackson.

The Johnson Spring Access is just off CR 638 and contains a parking area, canoe launch, and limited wading access. It is roughly 2½ miles below Gathright Dam. The Indian Draft Access is located on CR 687 just north of its junction with CR 641. Again, this access point has parking, a canoe launch, and limited wading room. The final access point is Petticoat Junction Access, which fits the same description as the two just mentioned. It is located on Mays Lane (gravel) just east of the lower CR 687 bridge across the river. The trout water on the Jackson ends in Covington at the WESTVACO pulp mill's low-head dam.

Water-release schedules for Gathright Dam are available by calling the Corps of Engineers' recorded message line at 540-965-4117.

40

Smith River

USGS Philpott Lake, Bassett • DeLorme 26

Not only is the Smith River the Old Dominion's oldest and best tailwater trout fishery, but it can also support the claim of being the best wild brown trout stream east of the Mississippi. Upon first glance, however, it is hard to conceive of this river as a truly world-class trout stream. Much of its course is through a suburban-to-urban environment, it is quite frankly filled with litter, and it flows only sluggishly through the lowlands of Franklin and Henry Counties in south-central Virginia.

Yet the icy waters released through Philpott Dam create ideal trout conditions for 25 miles downstream to the town of Martinsville. Along this stretch, brown trout have been thriving and reproducing for more than two decades. In fact, the VDGIF estimates that the Smith River comprises fully 60 percent of all the water in Virginia that contains naturally reproducing brown trout.

Recognition of the Smith as a haven for big bruiser brown trout came first in the summer of 1974, when the Virginia state record for the species was broken three different times on this tailwater. At the end of that summer the mark stood at 14 pounds, 6 ounces. After a 5-year pause, the Smith yielded a new record fish to Bill Nease of Martinsville, who landed an 18-pound, 11-ounce brown. Just to prove his catch was no fluke, within 2 months he had also caught a 17-pound, 12-ounce brown. Since those halcyon days, the Smith has continued to produce large numbers of brown trout weighing 10 pounds or more.

One unfortunate footnote concerning the Virginia brown trout record is that Nease's catch is now described as the "historical record" for the species. Several years ago the VDGIF revamped its record book because of some older, questionable records. Though there was no controversy connected with the Nease fish, it got swept into the historical category anyway.

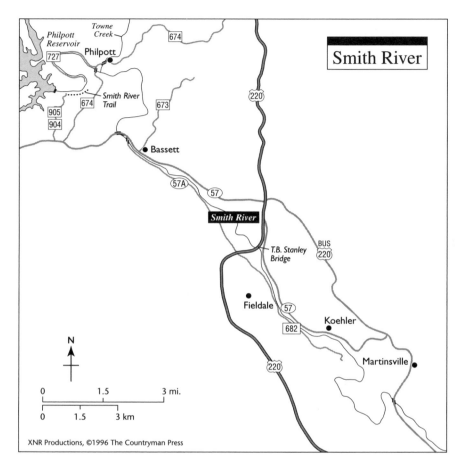

Although the Smith was originally stocked with large numbers of brook and rainbow trout, the plantings soon switched over to predominantly rainbows. Still, it was the browns that proved most at home in the river. Almost immediately they began spawning throughout the tailwater. Today there is some indication that the rainbows may also be spawning here, but the Smith is firmly established as a blue-ribbon brown trout stream.

While the Smith produces lots of browns of trophy size, it no longer gives up fish in the 14- to 18-pound range as it did in the 1970s. Several factors are suspected of contributing to this decline in monster fish. Early on in the operation of the powerhouse at Philpott Dam, large numbers of alewives were sucked through the turbines to float helplessly downstream. The brown trout gorged themselves on these drifting baitfish. Then, in the 1980s, the alewives for unknown reasons quit coming through the dam.

When the turbines are silent at Philpott Dam,
the Smith River shrinks to a veritable trickle.

During the mid-1980s a couple of major floods struck the Smith, and these are thought to have washed some fish downstream. Finally, there can be no doubt that the increased fishing pressure and the high level of expertise among spin-fishers have also dented the big-fish population in recent years.

Knowing that the Smith River tailwater contains quality trout, however, does not make the fishing easy. The Smith is a fairly wide stream, often spreading to 100 feet or more even during low water. Its course is a continuous string of riffles and pools, often so calm that they look as though there is no water movement at all. Almost all of the water is wadable, for even many of the deeper pools are edged by shallow, gravel shelves.

The long flat stretches of water make the fishing difficult. Under these conditions the trout are easy to spook. Even wading can be an ordeal because any waves you create travel far ahead of you to send the fish scurrying for cover.

When fishing the Smith, the rule of thumb is to cast to the middle of the stream for the freshly stocked trout, but to work the deeper holes along the shore—particularly those shaded by vegetation—for the larger fish. Do not overlook visible holding areas around logs, rocks, or even large items of trash, such as auto tires. They will often have a trout or two hiding close against them. On low water, flies need to be extremely small and spinners need to be fished very slowly to keep from spooking the trout.

There is a 3-mile stretch of the Smith downstream from Towne Creek (the VDGIF uses this spelling, but some maps use *Town*) to the CR 666 crossing at the village of Bassett that is open to fishing under special regulations. Through here only single-hooked artificial lures are allowed and the creel limit is 2 fish per day of a minimum size of 16 inches. This quality trout area receives no stockings. On the rest of the river, general Virginia trout regulations and creel limits apply. Since 1995 the entire Smith River has been open to year-round fishing.

When the turbines begin to run at the Philpott Dam powerhouse, the Smith River is transformed. The pastoral pools change suddenly to raging torrents. This is not a stream to wade during high water. Near the dam, a 3-foot wall of water will sweep down the river after the warning siren at the dam sounds. When power generation starts, keep above the high-water mark even when bank-fishing. It is, however, possible to leapfrog ahead of the rising water and get in more fishing before the surge gets downstream. The rising water takes an hour to get to Towne Creek, 2 hours to North Bassett, 3 hours to South Bassett, and 5 hours to reach the village of Koehler.

These periods of rising and high water are the times to fool the really lunker-sized trout on this tailwater. Casting Rapala-type minnow lures and bait-fishing with spring lizards or night crawlers are popular ways to target the big trout, particularly just below the dam. This action continues when the river level is falling. It generally takes the flow about 1½ hours to get back down to ideal low-water fishing levels.

Once the river is back at low levels, it is again the domain of fly-casters. The hatches on the Smith River are so massive in May and June that they have become legendary in the state. Kicking off with the appearance of eastern sulfur duns in the late-spring afternoons, other insects soon appear, including light Cahills, Hendricksons, caddis flies, and olive midges. In each case, however, the Smith's brown trout are noted for being finicky about what they eat. They will target the predominant insect to the exclusion of any of different size and color. And the size is often quite small, requiring hooks in the 16 to 20 range. About the only fly noted for attracting much surface action when no active rises are visible is the Blue-Winged Olive in sizes 16 to 26.

Later in the year, beginning in September and October, terrestrial insects become important trout attractors on the Smith. The best imitations then are beetles and ants. Cinnamon or black ant flies in sizes ranging down to 26 are deadly on the browns and rainbows.

There is access to both shores of the Smith at the foot of Philpott Dam. On the southern side of the river, a recreation area contains a parking lot and the Smith River Trail, which runs downstream for ½ mile. It is possible to walk along the trail and spot the fish in the clear water at nongeneration times.

To reach this access, take CR 904 (Philpott Dam Road) for ¾ mile north off VA 57 (Fairy Stone Park Highway). Next, turn right onto CR 905 (Dam Spillway Road) and proceed ¾ mile to the parking area.

On the northern shore of the river, ½ mile of land is open to the public. Parking, canoe launches, and rest rooms are provided here. To reach this park, take CR 727 (Stoneybrook Drive) west from the CR 674 bridge over the Smith. At 2¼ miles the road changes from pavement to gravel. The last ½ mile of road is on power-company land, but before this point there are some roadside turnouts and access to the water along CR 727. After this point there are a number of bridges across the river down to Martinsville. Most of these offer limited parking and river access. The most accessible are on CR 674 at the crossroads of Philpott; in the town of Bassett at the VA 57 and CR 673 (Bullock Drive) bridges; and at the T.B. Stanley Highway Bridge (VA 57A and US 220).

Additionally, just upstream of the town of Fieldale, CR 682 (River Road) parallels the southwestern side of the river and has a number of roadside turnouts providing access to the water.

For information on water-release schedules at Philpott Dam, call the Corps of Engineers' 24-hour recorded message line at 540-629-2432.

41
The Murky Crystal Ball

It would be nice if the future of Dixie's tailwater trout fisheries were as crystal clear as the water flowing down many of those rivers. Unfortunately, guessing is not a very exact science.

It can, however, be surmised that the great age of dam building is over in the southeastern United States. Although there will probably be a few more large reservoirs created in coming decades, the environmental impact of losing our few remaining free-flowing rivers is becoming too high a price to pay for such projects. The trend in the US is toward removing dams, rather than building more.

At the same time, the tailwater trout fisheries that we already have will obviously become more crowded with anglers. The Sun Belt states of the South are growing rapidly in population, and many of these new residents will become trout anglers looking for a place to wet a line. Wild mountain streams are a joy to fish, but they are also small, delicate, and difficult to reach. On the other hand, tailwaters are large, produce big fish, are relatively resilient, and are usually close to major population centers.

So it is a safe bet that our tailwater trout streams will become more popular in the future. This also means that more care will be needed to protect them. The downside of these rivers being near anglers is that they are also close to many potential points of runoff pollution. These flows are man-made trout fisheries, but they need to be protected from man-made problems as well.

Another by-product of creating these great tailwater trout rivers is the appearance of the Trout Unlimited chapters and fly-fishing clubs in the metropolitan areas surrounding many of them. Getting involved with these groups is one way the average angler can ensure that the resources endure. These clubs and chapters are the local watchdogs that monitor and fight for the individual rivers and fisheries.

For more information on Trout Unlimited chapters in your area, write to Trout Unlimited, 1500 Wilson Boulevard, Suite 310, Arling-

Can anglers provide enough protection to Dixie's tailwater trout fisheries to ensure that the resources will last?

ton, VA 22209-2310; or call 703-522-0200. To find out about fly-fishing clubs in your vicinity, contact the Federation of Fly Fishers, PO Box 1595, Bozeman, MT 59771, or call 406-585-7592.

Appendix

MAP SOURCES

Some of the publications listed below are available free of charge from public agencies, but others must be purchased. Contact the individual companies and agencies for details.

Arkansas Game & Fish Commission
Information and Education Division
2 Natural Resources Drive
Little Rock, AR 72205
501-223-6351
This agency publishes a book entitled *Fishing in Arkansas: A Fisherman's Guide to Public Access Facilities in Arkansas Counties*. The publication contains detailed maps of each county in the state, with special attention paid to access points on public waters.

Chattahoochee River National Recreation Area
Superintendent
1978 Island Ford Parkway
Dunwoody, GA 30350
770-399-8070
This agency distributes a brochure containing a detailed map of the tailwaters of the Chattahoochee River from Lake Sidney Lanier to the end of trout water in Atlanta.

Thomas Publication, Ltd.
County Maps
Puetz Place
Lyndon Station, WI 53944
608-666-3331
This private company produces books containing individual county maps. It presently offers maps of Arkansas, Kentucky, North Caro-

lina, South Carolina, and Tennessee. The maps are particularly helpful
in that they show county and state route numbers on secondary roads.

DeLorme Mapping Company
PO Box 298
Freeport, ME 04032
207-865-4171
Another private company, DeLorme produces an *Atlas & Gazetteer*
for a number of states. These are the most comprehensive maps
available from private sources. They show names for secondary roads
and numbers for forest service roads. Among the states discussed in
this book, the *Atlas & Gazetteer* is presently only available for North
Carolina, Tennessee, and Virginia.

South Carolina Wildlife and Marine Resources Department
PO Box 167
Columbia, SC 29202
803-734-3888
The SCWMRD publishes the *South Carolina Wildlife Facilities Atlas*.
This book contains individual maps of all the counties in the state, with
special emphasis on access points to public fishing waters.

Tennessee Wildlife Resources Agency
Central Office
PO Box 40747
Nashville, TN 37204
615-781-6500
This agency distributes a brochure entitled "Trout Fishing in Tennes-
see," which contains maps showing the locations of all of the state's
cold-water fisheries.

United States Geological Survey
Map Distribution
Federal Center Building 41
Denver, CO 80225
1-800-USA-MAPS or 303-202-4700
The USGS distributes free indexes to topo maps and order blanks for
those quadrangle maps for all of the states covered in this book.
Request the index for the states for which you need maps.

Index

Alabama, 35-36
    regulations, 36
    water release schedules, 40-41
    See also Sipsey Fork
Anglers, types of, 18-19
A River Runs Through It, 19
Arkansas, 13, 43-44
    record-holding fish, 58, 64, 66,
        83, 85
    regulations, 45-46, 55, 86
    See also Beaver Tailwater; Bull
        Shoals Tailwater; Little
        Missouri River; Little Red
        River; Norfork River
Arkansas Fly Fishers of Little Rock,
    54-55
Arkansas Game and Fish Commis-
    sion (AGFC), 16, 44
Atlas & Gazetteers, 15-16
Augustus, R. James, 140

Babusa, Marty, 157, 159
Baitfish, 12, 19, 134, 243
Bait-fishing, 18, 27, 61, 69-70, 76
    types of bait, 24
Bank-fishing, 27-28
Bass fishing, 8, 10-11, 19, 25, 43
Beaver Tailwater, 72-73
    access, 77-78
    stocking procedures, 73-76
    water release schedule, 79
Birmingham Fly Fishing Club, 37, 39
Blue Fox, 24
Bluegrass State. *See* Kentucky
Boats, 69, 87-88
    types of, 28-29

Branson, Missouri, 161
Bream, 11
Brook trout, 7, 13, 45
    record-holding, 64, 140, 209
Brown trout, 7, 11, 13, 45
    record-holding, 53, 64, 66, 85,
        156-157, 195, 218, 242
    regulations, 74
Bull Shoals Tailwater, 81-83
    access, 89-93
    stocking procedures, 83-86
    trout food, 88-89
    water release schedule, 93

Caddis flies, 20-21
Caney Fork River
    access, 192-194
    stocking procedures, 189, 191
    trout food, 191
    water release schedule, 194
Chattahoochee River
    stocking procedures, 97, 99-100
    trout food, 101-103
    water release schedule, 104
Chattahoochee River National
    Recreation Area, 16
Chironomidae. *See* Midges
Clinch River, 195
    access, 198-200
    stocking procedures, 196-198
    trout food, 198
    water release schedule, 200
Collins, Rip, 53, 56, 60, 65
Cooper, Van, 56
Cotton State. *See* Alabama
Crankbait, 25, 76

Crayfish, 24
Crustaceans, 23-24
Cumberland River, 119
    access, 123-124
    stocking procedures, 120-121
    trout food, 121-123
    water release schedule, 124
Cutthroat trout, 13, 45, 218
    record-holding, 66, 84

Dam construction, 7-8, 10, 11, 14,
    43
    weirs, 12-13, 197, 221
DeLorme Mapping Company, 15-16
Diptera. See Midges
Directions, following, 17
Dixie, 7, 247
Drag fishing, 87-88
Duck River, water release schedule,
    203

Eisenbarth, Elizabeth and John, 39
Elfrink, Kevin, 157
Elk River
    access, 207-208
    stocking procedures, 205-206
    trout food, 206-207
    water release schedule, 208
Else, Thomas, 66
Ephemeroptera. See Mayflies

Federation of Fly Fishers, address,
    248
Fish consumption advisory, 102
Fisheries, 8, 11-14
    future of, 247
    put-and-take, 10, 13, 74, 167
Fishing methods, 10-11, 27-29
Fishing in Arkansas: A Fisherman's
    Guide to Public Access Facilities in
    Arkansas Counties, 16
Float-fishing, 28-29, 43, 87, 146
Fly-fishing, 18, 19-24
Friends of the Little Red River, 56-
    57

Gathright Wildlife Management
    Area, 237
Gear
    fly-fishing, 19-24
    spin-fishing, 24-25
Georgia, 95
    regulations, 96
    See also Chattahoochee River;
        Toccoa River
Gott, Charles, 157

Hallmark, Melvin, 54
Hecker, Bill, 157
High-water fishing, 68-70, 87-88
Hiwassee River, 209, 211-212
    regulations, 211
    water release schedule, 213
Holston River, water release sched-
    ule, 216
Hunt, Ricky, 54

Insect forms, 20-23
International Game Fish Association,
    56, 65, 85

Jackson River, 237, 239
    access, 240-241
    regulations, 240
    water release schedule, 241
Jerkbait, 25
Johnboats, 28, 69, 87
Jones, Carl, 85

Kentucky, 111-112
    Barren River, 113-115
    Carr Fork, 116-117
    Dix River, 125-127
    Johns Creek, 128-130
    Licking Creek, 131-132
    Licking River, 133-135
    Little Sandy River, 136-138
    Martins Fork, 139-141
    Middle Fork Kentucky River,
        142-144
    Nolin River, 145-146

Paint Creek, 147-149
record brook trout, 140
regulations, 112
Rough River, 150-151
See also Cumberland River
Kentucky Department of Fish and
Wildlife Resources (KDFWR),
112, 113, 116, 125
Kitchens, David, 58

Lake Taneycomo
access, 158-161
stocking procedures, 155-158
trout food, 158
water release schedule, 161
Little Missouri River, 47-49
access to, 49-51
Little Red River, 53
access to, 61-63
regulations, 55-56, 62
stocking procedures, 54-55, 57-
58
trout food, 54, 59-60
water release schedule, 58, 63
Live Trophy Release Kit, 57

MacKenzie drift boats, 29
Maclean, Norman, 19
Mandernach, Frank, 66
Manley, Mike "Huey," 64-65, 85
Maps, 15-17
Mayflies, 21-22
Midges, 22
Mid-South Fly Fishers Club, 55
Miller, Jim, 83
Minnows, 24
Missouri, 153
record-holding fish, 156-157
regulations, 154
See also Lake Taneycomo
Missouri Department of Conserva-
tion (MDC), 153

Nantahala River, 169
access, 172-173

trout food, 170-171
National Fresh Water Fishing Hall of
Fame, 56, 65
National Park Service, 16
Natural State. *See* Arkansas
Natural trout habitat, 95, 163, 169,
175, 231
Nease, Bill, 242
Night-fishing, 76-77, 171
Norfork River
access, 70-71
stocking procedures, 66-67
water release schedule, 68, 71
North Carolina, 8-9, 163-165
Linville River, 166-168
regulations, 163, 165
rivers, 8-9
See also Nantahala River
North Carolina Wildlife Resources
Commission (NCWRC), 163, 166
North Fork River. *See* Norfork River
Nymphs, 21-23

Obey River, 217
access, 219-220
stocking procedures, 218
water release schedule, 220
Old Dominion. *See* Virginia

Palmetto State. *See* South Carolina
Peach State. *See* Georgia
Plecoptera. *See* Stone flies
Powerhouse sirens, 31
Prime fishing area, 10-11

Quality Trout Fishing Area, 197

Rafting destinations, popular, 103-
104, 172
Rainbow trout, 7, 13, 45
record-holding, 58, 66, 83, 156-
157, 218
Regulations, 15, 62, 74
Alabama, 36
Arkansas, 45-46, 55, 86

Georgia, 96
Hiwassee River, 211
Jackson River, 240
Kentucky, 112
Missouri, 154
North Carolina, 163, 165
Savannah River, 183-184
South Carolina, 176
Tennessee, 188
Virginia, 231-232
Riverside Fly & Tackle, 39
Rooster Tail, 25, 134
Rudolph, Scott, 84

Safety, 29-33
Salamon, Tony, 64, 66
Saluda River
    access, 179-181
    stocking procedures, 177-179
    water release schedule, 181
Savannah River, 182
    access, 184-185
    regulations, 183-184
    water release schedule, 185
Schoolcraft, Henry Rowe, 82
Scuds, 24, 157
Show Me State. See Missouri
Sipsey Fork, 37
    access, 39-40
    stocking procedures, 38-39
Smith River, 242
    access, 246
    stocking procedures, 243-244
    trout food, 245-246
    water release schedule, 246
South Carolina, 9, 175
    regulations, 176
    See also Saluda River; Savannah
    River
South Carolina Wildlife and Marine
    Resources Department (WMRD),
    175
South Carolina Wildlife Facilities
    Atlas, 16
South Holston River, 221-223

access, 224-225
    water release schedule, 225
Sow bugs, 24, 54
Spin-fishing, 24-25, 28, 60-61, 69, 76
Stickbait, 21
Stocking of fish, 13-14
    North Carolina, 164-165
    See also specific locations
Stone flies, 22-23
Sullivan, Raymond, 66

Tackle, 18
    See also Gear; specific fishing
        methods
Tailwater fishing, types of, 18-19
Tailwaters, anatomy of, 8-11
Tailwater trout fisheries, 14-15
    future of, 247
Tar Heel State. See North Carolina
Tennessee, 9, 187
    Duck River, 201-203
    Holston River, 214-216
    record-holding fish, 195, 209, 218
    regulations, 188
    Watauga River, 227-229
    See also Caney Fork River;
        Clinch River; Elk River;
        Hiwassee River; Obey River;
        South Holston River
Tennessee Valley Authority (TVA),
    7, 12-13
    Caney Fork River, 194
    Clinch River, 198, 200
    Duck River, 201, 203
    Elk River, 208
    Hiwassee River, 212, 213
    Holston River, 216
    Obey River, 220
    South Holston River, 221, 225
    Toccoa River, 107, 109
    Watauga River, 229
Tennessee Wildlife Resources Agency
    (TWRA), 187, 193, 195-197
    Duck River, 201, 203
Thomas Publications, Ltd., 16

Tilley, Frank, 85
Toccoa River
    access, 107-109
    stocking procedures, 105-107
    water release schedule, 109
Treble hook, 65
Trichoptera. *See* Caddis flies
Trophy-trout fishing, 64
Trout, 8
    record-holding, 53, 56, 58, 64-
        66, 83-85, 140, 156-157, 195,
        209, 218, 242
    See also specific types
"Trout Capital of the World," 81
Trout food, 20-24
    See also specific locations
Trout management, 74-76, 233, 235
Trout Unlimited, 75-76, 125, 177,
    212
    address, 247-248

United States Geological Survey
    (USGS), 15
US Army Corps of Engineers, 7, 13,
    61, 63, 66
    Beaver Tailwater, 79
    Bull Shoals Tailwater, 83, 93
    Caney Fork River, 194
    Chattahoochee River, 104
    Cumberland River, 119, 124
    Jackson River, 241
    Kentucky, 117, 128, 129, 132,
        136, 137, 144, 145, 147, 149,
        150
    Lake Taneycomo, 161
    Norfork River, 71
    Obey River, 217
    Savannah River, 184, 185
    Smith River, 246

Virginia, 231
    Back Creek, 233-236
    record-holding fish, 242
    regulations, 231-232
    See also Jackson River; Smith River

Virginia Department of Game and
    Inland Fisheries (VDGIF), 232
Volunteer State. *See* Tennessee

Wading, 29, 33
Waggoner, Leon, 85
Warren, Dee, 54
Watauga River, water release
    schedule, 229
Water level, surge conditions, 29-
    32
Water release schedule, 12, 29
    Alabama, 40-41
    Beaver Tailwater, 79
    Bull Shoals Tailwater, 93
    Caney Fork River, 194
    Chattahoochee River, 104
    Clinch River, 200
    Cumberland River, 124
    Duck River, 203
    Elk River, 208
    Hiwassee River, 213
    Holston River, 216
    Jackson River, 241
    Lake Taneycomo, 161
    Little Red River, 58, 63
    Norfork River, 71
    Obey River, 220
    Saluda River, 181
    Savannah River, 185
    Smith River, 246
    South Holston River, 225
    Toccoa River, 109
    Watauga River, 229
Water temperature, 11-12
    safety regarding, 32-33
Weirs. *See* Dam construction
White River. *See* Beaver Tailwater;
    Bull Shoals Tailwater; Lake
    Taneycomo
Wills, Jerry, 209
Wolf, Craig, 157
Wooten, David, 66
World-record trout, 53, 56, 64, 85
Worms, 24

Also from The Countryman Press and Backcountry Publications

The Countryman Press and Backcountry Publications, long known for their fine books on the outdoors, offer a range of practical and readable manuals on fish and fishing.

Bass Flies, Dick Stewart
Building Classic Salmon Flies, Ron Alcott (hardcover)
Fishing Small Streams with a Fly Rod, Charles Meck
Fishing Vermont's Streams and Lakes, Peter F. Cammann
Flies in the Water, Fish in the Air, Jim Arnosky
Fly-Fishing with Children: A Guide for Parents, Philip Brunquell (hardcover and paperback)
Fly-Tying Tips, Second Edition (revised), Dick Stewart
Good Fishing in the Catskills, Second Edition (revised), Jim Capossela, with others
Good Fishing in Lake Ontario and Its Tributaries, Second Edition (revised), Rich Giessuebel
Good Fishing in Western New York, Edited by C. Scott Sampson
Great Lakes Steelhead: A Guided Tour for Fly-Anglers, Bob Linsenman and Steve Nevala
Ice Fishing: A Complete Guide . . . Basic to Advanced, Jim Capossela
Michigan Trout Streams: A Fly-Angler's Guide, Bob Linsenman and Steve Nevala
Pennsylvania Trout Streams and Their Hatches, Second Edition (revised and expanded), Charles Meck
Trout Streams of Southern Appalachia: Fly-Casting in Georgia, Kentucky, North Carolina, South Carolina and Tennessee, Jimmy Jacobs
Ultralight Spin-Fishing: A Practical Guide for Freshwater and Saltwater Anglers, Peter F. Cammann
Universal Fly Tying Guide, Second Edition (revised), Dick Stewart
Virginia Trout Streams, Harry Slone
Wisconsin and Minnesota Trout Streams: A Fly-Angler's Guide, Jim Humphrey and Bill Shogren

We publish many guides to canoeing, hiking, walking, bicycling, and ski touring in New England, the Mid-Atlantic states, and the Midwest. Our books are available through bookstores, or they may be ordered directly from the publisher. For ordering information or for a complete catalog, please contact: The Countryman Press, c/o W.W. Norton & Company, Inc., 800 Keystone Industrial Park, Scranton, PA 18512.